# e-Commerce answers

Dear Rolf and Jackie

Wishing you all the very best for 2002.

Regards,

Mick Rumpley-Sturgeon

THE **big** BOOK OF

# e-Commerce answers

How to turn your website into a

money machine

TOM LAMBERT

*An imprint of* **Pearson Education**

London · New York · San Francisco · Toronto · Sydney · Tokyo · Singapore
Hong Kong · Cape Town · Madrid · Paris · Milan · Munich · Amsterdam

PEARSON EDUCATION LIMITED

Head Office:
Edinburgh Gate
Harlow CM20 2JE
Tel: + 44 (0)1279 623623
Fax: +44 (0)1279 431059

London Office:
128 Long Acre
London WC2E 9AN
Tel: +44 (0)20 7447 2000
Fax: +44 (0)20 7240 5771
Website: www.business-minds.com

First published in Great Britain in 2002

© Pearson Education Limited 2002

The right of Tom Lambert to be identified as Author
of this Work has been asserted by him in accordance
with the Copyright, Designs and Patents Act 1988.

ISBN 0 273 65628 7

*British Library Cataloguing in Publication Data*
A CIP catalogue record for this book can be obtained from the British Library.

10 9 8 7 6 5 4 3 2 1

Designed by Claire Brodmann Book Designs, Lichfield, Staffs
Typeset by Pantek Arts Ltd, Maidstone, Kent.
Printed and bound in Great Britain by Bell & Bain Ltd., Glasgow

*The Publishers' policy is to use paper manufactured from sustainable forests.*

# **About** the author

**TOM LAMBERT** is an international author, broadcaster, consultant, trainer, conference speaker and business journalist who is called, in America, 'the world's friendliest guru'. In Europe and Southern Africa his books and seminars have led him to be known to the quality business press as 'the consultant's consultant'. Clients who use his skills and knowledge in the hush-hush field of market dominance know him as the one consultant who can be trusted not to drop names, as do the chief executives who benefit from his mentoring services. He is recognized globally for his insights into strategic planning and particularly market dominance through 'bricks' or 'clicks' alone or a fully integrated strategy online or off.

Tom has held senior international marketing, executive and organizational development positions with blue chip corporations and has lectured at universities worldwide. He is currently Chairman of Coastal Sites (United Kingdom) Ltd. He mentors top executives and serves as adviser to the Chairman of the Board of Managing Directors for a major European bank in addition to holding non-executive directorships. As a consultant, Tom offers strategic advice to major corporations to enable them to develop ethical global dominance strategies. He also conducts training workshops in the fields of consultancy process as well as ethical sales and marketing based on customer and client psychology.

Tom has been the recipient of numerous business honours. He was awarded the appellation Certified Professional Consultant for 'unique and outstanding contributions to the profession'. He has been elected a Fellow of the Institute of Sales and Marketing Management and had the honour of being the first Fellow of the International Institute for the Development of

Creativity. He has served the Strategic Planning Society as a regional committee member, has been a full member of the Transpersonal Psychology Association and is currently a Member of the Society of Authors. He has been invited to become a Fellow of the Royal Society for the Arts (founded in London in 1754) and The Executive Club of Chicago.

# Contents

The Contents are in the form of the key questions that the book seeks to answer. In keeping with the working concept of the Internet 'key words' are emphasized to make it easier to find topics. This, the addition of 'see also' notes to direct attention to some key areas, the application of the odd scrap of reader psychology (about which the less said the better) and the design of the information on the page combine to make this an easy reference.

## INTRODUCTION AND SECTION ONE
### THE INTERNET OPPORTUNITY AND PITFALLS

This section provides the background and some of the tools for online and offline business success. You are advised to 'skim read' this section in order to become familiar with the layout and style of the book. You will also want to use at least some of the tools and ideas that are described.

Finding the answers could not be more simple or straightforward. Let your eyes wander down the page until you see a keyword or phrase that interests you and then read the whole question to test its relevance to your need right now. For example, you may see the word 'money' and 'training' and stop to read the whole question: How much **money** is wasted on **training**? Whether your reaction is 'that interests me' or 'what is the fool talking about', you know now where to find the answer. Trust me, it works and what is more you are training your mind to act as an analogy of a search engine.

# CONTENTS

# A note to **you** the reader

*Please excuse the liberty, but don't I know you?*

The key to customer satisfaction online and off is to try to understand the customer's situation, needs and wants and then go beyond satisfying them. The Pearson Group and I want you to be more than satisfied with this book – we want you to be delighted with it. We have designed this to be a valued resource that you will turn to again and again so please bear with me while I try to establish whether you are the person we think that we recognize.

## AS I SAY, I THINK THAT I KNOW YOU

✓   You are a busy professional all but overwhelmed with information and time is your scarcest, most valuable resource.

✓   You take your responsibilities seriously and you would love to read every worthwhile book on all the subjects that are important to your business, but time to read books is hard to find.

✓   You have been disappointed by books that contain one good and useful idea buried somewhere in 300 pages of anecdote, opinion and aside.

✓   You are convinced that your business could do better, but you need relevant, clear and practical information that you can easily find whenever you want it.

✓   You do not want to be a technical expert, but you do want to have the knowledge at your fingertips that will enable you to manage your technical people to achieve your business goals.

✓ *Above all you need proven and useful business information in a form that will save you precious time and make money.*

If I have been able to describe your needs, wants and situation accurately there is no magic involved. I have done no more than portray the executives and entrepreneurs that I meet on a daily basis as part of my job, but if I have described you correctly this book has been designed and written with your needs always in mind.

# HOW TO USE THIS BOOK

*Crazy as it may sound please* **do not read this book.**

Research shows that busy executives or entrepreneurs buy books and after an average of 29 pages need to put the book aside to get on with running the business or spending some meaningful, precious time with family or friends. Once they have put a book aside they rarely find the time to read the remainder. That is why we have designed this book to be used rather than read. It is made up of the key questions that serious and smart business people ask about building success and prosperity on the Internet, and the answers that they have found to be most useful in the real world. It also contains current and relevant case studies, self-assessment instruments, action plans, checklists and key research findings.

To get the most out of it please take a look at the contents for the question(s) to which you need an answer right now. Having got what you need or having been guided towards easily accessible detailed information put the book to one side until you want to refer to it again ... and again ... and again.

# Introduction

## WHY SHOULD I BUY THIS BOOK?

The new 'e-conomy' is (and you may make your choice, we live in a democracy at least of thought) either the greatest revolution since the printing press or the most hyped fragment of fizz since the South Sea Bubble. From the businessperson's point of view it hardly matters which judgement will prove to be correct in the long run. As Keynes said, 'in the long run we are all dead'. Those who do not understand the change that is taking place, however, will be 'dead'' in the business sense in short order. For, hype notwithstanding, we are living in a time of major and critical change. This book will help you to build your understanding the easy way.

In the short term hype makes 'stars' (consider the world of 'popular music') and until the stars turn into 'dogs' entrepreneurs and executives need to keep ahead of the game as it is, not as it ought to be. This is particularly true since 'stars' unlike 'cash cows' require major investment of time and money, and where there is investment the businessperson rightly demands a suitable level of return. Your competitors, known and unknown, at home and across the wide world are not waiting to see how things turn out. They are acting now to exploit every opportunity that the new economy provides. The only way to ensure a sustainable competitive edge is to get in there and perform so well that you set the rules by which others have to play the game. You need to be so effective in the exploitation of every opportunity that competition loses money, loses heart and withdraws from the attempt to steal your most worthwhile customers and your profits.

No one in the world of enterprise can ignore the growth of e-commerce or remain ignorant of its potential and pitfalls. It gives any company, from the one-person band to the mega-conglomerate the chance to beat competition into the ground. It has also provided an unprecedented opportunity to squander cash and other resources on an almost unimaginable scale.

## Profit remains the essential prerequisite of being in business

Rather than regard e-commerce as a new form of seventeenth-century Dutch tulip mania perhaps a comparison might be made with the railways. In the middle years of the nineteenth century rail travel was wildly hyped. Railway companies proliferated and attracted stockholders who pushed market values to unparalleled and unsustainable levels. Company after company spent other people's money wildly for a while, then crashed. This didn't mean that there was no future in rail travel. What it did mean, however, was that unthinking bizarre overinvestment in an novel idea rather than a business plan is always likely to be a financial disaster no matter how attractive the idea is in theory. The advent of e-commerce has meant that too many people have hoped to exploit any passing bandwagon with neither effort, thought, knowledge nor skill beyond that required to spend other people's money. Too many have assumed that because there is a new way of doing business the rules governing business economics have been set aside. Just because business can be done and is being done online is no reason to assume that Peter Drucker's assessment of profit is no longer true. Profit is as much an essential prerequisite of business survival and prosperity today as it was in the 1970s. Companies that fail to deliver a surplus eventually fail online or off. They always have and they always will. But there is every reason to believe that, spectacular crashes notwithstanding, the online revolution will prove to be at least as important to the global economy as the development of rail travel. Those who fail to become or remain winners will be spectacular losers. Your responsibility is to consider the potential risks and rewards, and implement the strategy that will make you such a convincing winner that the losers withdraw from the battle. If you want to know what this book is about in a word, it is about *profit*.

As I write, two telecommunications giants have reported their profits for the year recently completed. Nokia have driven profits up by 15 per cent in difficult trading conditions. Ericsson have lost millions and are firing 10 000 workers in an attempt to save themselves into a profit. Asked by journalists to explain the difference in performance, the head of Ericsson bemoaned the sluggish global economy and a reduction in demand for mobile telephones. His counterpart at Nokia explained how they made bigger profits in the same circumstances with roughly similar products. They managed the changing situation within the guidelines of a robust, but flexible business strategy. The key to success is, and always will be, to understand the volatile environment in which you operate and make timely adjustments as evolutions or revolutions emerge.

## The market grows more attractive daily

Moore's Law states that, 'the value of a computer network is the square of the number of people with access'. At the time of writing 350 million computers are ready for e-commerce and this number is expected to treble to more than a billion in only a little more than the time that it will take for this book to appear in the shops. One billion computers in workplaces and homes promise to deliver a great many potential and actual customers. Research shows that those who have access to the web, whether they are business buyers or consumers, have the greatest discretionary spending power and the least time in which to make their buying decision in the history of business. Those who try to display cleverness with no regard for the psychology of the online customer will drive away potential buyers in multitudes. Those who use technology to make the buying decision quick and easy will dominate the new economy.

## Doing more, much more, with less

A friend of mine used to be a vice president of General Electric. Each year she would have a one-to-one discussion of her results with Jack Welch. He would congratulate her on her considerable achievements. Then he would focus on what was really important to a business. 'This coming year how much more are you prepared to achieve with how much less?' That is what e-commerce is ultimately about – productivity and profits.

Productivity in the USA has finally, only since 1995, accurately reflected the level of investment in technology. After a disappointing decade or more of productivity increases of around the historical average of 1.2 per cent a year (apparently regardless of the national technology spend), the critical mass has at last been achieved and productivity per worker/hour has surged to 4 per cent a year and better. Costs in even the highest waged economies are falling dramatically through making more effective use of technology. Savings can and are being used to delight customers and build profits. The level of productivity growth driven by the new technology is far higher than that, for example, which followed the invention of the printing press or steam or electric power. This is a sea change and it is a sea change that you ought to be positioning yourself, as a business manager or entrepreneur, to exploit to the full. Unlike the USA, in Europe and in Asia the critical mass has yet to be achieved, but it will come and it will come soon. When it does, massive business growth will be possible at the lowest ever relative cost. The key question is *'will you be ready to exploit the opportunity or will you be left behind among those plaintively calling out "me too, listen to me please, me too"?'*

## If it was easy it might not be worth doing

There have been widely reported online failures not only involving callow, youthful MBAs with little or no experience, but also seasoned business professionals. It is a harsh world out there whether online or off. Take it on trust for the moment, if you will, those who have failed have simply got it foolishly and unnecessarily wrong. This book cannot tell you in detail what is the optimal strategy for you except for this; while dog continues to eat dog you need to develop all the skills relevant to a successful carnivore in a new environment. As the dinosaurs became the victims of the faster moving, faster thinking mammals, there must have been many a mammal that thought too little or acted too slowly and paid the ultimate penalty. This book is designed to provide you with the information that will enable you to think quickly and thoroughly and to act with flawless timing.

On St George's Day (23 April) 2001 a detailed report by the much respected IDC organization looked in depth at what is happening to e-commerce globally and concluded that any business turndown in the USA and any shake out of Nasdaq stock values is, and will continue to be, 'irrelevant' to the growth and importance of e-business in the medium term. A further detailed survey published in May 2001 showed that virtually half the population of 14 European countries had surfed the Internet between the months of February and April of that year and 10 per cent had made at least one purchase during that time. In the year 2000, European consumers spent $12.2 billion online, double the spending of the previous year. Internet commerce is expected, on the most conservative forecasts, to exceed $1 trillion in Europe alone by 2004. The new economy has grown, is growing at an accelerating rate and will continue to grow come hell or high water.  The key determinants of success online or off will remain what they always have been: a clear and compelling vision of where you want to be; a vigorous and flexible business strategy that will get you there; a determination to turn visitors into customers, customers into friends and friends into advocates for your business; a sensitivity to the customer's emergent needs that will make them want to stay with you for life; and a driving ambition to become and remain the best of the best. The challenge to online business in the short term is that of delivering satisfaction and savings in the B2B (business to business) world and boosting the confidence of consumers in B2C (business to consumer – what we once happily called 'retail'). A recent research report showed that 16 per cent of consumers who buy online still do not trust suppliers to deliver what is promised, while almost a quarter of those who will hand their credit cards to a waiter without a qualm still mistrust the online payment systems. They are buying less than they could, less in fact than they wish because, although they want the convenience, they lack the confidence. Growth in online business is massive, but the potential for growth is more massive yet. The Internet needs businesspeople who are experienced in the real world to create the environment in which the potential can be achieved.

No one who is seriously interested in making money for themselves or for their employers can afford not to become as informed as possible about the business opportunities and potential downside of an Internet presence. In a busy life you need a convenient, easy and time-effective way of becoming informed. This book is designed to fulfil that purpose.

In addition to answering the key questions that businesspeople ask 'experts' in the field, this book will suggest the questions that you, as managers, entrepreneurs and executives should be prepared to answer. Further it will provide you with a range of answers that may fit with and enhance your overall business and marketing strategy offline as well as on.

The author of this book makes an important part of his living advising top businesspeople in confidential mentoring conversations so that they can ask the right questions and refer to the salient facts at board meetings and beyond. He has struggled to become something of an 'anti-technical' technical expert who believes that business decision-makers should be provided with the facts that they need to make good business decisions on how best to exploit their technological resources for sustainable profit. Having a copy of this book is the equivalent of having daily access to two leading business mentors, one technical the other entrepreneurial, who provide specialist knowledge in jargon-free, easy to understand and easy to communicate terms. Schizophrenia, it seems, goes with the territory.

A strategic and tactical summary for online prosperity

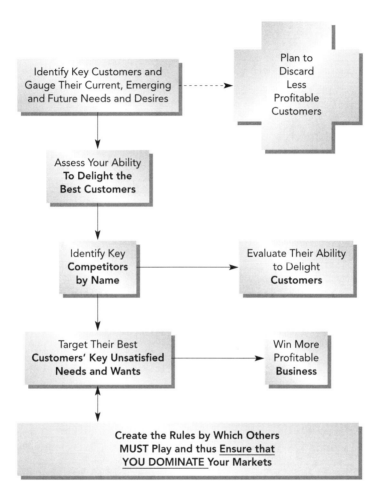

section

# one

# the internet opportunity
# and pitfalls

# FAD OR FUTURE

Why is the Internet unlikely to be a business fad that will
fade as quickly as it emerged?

Things could certainly look as if the future of e-commerce has been
excessively hyped. As I write this, my sources report that 212 major
Internet companies have folded in this year with the loss of 50 000 jobs.
Whilst a few days ago I heard one dizzy woman, who became a paper
millionaire overnight, breathlessly express the opinion that it was 'fun' to
spend some £38 million of other people's money and was looking forward
to her new career, as so many such business disasters seem to expect to do,
as a highly paid conference speaker. To keep this in perspective, however,
the Department of Trade and Industry in the UK is currently discussing a
turnaround programme for 'bricks and mortar' companies that are in
trouble and is telling consultants that they have 2000-plus companies on
their books that are in need of urgent help. Against this a little over 200

badly planned, badly run attempts at making optimism triumph over reality worldwide does not seem so bad – bad as it is for those that have lost their investment and those that have lost their jobs. But facts must be faced. Bad business decisions and their consequences are not unknown in the real world.

### Some recent layoffs in the real world

| | |
|---|---|
| Disney | 4000 |
| General Motors | 10000 |
| Motorola | 10000 |
| Proctor and Gamble | 9600 |
| Marks and Spencer | 4000 |

If you think that business risk has suddenly been transferred exclusively to the Internet, think again. E-commerce is the fastest growing, most economical means of trading that has yet been invented. It will go through a period of 'shaking out' of bad ideas and badly run companies. There will be casualties, but it will prosper. As this goes to my publisher experts are arguing that dot coms have already experienced their nadir, the decline has 'bottomed out' and the only way is up. I suspect that they are seeing the 'green shoots of recovery' a little prematurely, but in this at least they are right; the future of e-commerce, shorn of some current and past idiocies is secure.

See also:   How fast is the web growing?

How fast is e-commerce growing?

Where is the greatest growth likely to be?

Are investors really losing their shirts online?

Who is succeeding online?

# GROWTH AND OPPORTUNITY

## How fast is the web growing?

There is a mass of data all showing unprecedented growth. To the businessperson two basic areas are of interest: the growth of the potential market and the growth of competition.

The number of commercial sites in the UK was estimated in 2000 to be around 400 000. By next year (2002) it is estimated that at least 700 000 firms will be online in this country alone. France and Germany, each starting from a lower base will see at least similar growth. In spite of a business downturn in the USA the growth of online business continues apace and it is estimated that 80 per cent of companies across the world will be online by next year. The question that should be exercising the minds of businesspeople will be: *'With so many sites online how will customers find mine?'*

*See also:*  Why is the Internet unlikely to be a business fad that will fade as quickly as it emerged?

Where is the greatest growth likely to be?

Are investors really losing their shirts online?

## How fast is e-commerce growing?

*High numbers – low profits (for some)*

Amazon.com is pulling in an average of over 2 million buyers a month and in January 2001 1.3 million people in the UK visited recruitment sites alone according to research by NetValue. Forrester research indicates that energy trading online grew by 750 per cent between 1999 and 2000. It is unlikely in the extreme that such trends will suddenly reverse. Jeff Bezos the charismatic boss of Amazon has great belief in the growth potential of B2C sales. In a report to shareholders (April 2001) he forecast that 15 per cent of all retail buying would soon be online. On the same day it was reported that the boss of Blackberry, an online systems provider, delivered considerably higher sales and profits than forecast and described the 'downturn' in US business as 'mythical'.

By April 2001 one in three homes (9 million) are estimated to have online access in Great Britain, a smaller proportion than in Denmark or the USA, but more than in France or Germany. The potential market continues to grow and one day, perhaps, the hordes of new customers will be offered the quality of service that they deserve. Then e-commerce will begin to realize its massive global potential. Every firm that ensures delighted customers at the end of each transaction is contributing not only to its own success, but also to the long-term economic well-being of us all.

*See also:*     How fast is the web growing?

If we are considering breaking into new markets using the Internet, are there any indicators of countries that we might aim for first?

## Where is the greatest growth likely to be?

If you are in a service industry you should be looking towards the future with equanimity at least. According to recent research by Dataquest services to e-business alone are set to increase from $23.6 billion in 1999 to $157.9 billion in 2004. Even allowing for a touch of optimism in terms of projection, it seems better than a racing certainty that online business will flourish and will help total trade to grow at a quite dazzling pace.

*See also:*     Who is succeeding online?

What are the business barriers to growth?

## Who is succeeding online?

**Mini Case Study** **Flying high**

Starting as a traditional bricks and mortar business in the very early days of e-commerce easyJet has progressed to the point where they did 85 per cent of their total business on the web in January 2001. Meanwhile they have successfully diversified into a range of businesses with the latest, the felicitously named easyMoney, taking off in the spring of 2001. The key to their success is to avoid overall 'branding', but to have a robust business plan that enables them to re-engineer each business according to the needs of the enterprise and its customers.

## What are the business barriers to growth?

**Mini Case Study** **The banks do it again?**

One problem that will hit individual companies, and possibly whole business sectors, is the crazy belief some cling to that having a website and a plethora of products to put onto it is enough.

Jupiter Media Metrix research (11 April 2001) suggests that executives in many online banking companies are suffering from a death wish for their enterprises. They continue to think that they know better than the customer what the customer 'really' wants.

**WHEREAS**

✓ A mere 25 per cent of banking executives thought that security online should be a priority.

✓ *Fifty-nine per cent of customers made it clear that for them security and trust issues were their number one concern.*

✓ Only 18 per cent of bank executives believed that improving the layout, design and usability of their websites was an issue.

✓ *Eighty-three per cent of potential buyers still 'walk away' from websites that are too smart for easy use.*

✓ Fully 57 per cent of bank executives stated that concentration on new products online was the top priority.

✓ *Fifty-two per cent of customers made it clear that they wanted better customer service with the products already online rather than new products.*

You ignore your customers at your peril as much online as off. No industry that thinks it knows better than the customer that it relies on can succeed if even one competitor decides to listen to the customer and respond to their concerns. In the UK the banks think that they have the upper hand with only one bank for 140 000 potential customers, but in North America there is one bank for every 11 000 customers.

When I lodge a cheque in my small-town American bank I can check that it has been credited to my account uncleared using the ATM (automated teller machine) as I leave the counter. The next working day I can draw against it. That is the service that customers in the USA expect and receive. Eventually, speeded perhaps by online capabilities, that level of competition will spawn a degree of sensitivity to customer need that will readily transfer across the Atlantic. Then it will become a case of traditional banker beware.

☞ *See also:* What is the cost of inadequate planning?

How should online and offline shopping experiences relate?

## Are investors really losing their shirts online?

*Investment remains for the long term*

The rise and fall of some daft dot coms have been hyped in both directions. Sometimes the injection of the odd fact can put things into perspective.

Mary Meeker, the leading business analyst and early prophet of online business, produces an annual report on the progress of stocks and shares of dot coms. The lady remains optimistic. Investment is a long-term game and over the long term the picture is very different from that painted by the popular press. It is true that if you look at dot coms that went public in 2000 no less than 77 per cent are now trading at below their launch price. Share values of IPOs (Initial Public Offerings) since 1980, however, have increased by $2000 billion and 82 IPOs have risen in value by more than 1000 per cent. In spite of recent panics more than half of new (2001) online public companies are currently (April 2001) trading higher than their IPO price. The shake out of rubbish appears to be working. Online business continues to be a major creator of wealth. The lesson to be learned is the lesson that is repeated again and again in this book.

✓ The economy is changing, but the laws of economics are not. If you cannot make a profit you are not in business. You are indulging in the long established hobby of urinating other people's money down your leg and getting a short-term feeling of warmth.

✓ Companies with a worthwhile strategy, a clear customer focus and high quality products or services will prosper online or off. Those that lack any of these will eventually fail no matter how much money is thrown at them.

✓ There is an unavoidable shakeout of bad ideas and good ideas badly thought through.

✓ Investment remains a high-risk business, that is why rewards are potentially so high and anyone who chooses to follow the hype of inexperienced youngsters with only newly minted MBAs to rely on in a real and increasingly tough world probably deserves even more sorrow than they get.

As Richard Pascale is quoted as having said: 'Who wants to be clutching the hands of a couple of newly minted MBAs when gazing into the abyss?' Meeker's research suggests that if we are looking into a big hole in the ground it is a hole entirely of our own making.

During the final preparation of this book with my publisher, the leading venture capital company 3i announced its results for the year ending 31 March 2001. They saw an increase in profits from £350 million last year to £453 million this year. In respect of investment in technology they stated that 'the sector still offers strong potential for growth'. They literally put their money where their mouth is, so things may not be as black as they are painted.

*See also*:  Who is succeeding online?

Why does European e-commerce continue to lag behind that of the USA?

# THE PURPOSE OF TECHNOLOGY

## What is the role of technology?

*It is here to stay*

Regardless of problems, you need to make the strategic assumption that technology has an important role to play now and in the future. The technology has been tested and it works. Business buyers and consumers are doing their buying online in crazily increasing numbers in spite of their justified concerns. There really is a new economy. We have to learn quickly how to exploit technology successfully, because if we do not our competitors will. That is inescapable. You must not, however, allow your business judgement to be influenced by hype or panic. You need to base your business decisions on fact. Companies and organizations founder through assuming that a website is an easy way to quick riches. It does not work like that. An e-business is a business like any other in that those that plan best prosper most. This book will help you to plan and operate a well-founded e-commerce operation. It will also suggest ways in which you may make the best use of technology throughout the business to improve productivity and reduce costs.

*See also*:   The Introduction (for the effect that technology is finally having on productivity and profits in the USA).

What are the effects on business of the assumption that the Internet is best left to technical people?

## What do 'coal face' managers need to know about the Internet?

Executives, entrepreneurs and managers need to have a clear working understanding of how the Internet, investment in technology and e-commerce work, and what business opportunities, competitive advantages and threats they offer for their companies. Moreover, they need a source of information and opinion that is easy to access.

They do not have the luxury of sufficient time to plough through masses of words in order to find what they need for that critical meeting that starts at nine o'clock this morning. They need to easily access the answers to the questions that are important to them right now. That is what this book is designed to deliver.

*See also*:   Why can't I simply delegate the decisions to the technical and marketing experts that we have in-house?

What are the new rules of the new economy?

What is wrong with traditional marketing techniques?

What is the cost of inadequate planning?

Can we trust the predictions of so-called gurus – like you?

## What are the new rules of the 'new economy'?

*It is a new economy – with many old rules*

The Internet is creating a new business economy in which some rules are changing while many remain the same. Things will evolve, but the effect on business will be massive and permanent. Consider one relatively small area of online business so far, retail sales. In spite of the difficulties so often strewn in the way of online shoppers by badly designed websites and ill-planned online strategies and offline infrastructure, online direct sales in the UK between January and October 2000 doubled, while in the more mature market of the USA sales increased by 62 per cent over the $17.3 billion in B2C sales made in 1999. In the last three years online sales in the USA have increased by 580 per cent.

Forester Research figures show that the online customer grows in value over time. Whereas new customers buy only nine times a year, this rises to an average of 20 times a year once they have been online for five years or more. Even the stunted and questionable field of mobile e-commerce is gathering momentum. Current research suggests that 85 per cent of firms in Europe and the USA state that they regard mobile e-commerce as 'an important factor in their future business'.

The rule that all business thinkers and entrepreneurs need to be aware of is this: 'When things happen in the new economy they happen faster than we ever used to imagine possible'.

Trends in the weaker areas of the marketplace make it certain that businesses dependent on the new economy may have to learn to manage a whole range of glitches, blips and disasters in the early days, but the potential of e-commerce is massive and it is here to stay, optimistic hype or pessimistic bathos notwithstanding.

*See also:* What is wrong with traditional marketing techniques?

## What is wrong with traditional marketing techniques?

*Traditional marketing may not be the answer*

It is partly through getting the answer to this question seriously wrong that some dot coms have collapsed so dramatically. Expenditure on advertising has simply exceeded total revenues. Growth of the web means that the competition to be seen online gets more difficult daily. Advertising online or off is not working as far as getting a sufficient number of customers to beat a path to your door is concerned, no matter how clever or strident that advertising may be. You need to consider a comprehensive marketing strategy that reflects the needs and expectations of your customers, current and potential. I suggest a low-cost approach:

✓ Make sure that your website address is clearly shown on every piece of paper and every e-mail that leaves your company, and is mentioned in every communication that you make – slide presentations, letters to the press, press releases or anywhere that your imagination may suggest.

✓ Use 'free ink' as much as possible, issue press releases, business articles and even letters to the press to promote the status and reputation of your business, and make it a habit to invite people to visit your website.

✓ Build a reputation as being 'the people for' whatever it is that you do so that people choose to use your website for information about your sector.

✓ Build a website that is a superior salesperson online.

✓ Use search engine positioning to ensure that you get onto the first two pages of the major search engines. Do not let your website be listed among the 'also rans' – there are millions of them.

✓ Avoid trying to get noticed by every little search engine that exists. They all have different rules and algorithms, and satisfying them all is a practical impossibility. Go for the main ones that your customers use. You will find them listed on www.coastalsitesuk.co.uk.

✓ Seriously consider the relatively small extra one-off cost of being listed by the main directories. Directories act like search engines except that they do not keep changing the rules, so although getting the right initial listing is tricky, once you are there you stay there.

✓ Ensure that, having achieved a high position in the search engine listings, you stay there through constant maintenance of your site.

✓ Having attracted and delighted customers, invite them to keep in touch through opt-in e-mails and to become advocates for your company by making it easy for them to pass on your informative and timely communications to others.

✓ Seek out strategic partners who serve a similar customer to those that you value most and establish affinity marketing programmes whereby they tell their customers, as a service to them, of your products or services.

✓ Ensure that although you may promise much you deliver more in terms of customer satisfaction. Get your 'customer delighting' infrastructure in place before you sue for business.

*See also:*   What is 'infoclutter'?

Does online advertising work?

What is the most effective way to market a website?

## Why can't I simply delegate the decisions to the technical and marketing experts that we have in-house?

The alternative to building your own knowledge is to have the technical people, or worse, advertising agencies or marketing departments making the business decisions that should be the sole province of the front-line management team. Current research shows that 74 per cent of marketing budgets are being used to attract customers to websites, but on average only 2 per cent of those that visit stay to buy and only one in ten of those comes back to buy again. That is what happens when the decisions that are made cease to be strategic business decisions and e-commerce initiatives are driven by technology for its own sake.

As for the marketers, too many are still imprisoned by old approaches to marketing that dictate that problems will go away if you throw money and advertising at them. The result is that some of the big names online are presently spending $1.25 on offline advertising for every dollar that they get back in revenue. Shouting louder while forgetting the message does not work any more – if it ever did.

Online advertising is not working either. Banner ads could once be relied upon to pull a 5–10 per cent response. Current research shows that the rate is now around 0.8 per cent or less. With a great many more people on the web a small percentage is still a lot of clicks, but given that potential cop out will your marketing people consider all the alternatives and there are, as this little book will show, many, unless they are told to do so?

Is it any wonder that those companies that are lucky enough to have attracted unthinking investment of hundreds of millions when the hype was at its height are recording higher losses the more they sell. Marketing is vital. I would say that, I have been in the business of marketing for almost 40 years. But marketing must be firmly rooted in a solid strategic plan and strategic planning is the business of the whole business. If you are an executive or entrepreneur that means you. Come to that, marketing is the business of the whole business. Specialists tend to become too specialized. That means they too often lose sight of the big picture as they gaze myopically at their own little area of expertise and past success. The big picture and the leadership that takes an enterprise from where it is to where it wants to be is no less important today than it has been in the past.

*See also:*   Does online advertising work?

What is the most effective way to market a website?

## Why does online business seem to flourish when part of a 'bricks and clicks' enterprise?

*It is not only the technology that makes the big difference*

I do not claim to be the only person promoting the thought that online business demands a thorough understanding of business principles and a 'mature business team' at the top. Peter Keen who has held professorships at both MIT (Massachusetts Institute of Technology) and Harvard has surveyed the global e-business scene in detail and has concluded that, 'The same technology is available to everyone, but in Europe e-business is four years behind the US'.

He makes clear that the key reason why Europe lags behind is because good old-fashioned business skills have not been applied to the good ideas or, until recently, abundant capital. One thing is absolutely beyond question; where the business skills are lacking the capital is unlikely to be forthcoming in future. The business team is as essential as the bright idea or the venture capital injection. Technical experts are unlikely to understand such aspects of a business as financial controls, scalability, branding and pricing. They are unlikely in the extreme, in a specialism where the speed of change is dazzlingly fast to look far enough down the track to think strategically. Keen is not alone in his views. The venture capitalists are showing through their actions that they are no longer prepared to put their money into a bright idea backed only by technology and optimism. Hans Hauser, the doyen of hi-tech development and investment is ensuring at his Entrepreneurial Centre at Cambridge (England) that would-be web billionaires are fully versed in the mysteries of running a business in the real world.

And you would be well advised to ignore the bandwagon leapers who are promoting the concept that technology is what it is all about and that businesses should dump strategic thinking in favour of acting on impulse like eighteenth-century privateers who sailed the high seas hoping that a ship that they might plunder will turn up on the horizon. As Hauser makes clear, at the end of the day a business succeeds or fails by generating and using money. It is far too easy, if you do not have a clear idea of where you are going and how to get there, to throw money at ever-changing technology, mirage-like opportunities and desperation advertising. That is in summary what has happened to those online operations that have lacked sound business sense.

This book is presented therefore in a practical, jargon-free, easy to use, how to do it format that is designed to answer the questions that busy businesspeople ask about doing business online and exploiting technology intelligently. It helps to put the management of the business back where it ought to be, in the hands of the business manager. The 'techies' have every reason to be proud of their skills and to delight in what technology can do. The manager, however, must make the business decision of how that wonderful potential is to be exploited to create and keep worthwhile customers.

*See also*:  Why can't I simply delegate the decisions to the technical and marketing experts that we have in-house?

How should online and offline shopping experiences compare?

## What is the difference between 'e-commerce' and 'e-business'?

E-business refers to all aspects of a business where technology is important. These may include knowledge management, design, manufacturing, research and development, procurement, finance, project planning, human resource planning and the rest.

E-commerce is that part of e-business that relates directly to sales and marketing. So e-commerce is part of the all-encompassing world of e-business. Some would claim that it is the most important part. As an example Peter Drucker has for long argued that only marketing and innovation drive the profits of a business, 'all of the rest are costs'. They are necessary costs of course, but costs nonetheless. If you agree with Drucker you will believe that the balance of this book which provides a comprehensive, non-technical understanding of technology in business with the emphasis firmly on sales and marketing is the correct one for today's business managers.

☞ See also: Is the Internet likely to become a preferred medium for training?

# THE PEOPLE DEVELOPMENT QUESTION

## Is the Internet likely to become a preferred medium for training?

> *The sorry state of education and training means that, in effect you confront panzer divisions with the home guard.*
> (Peter Morgan)

The Internet has yet to prove its value as a medium for training, although the potential is clearly great. As I write, some 70 million people worldwide are using the Internet to access training and IDC (International Data Corporation) projections suggest that the online training business will be worth $24 billion within three years. That does not change the fact, however, that popular as training may be with business and individuals much of what is done in the real world has little or no effect. Before I get excited about the web as a training and development medium I will want to be satisfied that it is able to deliver quantifiable business results. There is a very real difference between training for a specific business purpose and education. Education is worthwhile for its own sake, training is only meaningful when you can do something with it and that 'something' works in the real world, contributing to the achievement of worthwhile business objectives.

*See also*:    What are Lambert's Laws of Training?

How much money is wasted on training?

## What are Lambert's Laws of Training?

### Lambert's Laws of Training

1. All training and development should lead to measurable outcomes that contribute in a preplanned way to the attainment of strategic goals. And those outcomes must be routinely tested in the real world of work.

2. Training and development objectives must define precisely what the participant *will* do after training. Not what they 'will be able' to do. 'Will be able' is a cop-out for trainers who wish to place the responsibility for learning on the trainee rather than shoulder it themselves. Training objectives must specify in sufficient detail the required post-programme behaviours.

3. Those who are to perform together must be trained together.

4. Where work teams cannot be trained as a unit, groups of at least two must train together to ensure the development of a learning club. The club must always be open to new members.

5. All employees must be taught the skills of peer coaching and given the time and encouragement to use them. Peer coaching has been shown to be the key element in the consistent application of training in the workplace over time. Tools, including behavioural checklists must be provided to ensure effective coaching.

6. Managers must be taught to become role models of desired behaviours and professional coaches and supporters of the peer coaches within their teams.

7. Trainers and learners must be fully advised of how the desired programme fits with company strategy and operational tactics. The expectations of post-programme performance must be made clear to all by their supervisor before attendance on a programme.

8.  Trainers must be flexible in meeting the participants' behaviour goals.
9.  Trainers must be committed to their own lifelong learning strategy.
10. Core competencies must be leveraged to develop new products, services, use of resources and above all, ways of doing business.
11. Training must be delivered as part of a lifelong learning strategy 'just in time' to be applied in the workplace.

Contrary to what politicians may claim, you do not necessarily need more training. You need better training. If business experiences high-quality training which develops the skills and knowledge critical to the strategic plan and ensures that people exercise and hone those skills, then, and only then, will business seriously demand and use more training.

In spite of the great promise of the Internet I am by no means convinced that it yet would be able to satisfy the above even in the most skilled and committed hands, but the day will almost certainly come. Meanwhile the value of training offline remains for the most part just as questionable in the eyes of those who take training seriously.

## How much money is wasted on training?

*How much do you currently waste on training?*

Companies are in general great believers in training. It is a pity that their belief does not guarantee an adequate return on their investment. Research, carried out some years ago at the University of Columbia, New York, showed that according to the methods used training delivers between something less than 5 per cent and 13 per cent of what is taught to the workplace to be used by individual employees or teams. To make matters worse, Xerox completed research around the same time that demonstrated that of the learning transferred to the workplace 87 per cent is lost within the first 12 weeks. In short, the average return on the investment made in training lies between 1 and 2 per cent. It is a reasonable question to ask any businessperson whether, and under what circumstances, they are prepared to invest for a return of less than 2 per cent.

**Bruce Joyce's research, Columbia University**

| Training methodology | Transfer to workplace |
|---|---|
| Chalk and talk | < 5% |
| Explanation demonstration | 5%–7% |
| Experiential learning | 11%–13% |
| Real World Practice can deliver up to | 80% |

(but this is only of value if when it is transferred to the workplace it achieves measurable results. There is little gained if you use what you have been taught in the conference room, but it does not work or is not allowed to work in the office or factory.)

Note   Seward and Gers have shown that Real World Practice (supported by effective peer coaching) delivers better than 90 per cent and keeps it at that level for the full extent of a longitudinal study lasting 12 years. (See my *Making Change Pay*, published by Pearson Education.)

## MARKETING ONLINE: SOME PRELIMINARY THOUGHTS AND FACTS

### Is it simply a matter of being first to market with a creative idea?

The examples of first to market making massive personal fortunes (on paper at least) without delivering a cent in profit should not blind you to the fact that thought is an essential business process and thinking 'me too' is hardly thinking at all.

Lastminute.com has made estimated personal paper fortunes of £26 million and £18 million for its co-founders, Brent Hoberman and Martha Lane Fox, meanwhile those who bought its much hyped issue shares have lost, as of today, £71 million and the situation is getting worse. There are times when investors do not seem to be very bright, but they are unlikely to remain stupid enough to throw money down what appears to be a bottomless pit for much longer. Once bitten should ensure that we are at least once, better yet twice, shy. Finance for 'no brain' start-ups will get tighter and will increasingly depend on having, as it did in the old days, a good business idea and a flexible real world strategic and tactical plan to support it.

Of course lastminute.com may survive and even prosper, but it faces a major problem to which no one as yet has the solution. The more successful it is in building its database the more money it spends. The more it spends the greater its losses, The greater its losses, the shorter becomes its potential life cycle. For many of the web *wunderkind* profit will remain a dream for the future while assets are dissipated in misguided marketing. As I stated above, a report published in February 2001 indicates that some dot coms are spending $1.25 of their investors' money on advertising for every $1 that they win in revenues.

*See also:*   Why is market dominance essential?

How do I identify new opportunities? What are the global trends?

## Can companies make solid fortunes out of merely building a customer database?

Companies that believe that business on the web is little more than building a massive database of customers and would-be customers need to be absolutely clear about the cost of such an operation. If you run out of cash before the burgeoning customer file becomes profitable you do not have a thing.

It is not as if the database is of value in its own right. The receivers of more than one American operation are in court at present trying to persuade a judge to let them sell the names that they have collected. Since those names can be collected only by giving an undertaking that they will not be sold to any third party the chances of success are small.

Add the fact that the businesses that carry e-mail (Internet Service Providers – ISPs) are prepared to pull the plug on those who send unsolicited mail (spam) over the Internet and the position looks bad even for those who have yet to run out of cash.

*See also:* What is the difference between 'e-commerce' and 'e-business'?

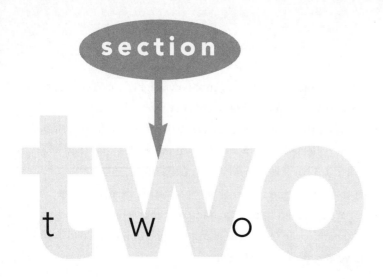

section

t w o

tools and techniques for

success

# PLANNING: THE ANTIDOTE TO PATHETIC PERFORMANCE

## What is the cost of inadequate planning?

As I write, priceline.com have issued a 'revenues warning' (they have yet to deliver a profit) and their stocks have tumbled. The e-conomy is now providing new approaches to value based on old ideas such as profitability and competence.

The demise of boo.com is another clear example of the combination of zero thought with rather too much imagination. Although Anthony Coleman will probably continue to do well out of conference appearances, he may have to change his tack from 'taking a look at the new world of business' and change to 'how we got it wrong'. The lessons may be salutary.

This is not to underestimate the value of creativity, but in cyberspace as in the real world a creative idea must be a sound business idea delivering to customers something that they want, even if they never knew that they wanted it until the idea was born. Business skills and business planning continue to be essential.

*See also*:     Can companies make solid fortunes out of merely building a
customer database?

How should online and offline shopping experiences relate?

Why do those who are first to market fail?

**Mini Case Study**    **Throwing it away**

At the end of 2000 the incubator, CMGI, had announced record losses of
$636.6 million for the third quarter. Many viewed CMGI as the *wunderkind*
of the new economy. Incubators would ensure the success of the dot coms
that they funded by providing business expertise, technical skills and
mentoring in addition to cash.

A great idea, so what went wrong? For a start, too many incubators sprang
into existence. Between 1997 and 2000 the number of incubators rose from
24 to 213 and with an industry growing at that rate business, technical and
any other expertise was a scarce commodity. Many of the dot coms that have
failed so spectacularly had nothing that remotely looked like a business plan,
but in the excitement spawned by hype funding was easy to get and
unfettered optimism enabled people to believe that they could cut corners on
business basics. In the Alice Through the Looking Glass world of dot com
fever, where ignorance and something close to stupidity were valued as long
as they were connected to an online initiative, even those who had driven
their own dot coms into the ground could raise the astronomic sums required
to launch an incubator. *Fortune* magazine followed the fortunes of four newly
minted MBAs who managed this feat and went on to offer their lack of
knowledge, but considerable funding, to others as naive as themselves.

There are, of course experienced and able incubator companies such as
those developed and frugally managed by the major consultancies, but the
combination of business nous and money remains something of a rarity.

*Executive or entrepreneur the lesson should be plain. The Internet is not a royal road to easy prosperity. If you want to make it online, the disciplines of business still apply. It may be a new economy, but that does not mean that the laws of economics have been revoked.*

## Have any of the big names in e-commerce really thought it through or are they all part of an enormous dot com bubble?

**Mini Case Study** **Lateral (and secret) thinking?**

Amazon.com is perhaps a surprising exception to the no-thought entries into the cyber marketplace. They have a plan or two, but they are keeping their cards as close to their chests as constant scrutiny by the world's press allows. It is suggested by some observers that if they were to limit their activities to book and video sales they could be making profits of $10 million a month by now (October 2000). But there is more to their plan than that.

Most experts agree that they have two key and potentially massive value long-term opportunities. They are building the world's biggest database of retail buyers and their buying behaviour, and they stand ever ready to cut out the publisher of popular books. Seth Godin has argued convincingly that once they have built up an immense following of buyers of say, Frederick Forsythe, Stephen King or Danielle Steele novels they will be able to go to the author with the kind of advance that very few can or will refuse, and will commission the next book on an exclusive basis, forcing fans to buy from them alone. Thus they can build their database further and increase their chances of dominance of a key sector of the massive communications market.

If Godin is right this is a high-risk high-return strategy for a company that, as I write, is expanding rapidly beyond its core business and showing every sign that mounting debt will overtake its, admittedly huge, cash reserves (well over $100 million) before they finally achieve a meaningful profit. But whatever the timing of the arrival of profitable business they have a strategy. It may prove to be the wrong strategy, but it is a dominance strategy.

The danger that they face may be their growing desire to use their unparalleled customer database to sell as wide a range of goods and services as possible. People close to Jeff Bezos the CEO (chief executive officer) and founder of Amazon say that he has ambitions to be the 'biggest, best multi-category online retailer in the world'. This could be why he is reported to be talking to WalMart, the world's biggest bricks and mortar retailer in March 2001, with a strategic alliance in mind. This could lead to a dissipation of effort that could prove to be costly. The same sources suggest that Jeff and his team have the 'technical expertise', all that they lack is the 'sales and the money'. Some industry specialists suggest that the book sales part of the business is already highly profitable and that those profits are being applied to funding growth in other areas where huge losses are still being made. In the long run Amazon's strategy will be plain to all, but of one thing we may be sure, they would not have survived so long or borne such losses with apparent equanimity unless they had a strategy firmly in place.

Of course, it is as possible to have the wrong strategy just as it is to have the right one, but without a strategy any firm is doing little more than whistling in the dark and hoping for the best. Do not let the wild-eyed proponents of the idea that the world is moving too fast for strategies these days fool you. If you do not know where you are going you are unlikely to get there – or anywhere else that you would want to be.

See also:   Why is market dominance essential?
            How flexible should an online dominance strategy be?
            What are the key steps towards a market dominance strategy, online or off?

## How should online and offline shopping experiences relate?

### Research PricewaterhouseCoopers, 6 March 2001

Amazon has 'announced' that their strategy is to become the world's biggest online e-tail operation. They may find this research useful.

In summary PwC (PricewaterhouseCoopers) found in a study of 540 online buyers that they bought when: 'the features make an online shopping experience more like on-land shopping'.

According to the researchers what the 'e-tailer' (online retailer) should concentrate on was not the technological bells and whistles, but 'developing full-bodied search engines and offering detailed product and availability information'. Putting this another way, customers want to be able to readily find what they want and to have full information about products and terms of doing business easily accessible. They want convenience.

Seventy-seven per cent of respondents said that they used search facilities and 43 per cent ranked efficient search 'functionality' as the most important online shopping feature.

Forty per cent said that product information was most important and here is where technology can help. In order to make the experience as close as possible to real-world shopping, zoom-in facilities and three-dimensional viewing of products is deemed by PwC to be useful because 44 per cent of customers said that the ability to get right up close increased the probability of making a purchase.

Only 19 per cent of buyers ever used e-tail 'wish lists' (lists of 'recommendations' ostensibly based on the demographics of the customer). These seem like a good idea unless you remember that one publisher created a bestseller by recommending the same book to all prospects quite regardless of their stated interests (a book described by an Irish friend of mine as, 'Starting by making you miserable and then going on to make you feel worse and worse').

The last word from PwC: 'E-tailers must monitor how consumers use current site features and not be afraid to remove those that do not expedite or add value to the shopping process.'

Readers who are seeking to develop their retail business online may wish to compare this report with the Wisconsin study that showed that anything that distracts the buyer from the vital business of gaining information as a basis for the buying decision causes them to leave the site in disgust and seek what they want elsewhere. They may also know of a 60-year study by the University of Columbia, New York, and the Sales Analysis Institute of Chicago that showed that when a buyer is interested in assessing any product or service there is virtually no limit to the amount of relevant, timely information that they will find useful. But the thirst for information follows the level of interest; it does not always promote it. So first make it clear to all customers that your online site is easy to use and there to help them to meet their goals.

☞ *See also*:    What are the business barriers to growth?


## Why does European e-commerce continue to lag behind that of the USA?

There is no simple answer, but a number of factors come together that between them are threatening to ensure that, economic blip in America notwithstanding, the gap is more likely to widen rather than to narrow in the short term.

✓ There is less investment in IT (information technology) generally in Europe than there is in the USA. The latest figures available cover the years between 1997 and 1999, but unless there has been a positive sea change in Europe they make sad reading for those of us who believe that eventually worker productivity and economic growth go hand in hand with IT investment. In the period in question investment in IT within the manufacturing industry in the USA rose by 3.8 per cent a year while in Europe it increased by 2.8 per cent. As far as transportation, utilities and communications are concerned, the US economy saw a 7.7 per cent increase in investment against only 2.5 per cent in Europe. Meanwhile, productivity in the USA has soared by 4 per cent a year and struggled to reach 1.5 per cent in Europe.

✓ In March 2000 Eurobarometer reported that only 27 per cent of European firms had a functioning website with an owned domain name, while 30 per cent had Internet access but no website and 29 per cent had no Internet access. The situation throughout Europe is improving rapidly, and nowhere more so than in the UK where the majority of SMEs (small and medium enterprises) now have some sort of presence online. But the USA, as usual, has failed to oblige by standing still.

✓ Denmark, the Netherlands, Sweden and Finland have led the Internet revolution in Europe, with Britain catching up to a degree recently. Germany and France too are now making rapid progress, but the USA still refuses to stand still.

✓ Internet access, like all telecommunications, is less expensive in the USA than in several parts of Europe.

✓ The attitude to risk in the USA remains more liberal.

Taking Europe as a whole, we will continue to lag behind the USA in several countries for years to come, but we should be ever mindful of what small nations, including Finland and Denmark, have achieved and invest in the future on a country by country basis. We should also recognize that we have in the European Union a bigger total domestic market than the USA and, following the Scandinavian countries and Canada's lead, we should be looking at how best to work together for the good of all. In the mean while executives in our individual businesses, large and small, might consider it wise to look further than the competitor next door when considering investment opportunities.

*See also*: If we are considering breaking into new markets using the Internet, are there any indicators of the countries that we might aim for first?

Where is the growth likely to occur?

# MARKET DOMINANCE: THE ONLY GAME IN TOWN

## Why is market dominance essential?

In a global, customer-centric economy market dominance is the only approach that makes sense. The simple fact is that if you do not make the rules by which others must play, someone else will be making rules that will turn you into a follower expensively trying to catch up. You do not need to be a global player to dominate your market. Simply select with care the niches, sector(s) or segment(s) that you can dominate and use your success there as a springboard for growth when you are ready.

*See also*: To have a dominance strategy do you need to be first to market?

What pitfalls of being first to market should I avoid?

## How flexible should an online dominance strategy be?

**Mini Case Study** **Changing strategy**

The story of Sabre is one of the success stories of the World Wide Web. From the very early days they were pioneers in Internet trading offering inexpensive flights to their many customers. As the American economy prospered so did Sabre, but now (1 March 2001) they are taking timely steps to continue to prosper in a rapidly changing world. After massive growth the American economy is heading for a downturn, and an economic downturn has a major effect on travel, particularly business travel.

Sabre has established a portal for travel agents (eVova Webtop), that is designed to take them beyond the search for cheaper flights and to re-establish customer service as the prime success factor. They firmly believe that the travel industry needs to free itself from the shackles of constantly searching out the best deal to concentrate on value-added services such as expense management and event planning. Since the best deal is in ever-greater demand as the economy experiences a 'blip', that relatively straightforward activity must be made increasingly more simple so that the concentration is on establishing and delivering what the customer wants. Their strategy is that although workings continue to be important on the Internet, service must always come before mechanics. With the anticipation of a decline in the market there is a growing and vital need for the industry to listen carefully to the customer and to respond quickly and effectively to emerging needs, and this new portal is designed to enable enhanced customer responsiveness through readily accessible information and training.

Another pleasant change from mindless, messageless advertising on television is that of expedia.co.uk. They actually tell you why you should use their site and their services.

*In a rapidly changing world the ability to re-tune a robust strategy to exploit new circumstances allied with a commitment to serve the customer's emerging needs and wants remains the key determinant of success, whether online or off.*

*See also*:  What should you do if you are first to market?

What should I do if I cannot be first to market?

## What is a dominance strategy in e-commerce terms?

If the Amazon plan is what it is believed to be (see page 25) and if it works they will be setting the rules by which everyone must play in their chosen sector. That is a dominance strategy. A dominance strategy online or off requires that you establish the rules by which all your competitors need to play if they want to compete. At the same time by developing and sustaining the highest level of customer understanding you fashion your offering to attract and retain the most profitable customers while you rid yourself of those who are more trouble to serve than they are worth.

If amazon.com become the only source of the latest blockbuster novel, more and more of the market is forced to come to them as sole supplier and their power in the market increases. If it fails, a number of people will have lost a vast amount of money. The business and legal ramifications, as recent Microsoft experiences show, are complex in the extreme. But the point is that e-commerce is delivering new forms of opportunity and new types of threat to business.

The lesson is clear. *Think before you go on line. You may be missing a simple ingredient that would make you rich beyond the dreams of avarice or, conversely, what seems a clever idea may turn out to be a wildly expensive pipe dream. Only a cohesive and comprehensive strategy will enable you to judge whether you have a plan or a fantasy.*

## So the key is not just to have an Internet strategy, but to extend that into a market dominance strategy?

I believe so, anything less and you are simply a follower trying to play the game to someone else's rules, but first you must have a cohesive strategy that melds your 'brick-based' business with your 'click-based' business. It is unlikely that you can implement a web strategy that is inconsistent with what you are trying to achieve offline.

Your web strategy cannot be left to chance. Once you have thought it through you can use some of the same tools that work in the so-called 'dirt world' to ensure that you prosper in every part of the business.

You can go for 'bricks' alone or 'clicks' alone, or you can develop a judicious blending of both, but you need to be clear why you are doing what you choose to do.

*See also*:   What are the key steps towards a market dominance strategy, online or off?

## What are the steps towards a market dominance strategy, online or off?

> A **market dominance strategy online** will be the same in terms of its key principles as that which you need in the 'dirt world'.

✓ Paint the 'big picture' in detail – where you want to be and why you want to be there – so that every stakeholder in the business can clearly state 'what's in it for me' and will give 100 per cent all day every day.

✓ Specify those customers who are likely to give you the most profit with the least hassle.

✓ Identify their wants, needs and desires, including their psychological and information needs now and as far as you can into the future.

✓ Target the customers that you really want to serve. Communicate with them and show precisely how you can satisfy their wishes better than any competitor. Provide credible evidence for your claims so that you do not have your customers or prospects think, 'they would say that, wouldn't they'.

✓ Deliver a level of information, support and service that makes it too much trouble and too risky for the customer to consider looking elsewhere.

✓ Keep in touch with your customers and grow the quality of everything that you do with the customer always in mind.

✓ Encourage all your people all the time to find ways to deliver more at lower cost to their customers.

✓ Have your top people constantly in touch with customers. Never leave customer contact as the exclusive domain of the salesperson. Good customers are too important for senior management to neglect them.

✓ Predict and plan to satisfy emerging needs and wants faster and better than competition can.

✓ Invite your customers to be first your friends and then your advocates. Make them want to be customers for life. Research shows that retained customers invariably deliver higher profits than new acquisitions, with the exception of those that will always be a pain in the butt. These you should discard, not least so that they go and bother your competitors.

✓ So identify those customers who are more hassle to serve than they are worth and find ways to be ruthless in getting rid of them while you still appear to care. Reputation and image are important in business so look efficient and effective, but not without a human face even when getting rid of unreasonable customers.

✓ Be frugal with all resources except when it is in the interests of your most worthwhile customers to be generous.

✓ Never be afraid to get into new markets as your customers needs and desires change, but build your capabilities in advance. Never risk upsetting previously delighted customers by putting all your resources into attracting new business.

✓ Ensure that your strategy is flexible and revisit it every day in your mind to make necessary adjustments. The exercise is beneficial.

# INTERNATIONAL TREND ANALYSIS

How do I identify new opportunities? What are the global trends?

*Defence is for times of lack, attack is for times of plenty.*
(Sun Tse)

*… those who render others helpless without fighting are best of all.* (Sun Tse)

Here are the main current international business, social and economic trends to give you some practical ideas for growth and prosperity.

*Global trends have been identified*

These trends include:

- A shift from producing goods to producing, processing and distributing information, particularly information that can be cheaply disseminated using current technology. The Internet is the cheapest publishing medium yet devised.

- The growth of personal care activities, counselling, health and beauty care, tourism, spiritual and psychological needs. Ask yourself, 'can I be a friend and guide to my customers providing desired and timely information above and beyond mere product knowledge without it becoming a distraction from my core business? Or should helping my customers this way become my core business?'

- Global competition in domestic markets – 'glocalization'. The Internet opens up the world to you. It also opens up your world to competitors anywhere. That is why you need to be aware that you must make the rules by which others have to play.

35

- A shift from centralized decision-making toward devolution and greater local autonomy. You may need to consider, market by market, just how local your global strategy must be, but avoid 'going native' for its own sake.

- A shift away from governmental provision of social care towards self-help and 'care in the community, by the community'. Strangely enough this new trend, were it not for its economic motivation and the lack of care that modern life seems to have engendered, would be a return to the 'good old days' of which my parents' generation still mourn the passing.

- A shift from formal hierarchies to informal networks bound by a shared perception of common interests. Actively look for strategic allies and learn from each other's experiences and communications with worthwhile customers. The advent of a new technology does not necessitate the reinvention of the wheel.

- Growing inequality of resources between the northern and southern hemispheres. What if anything can your business offer to the developing world? What, if anything, does your business owe to the developing world? Where does your enlightened self-interest lie?

- Growing inequality between rich and poor in the so-called 'developed' nations. To date e-commerce has concentrated on numbers – as yet they are largely numbers of the more affluent, but in many states of the USA online access is free to all in public libraries. In Europe it is increasingly cheap in Internet cafés. Credit companies appear to be encouraging us to 'spend, spend, spend' whether we can afford it or not. What does this mean for the future of your business? Should you be attracting hordes of potential customers or exploiting an exclusive niche made up of those genuinely able to pay for that 'vital' difference?

- Consumers having a vastly greater range of options to choose from than ever in the past. How precisely will you attract and retain the customers that you want? Online trading works best when the customer so readily finds what they want on your site that they have no reason to look elsewhere.

- The growth of religious fundamentalism. Is this a threat or opportunity for your business?

- The growing interest in getting PCs (personal computers) distributed and used in every corner of the globe, which means that some people will be using a computer online before they make an ordinary telephone call. On my first trip to South Africa I was amused to find that the telephone had become almost the exclusive property of the servants in many households. As banks of public telephones were made available in the townships people called up their friends when they had little or nothing to say, but all the time in the world to say it, and their friends were often working in my friend's houses. What we are given access to we use. Will this affect your business?

Any of these may create new market opportunities or threats. Keep your eyes on developments and always be ready to adjust your strategy to fully exploit worthwhile trends or to defend yourself. The contact that the Internet enables with loyal customers will inform you of those trends that are essential knowledge to you and for your business. It is also a wonderful way to keep abreast of trends as they begin to emerge. You would not be the first, for example to build a global network of individuals who would share information about emergent trends in their part of the world. Faith Popcorn has written three excellent books and has developed an enviable career as a conference speaker and consultant by identifying and predicting trends.

*Webstats – global*

✓ Greenfield online research indicates that 72 per cent of online customers made at least one online purchase during the last quarter of 2000. Even in a slowing global economy the increase in retail online sales was 92 per cent in 2000. At the same time, however, a new report by McKinsey underlines the need to have an effective fulfilment strategy.

✓ ActivMedia Research reports that analysis of the results of B2B firms online show that some patience (and some investment) is required in the early stages of online operation, but firms become increasingly profitable the longer that they stay online. This report melds with one by Forrester that indicates that the savings from being online also grow over time. Estimated average savings of 4 per cent of operating costs this year are expected to double by 2003. Companies cannot sit back, however, and watch the savings accrue. There must be a concerted effort to maximize savings while giving better service to the customer. That is why strategic planning allied to flexible tactical action is, and always will be, essential online or off.

✓ Research by the *Guardian* newspaper (March 2001) indicates that about half the adults in Britain now enjoy access to the Internet. This has grown from less than a third of adults in 1999.

✓ Not surprisingly the rich are better represented than the poor online, with 73 per cent of earners being online as opposed to 21 per cent of the unemployed.

✓ The gender gap is closing, with women users now only ten points behind males and the number of women with online access in Great Britain has risen from 1 288 000 to 4 656 000.

✓ Ancient types like me are increasingly using the web, with the so-called 'silver surfers' now numbering 2 235 000 in the UK.

The USA and the Scandinavian countries still are ahead of the game, with Germany, France and the rest of the EU steadily catching up.

☞ *See also:*   How can we optimize the return on our web presence investment?

What do (or should) top consultants ask clients to think about?

If we are considering breaking into new markets using the Internet, are there any indicators of which countries we should aim for first?

# THE PROFITS AND PERILS OF BEING FIRST TO MARKET

To have a dominance strategy do you need to be first to market?

*Those who are first on the battlefield are at ease.* (Sun Tse)

*Dominance really is the only game in town*

In a recent survey of major businesses less than 30 per cent could take and respond to an order placed via their wildly expensive websites. Only 25 per cent are even thinking about using B2B to improve their procurement. Around 80 per cent see e-commerce as a minor add-on to their business at best. Mike Mazarr asks an interesting question: 'How many of these folks will still be around a decade from now?'

If e-commerce really is the point of departure for a new economic structure and if it is being so badly used at present, it is open season for creative and early market dominance at minimal cost. What are you doing about the opportunity?

*Number one in the marketplace does not have to mean first to market*

There are many advantages to being first into the market.

- You become recognized as the supplier of the product or service that you were first to develop. There was clear marketing value in all vacuum cleaners being called 'Hoovers' or computers being spoken and sung of as 'IBM brains'.

- You have an opportunity to make it so difficult and expensive for competitors to enter the market that they lose money and withdraw.

- You have a strong possibility of being able to charge premium prices and make exemplary returns before competition finds its feet. Consider the pharmaceutical industry and the advantages of patent protection that it has enjoyed, but that may be weakened by the recent cessation of price controls.

*See also:*    The whole of this section.

## Why do those who are first to market fail?

So why do the innovators so seldom come out on top in the long run? If entering a marketplace shouting 'me too' does not work, why do companies who enter late with 'me too' products frequently overtake those who once had the market to themselves?

Some of the reasons include:

- First to market is often product rather than service driven. For as long as they remain the only game in town, first to market will attract all who want, and can afford, their offering, but when a customer-driven alternative emerges the effect can be swift, dramatic and sometimes fatal.

- Early success leads to complacency, the belief that 'we have the formula for success – we cannot fail'. In the immortal words of Bob Mager, 'nothing fails like success'.

- Emergent customer desires are often ignored on the basis of 'we are number one, we know better than the customer what the customer really wants'. Consider how British banks treat their customers or how Bedford Trucks went from being number one to oblivion.

**Mini Case Study** **Bedford Trucks**

Bedford Trucks, a British subsidiary of General Motors was the world number one manufacturer of trucks and buses. When the European trucking industry changed so that journeys became transcontinental, the need for a different kind of truck emerged. Bedford thought that they had the answer. American trucks are, almost by definition, transcontinental, so why not use the American power train? The reason why using the power train was inappropriate was complicated, but in very simple terms it came down to the need that the customer had for fuel economy. In America fuel was, and is, cheap, that is not the case on the European continent. The fuel consumption figures for the new vehicles were such that the trucking industry would not buy this truck at any price. Sadly, Bedford thought that they knew better than the customer and persisted, throwing advertising dollars at the problem. (I hope this offers a parallel with some online endeavours that rings warning bells to the alert businessperson.) A once great company paid the ultimate price. Many do, that is why the average life of a mature company is now measured in years rather than decades.

## What pitfalls of being first to market should I avoid?

**Checklist** **The 'first to market' pitfalls**

✓ If the organization is designed around the product it cannot be responsive to changing customer demands even if it wishes to serve its customers well.

✓ There is pressure to recoup development costs as quickly as possible, which means that all customers are welcome – the good, the bad and the ugly – and that leads to retaining customers who are simply more trouble than they are worth.

✓ Revenues, rather than profits become the key measure of performance – another reason why bad customers are never jettisoned. Top companies who thrive and prosper consistently over many years are ruthless in weeding out the unwanted customer and equally diligent in keeping the worthwhile customer for life.

✓ Expenditure on research and development is high and is focused on what can technically be done rather than what will sell.

## Mini Case Study Matsushita

Some years ago Matsushita developed a small-screen television to entertain 'homemakers' (are we being politically correct?), while they were doing the jobs in the kitchen which can reasonably be referred to as 'drudgery' (is 'drudgery' a politically correct word? Or are we now in the business of pretending that peeling spuds is somehow inspiring?).

The small, portable television that emerged, very late from R & D (research and development) was both beautiful and state of the art. It had every conceivable bell and whistle. It also had a price tag more than double that which market research had shown to be the expectation of the market and it came out of the R & D department too late to be in the marketplace for the peak selling season.

Research and development engineers hate to let products go if they do not carry all the state-of-the-art refinements that can be built in, and market opportunities are lost.

The pharmaceutical industry was, for many years, the worst example of this tendency. Research chemists (with PhDs and an abiding belief in scientific values) were reluctant to pass products to chemical engineers (with

MScs and considerable scientific training). These, in turn were not happy to turn things over to production engineers (master's degrees in engineering), who hated to pass their late delivery baby to production (some of whom, God help us, had no degrees at all).

## What should you do if you are first to market?

- Have a strategic plan in place that will enable you to develop and sustain strategic dominance through the development of loyal customers into enthusiastic advocates.

- Remain genuinely customer centred at all times. That means designing or redesigning the organization to be able consistently to communicate and respond to customers quickly and effectively. Today's technology provides the tools.

- Be merciless in getting rid of customers who are more trouble than they are worth. Or if you must keep them for the sake of appearances, at least find a way to charge them all that it costs to keep them happy.

- Require your salespeople to bring in highly profitable new customers. Do not let them swan around 'servicing' the ones you already have and acting as order takers. Too many salespeople 'pop in for a chat' and honestly believe that they are 'looking after' their customers. I have news for them. I can assure them that even the customers regard them as a pain in the fundament and are simply too polite to mention it.

- Assess your people's training needs and use the assessment as a training opportunity in its own right. Break down the job into:
    Job purpose – what company objective do the outcomes of this job satisfy?
    Key accomplishments – what exactly must be done by any and all jobholders to achieve the job purpose?
    Standards of performance – how well do the key accomplishments need to be performed to satisfy the job purpose?

Competencies – how can we profitably apply existing competencies to better exploit the best market opportunities today? What competencies do we need to build to exploit the most exciting and profitable business opportunities of the future?

*Make your training work. There is solid incontrovertible evidence that the transfer of learning to the workplace can be raised from a miserable 2 per cent, to better than 90 per cent through peer coaching and management support.*

● Keep a tight rein on R & D costs. Research and development should be market and strategy driven. To be otherwise means that the horse is following the cart.

● Be frugal with expenditure. Research by Arie de Geus of Harvard shows that long-lived companies, those that prosper for centuries rather than a handful of years, are flexible, learning communities that are careful to always have the money available to pursue market opportunities as they arise.

● Never let your people, at any level, believe that they have the formula for success. The world is changing too rapidly for any formula to work for long.

● Involve everyone in the business in the marketing and strategic process.

● Do nothing in a business unless:
    There is a compelling strategic or tactical reason for doing it.
    It will pay for itself in a reasonable time.
    It can be explained in clear, easy to understand and inspirational words to those who must make it work.

## What should I do if I cannot be first to market?

Do all of the above and:

● Develop a strategic plan that will enable you to dominate a carefully chosen niche, sector, segment or global market. Make online business a part of your strategy, but avoid letting e-commerce drive the strategy for its own sake.

- Identify with precision the aspirations as well as current needs of the most desirable customers in that market.

- Compare your capability to deliver those aspirations with that of your competitors.

- Build on your strengths in relation to market needs and desires.

- Identify those key, profitable customers who you can capture from competition by exploiting your strengths and competencies, and leveraging competition's weaknesses.

- Seek and gain a mandate from your customers to consistently supply them with information, entertainment and opportunities that are personal, expected, relevant and useful.

- Use your competencies to rapidly respond to customer needs, wants and desires.

- Build effective strategic alliances to acquire new, high-quality customers.

- Understand technology to the degree that you must, that is, to the level where you can use it to make money and secure the ongoing prosperity of the business in an increasingly volatile marketplace.

- Serve all your worthwhile customers with such responsiveness to their needs that you establish the rules for doing business in your chosen markets.

First to market or 'Johnny come lately' this is what a truly strategic approach to e-commerce gives you the power to do at lowest possible cost.

*See also:*  To have a dominance strategy do you need to be first to market?
All this section.

## So it's a simple case of 'planning rules' – OK?

Planning always is vital in business. Tactical planning is a matter of doing the right things now and strategic planning is ensuring that you are still doing the right things ten years or more down the track. The importance of having the right plan is that it will give you a much better than fighting chance of still being around ten years later.

Most businesses that founder do so because they lose focus and squander scarce resources where they will do no good, because the plan was insufficiently robust and too inflexible. Arie de Geus has made the point clearly in his study of long-lived companies that those that are frugal with resources until they spend wisely in strict accordance with their flexible strategic plan survive and prosper while others emerge briefly only to go 'belly up' after a brief blaze of glory – a blaze of glory that is becoming briefer by the day.

E-commerce is simply another part of the business. It is about marketing and sales, not technology and marketing and sales must be planned or people will degenerate into 'popping in for a chat'.

# THE TOOLS IN DETAIL

## What are the planning tools?

E-commerce is a business enterprise. The normal planning tools are essential, but in this case there is more. Starting with the normal you need to believe that your business can be world class. If you have a single loyal customer you are doing something right. By leveraging your strengths you can set the rules by which others have to play and, when they play by your rules, you win and go on winning. A General Electric does it on a grand scale. Many small enterprises do it one small step at a time. Here is how it is done.

- ✓ First and foremost ensure that the decision makers in your firm share a burning desire to be the very best in the business.

- ✓ Build a clear vision of exactly where you want to be in six months, a year, three years, ten years hence. A vision so compelling, so inspirational, that it will get every one of your people to the barricades when needed.

- ✓ Communicate that vision until everyone has a shared view of a future that they lust after. Have them tell you what is in it for them and challenge them to go out and get it.

- ✓ Find out what would attract the best people in the business to you and go and do it.

- ✓ Regard your vision as achieved and always 'walk the talk' of success in front of employees, customers, suppliers and other stakeholders. (Current research into leadership suggests that the great leaders first create a mythology around themselves and then make it reality by living it. That is the power of 'walking the talk'. Just as 'imagined evils soon become realities' carefully thought through triumphs do no less.)

- ✓ Be sure that you know your customers' real needs. Do not think in terms of products or services, but think of the customer satisfactions that you deliver. Specify where you beat competition and build on your advantage. Work to leverage your strengths before worrying about your weaknesses.

- ✓ Identify those segments or niches where you are, or can be, the best.

- ✓ Build a strategic plan and use benchmarking of the best in any industry not to play 'catch-up', but in order to leapfrog the competition.

- ✓ Analyze all the customers who are in your market and establish who are worth dealing with, and who are more trouble than they are worth.

- ✓ Politely, pleasantly, but very firmly dump those customers who give you hassle rather than profit. Let your competitors steal them. Let the nuisance customer weaken your competitor, not you.

✓ Analyze your competitors, by name, in a head-to-head comparison between your offering and theirs strictly in terms of how well you each satisfy the most important customer wants. Remember in the days of sexual equality and plenty that what used to be MAN (Money, Authority and Need) is now WOMAN (Wants Override Money Authority and Need).

✓ Identify those of the competitions' customers that you would give your eye teeth to serve and focus your sales effort on them using your relevant strengths to win their business.

✓ Commit yourself totally to doing everything better, faster and cheaper every day. Find the best sources of information and advice and implement what you find.

✓ Set standards of real customer service that makes the competition shake with fear.

✓ Turn your best customers into advocates for your business. Have a systematic approach to referrals. Make sure that your best customers know how much you appreciate it when they return the favour of state-of-the-art service, but never pay for what they give willingly. Payment demeans the gift. A simple 'thank you' is more effective than a rich gift.

✓ Treat your worthwhile customers as if they were your only hope of survival in an unforgiving world.

✓ And, in Winston Churchill's words: 'Never, never, never give in.'

I have spent the last few years helping small companies and huge corporations all over the world to do the above. They have two things in common: that burning ambition that I wrote about above and they take pleasure in 'kicking ass' (as my friends in the USA express it).

## What is the difference between market planning and strategic planning?

*Strategic marketing*

# *All strategic planning is market planning.*

If Drucker is right when he claims that only marketing and innovation takes a firm from where it is to where it wants to go, then planning the medium- to long-term future of the business is essential – if the business is to have a future! Innovation is part of the marketing strategy. A firm innovates to get new services and products to the marketplace, to get them there quicker and to get them there cheaper.

The purpose of strategic planning is to create a medium- to long-term set of actions that will ensure that the firm grows in terms of quality, productivity and profits. To do this effectively the focus may or may not be on growing in the sense of physical size, product range or sales. It is perfectly possible to grow smaller and richer at the same time by serving a carefully 'culled' group of the most worthwhile customers with the best imaginable products and services in your field.

The key difference between 'normal' strategic planning and market dominance planning is that dominance planning is aimed specifically at weakening competition by targeting their most profitable customers while the dominant company 'fires' their own least profitable to be served by a weakening competition. This creates a situation in which competition is always forced to play 'catch-up' at great expense and eventually has little alternative other than to lose money or withdraw. Some of the more profligate examples in e-commerce demonstrate just how ready some firms are to lose money – but few can lose money for long. Profit is a prerequisite of business survival. Profit is a little like Bill Shankly's much quoted description of football as 'not a matter of life and death, it's more important than that'. When it comes to dominance planning another thought of Shankly's might be appropriate: 'Lacking an education I was forced to use my brains.'

## What is the detail of the planning process?

*The process*

The ideal future of the company is defined in detail. Questions discussed and answered include:

- How 'big' will we be in terms of revenues, products, profits, numbers employed, distribution methods, productivity and quality?
- Who will be our customers?
- Who will be our team?
- What will outsiders say about our company?

The here and now is analyzed. Traditionally this has been through the medium of a SWOT analysis (Strengths, Weaknesses, Opportunities and Threats). Recent research shows that SWOT is ineffective for procedural and psychological reasons. My clients prefer to consider:

*Concerns*: the problems that specifically get in the way of attracting the right customer are defined and solutions are sought. Where possible the solutions are developed by those people who have most to gain from solving the problem. Only concerns that are a barrier to customer attraction and retention are significant enough to be resolved. The main thrust of effort must be on exploiting strengths. War stories, grievances and trifling niggles are beneath the notice of real business people at any level.

*Opportunities*: the current and foreseeable business environment is scanned to identify specific market opportunities that will occur both right now and up to 15 years into the future. This long planning horizon makes necessary a high degree of flexibility. (Arie de Geus' [Harvard] research into 'survivors' shows four essential attributes:

- a genuine learning organization
- long-term strategic planning
- flexibility in execution
- frugality with essential resources.)

If you intend to use the advantages of e-commerce to expand your business internationally or even if your ambitions are limited to domestic growth you should think seriously about global business trends, and for each market consider the political, social, economic, technological and legal environment in addition to making a careful appraisal of the capabilities of competition in any market.

Your decisions must be clear to all:

- Which opportunities will we exploit now?
- Which will we exploit in the future and what steps do we start today in order to be in a position to make the most of them?
- Which do we not expect to exploit at all – why?

*Strengths*: many years of research and experience proves that leveraging strengths is far more productive of profit than is curing weaknesses. The strengths that the firm has or can easily build or acquire are related directly to the opportunities in the business environment.

- Think in terms of the strengths, competencies, skills, behaviours and knowledge that you have and that will enable you to take advantage of today's most profitable market opportunities.
- Consider what new strengths you need to build or acquire to take full advantage of today's best opportunities and plan to realize them.

- Assess the most promising opportunities of the future and identify how current strengths will enable you to exploit them.

- Identify what strengths you will need to build for most profitable future success and decide how you will build them.

- Consider the strengths, competencies, behaviours, skills and knowledge that you need to build in order to dominate the most profitable markets of the future and start to develop them today in order to establish the rules by which others have to play.

*Threats*: are categorized as

avoidable – those that we can avoid if we take timely steps now;

contingent – those that we cannot take immediate measures to prevent, but we can identify reliable indicators of coming danger and can roll out a plan when necessary. The plan includes tactics to avoid the avoidable and contingency plans based on warning signs to ensure that the business is not taken by surprise.

The final steps of the Here and Now analysis are:

*Customer analysis*: a clear identification of what the most profitable customers want from the firm in order of relative importance to customers. Avoid falling into the trap of thinking that customers will want what you think that they ought to want. When dealing with other people the greatest danger is to think; 'You really oughta want ... '

*Comparative analysis*: a comparison between the firm and its key competitors (by name) to test how well the firm measures up in meeting customer wants. Competitive advantages of the company are clearly identified, communicated and used by the sales and marketing team to target highly desirable, highly profitable customers.

*Competitive analysis*: the key competitors' best customers are analyzed and a plan is developed to build and use competitive advantages, key strengths and competencies to win conquest business while ensuring that the firm's own best customers are retained.

### Back to the future

Any company which wishes to mobilize all its people to work together for success needs a clear vision. The vision is a short, but inspirational statement of where we are going. Tom Peters says it must get everyone to the barricades when the need arises or it is meaningless.

The mission which develops from the vision, is more detailed, but equally inspirational. It tells all stakeholders (employees, customers, shareholders, suppliers, customers and the local community):

- what customer wants we exist to satisfy;
- what makes us different (and better) than competition;
- why the customer should come to us first – and stay with us;
- what challenges we welcome so that we will grow in skill, knowledge, customer sensitivity and productivity, etc.;
- what we believe in (the key values we all share);
- how stakeholders are treated by all our people all the time;
- the basis on which decisions are made so that all our people can use their initiative in the interests of the customer and the firm.

If a plan is to be flexible a number of alternative strategies must be recognized. From those available we choose and define the best strategy.

The chosen strategy dictates a full range of strategic and tactical objectives which are:

- Specific and superior: they say exactly what we will do and we ensure that what we will achieve is better than the best of the opposition.

- Measurable and meaningful: select objectives that make a significant contribution to achieving the Mission and Vision and place us well ahead of our competition so that they are forced to try to catch up.

- Attainable and agreed: they must not be 'pie in the sky' wishful thinking and those who will achieve them must accept and be excited by the challenge of attaining them.

- Realistic and radical: they must be attainable with the resources that we have or can build or acquire and they should be built on thinking the business anew to create the ideal.

- Timed and transformational: we must be able to provide a basis for progress to be checked and that progress should play a part in building a unique, compelling, customer centric business.

Finally, a detailed step-by-step tactical plan ('an ounce of action is worth a ton of theory') is developed with clear authority and responsibility built in, which will take us from where we are to where we want to be in the time frame of the strategy.

*Notes*

1. This is a comprehensive overview of the marketing strategy process, not a fully detailed game plan.

2. We have all the essential tools and techniques at our disposal in many publications including my own *Key Management Solutions* (Pitman/Financial Times).

3. All the tools have been tested in the field with a wide range of companies in almost all cultures. They always work if properly used.

Strategic marketing may seem a little esoteric, but as I tell my clients: 'If you have so much as one good customer, someone, somewhere is plotting to take that customer from you. You had better plan to beat them to the punch.'

### Some important strategic marketing terms

Cash cow: a mature product/service that brings in excellent revenues with minimum investment.

Star: a relatively new product/service that brings in large revenues, but is subject to heavy promotion and investment.

Question mark: a new product or service that has yet to recoup its investment in the marketplace and is at present regarded as 'promising' although not without risk.

Dog: a product or service that is incapable of bringing in high revenues no matter how well promoted. Many of the 200 e-commerce operations that folded in the last few months had 'dogs' for products and no strategy better than 'spend, spend, spend' on pointless promotion.

Product life cycle: the process by which a cash cow eventually becomes a dog.

Marketing definition: an *integrated* (everyone must be involved) activity to *create*, *identify* and *satisfy* customer wants *at a profit*.

Note: Marketing involves the whole business – it is the whole business. It creates wants as well as identifying them. It must be a profitable operation and an investment in success. Everything that you do that fails to bring customers beating a path to your door is cost.

Please take a look at the Glossary when you have a moment for some further definitions and thought starters.

## What is the key difference between tactics and strategy?

A tactical plan ensures that you are doing the right things today. A strategic plan ensures that you will still be doing the right things ten years from today.

## What are the elements of a tactical marketing plan?

*The bits and pieces of tactical marketing*

- Market testing – market testing is to be preferred to market research where it is practical to offer a new or improved product or service to the market and see if it is snapped up. By placing your offering before real customers at minimal cost you get a clear response – they buy or they do not buy. If they buy, you know that the market welcomes your offering and you make a little money from day one.

- Market research – market research is only reliable when the right questions are asked of the right people. Unless you have internal access to considerable skill in this area it is one that is usually best left to qualified professionals.

- Direct selling – all aspects of selling should be planned, the message as much as the media. Be sure that your sales team is conveying the right message to the customers with the greatest profit potential and that salespeople are consistently building the reputation and image of the business in the eyes of the customer. Only if they do this can you expect customers to grow in confidence to where they become the most effective salespeople for the company. If your website is your online salesperson it must be easy to use and it must be an exemplar of the quality to which you are committed.

- Direct mail – If you write your own direct mail pieces I suggest that you invest in a book by a leading expert such as Drayton Bird or refer to the appropriate section in my *e-Market Dominance* (McGraw-Hill, 2001).

- Advertising – make it an objective to find low-cost, no-cost alternatives to advertising and never throw money at advertising if there is no market for what you offer. As many a dot com has belatedly discovered, advertising to people who simply are not interested does not cut it any more, no matter how clever the ads may be.

- Point-of sale merchandising – Where, how and at what height you display your offering is a highly skilled business, as is package design.

- Merchandising – people love a bargain. Some years ago some coupons were misprinted so that they offered 'nothing off' the price of the goods. Sales rocketed nonetheless. Carefully planned and executed merchandising can be powerful, but be careful not to make offers to new buyers that upset your existing loyal customers or to pre-buy business that you would have enjoyed anyway.

- Public, employee and press relations – nothing is such an apparently honest broker as well-written 'free ink'. But obey the rules:
  Do not badger the editor to publish your deathless prose.
  Write news not advertising puff.
  Be sure that the date of release of information is clear.
  Supply good quality pictures where you can.
  Mark the back of any picture clearly to ensure that the busy journalist knows what photograph goes with what piece.
  Clearly indicate a contact number from which more information can be obtained and, having done so, make sure that someone knowledgeable and capable is there to respond to calls.

- Budget and cash flow projections – avoid optimistic cash flow projections. More companies go belly up from the late arrival of cash than from lack of profit.

- Manufacturing mix and volumes – customers, not convenience should dictate build schedules.

- Total quality programmes – remember that what cannot be measured is difficult to manage. If you want to be world class measure and improve constantly, but do not improve beyond the needs, desires or expectations of your customers without good reason for doing so.

- Distribution and fulfilment – many online failures result from angry customers who feel, and are, cheated by poor fulfilment of their orders. Get your infrastructure right from the start or your reputation will be in ashes.

- Customer satisfaction and customer relationship programmes – try testing your levels of customer satisfaction not through surveys, but by asking your best customers to find you more customers like them.

- Feedback, evaluation, review and necessary change – plans must be robust and flexible, build your feedback system into the plan from the word 'go'.

Starting on page 64 is an opportunity to look at where you start from and where you are going in some detail. The importance of strategic and tactical planning for online success cannot be overemphasized. No one can plan and implement your success but you. We can only provide the background information and the tools. (For a full strategic and tactical toolkit, online or off please take a look at my *Key Management Solutions* published by Pearson Education under the Pitman/Financial Times imprint.)

## How do we avoid losing money online?

In April 2000 the value of the Nasdaq Composite stood at a proud 5000 points and there was a growing happy band of new Internet millionaires. By March 2001 the value of dot coms overall had tumbled to less than half of that which they enjoyed a few months before. Some had joined a new club. The 'Ninety Per Cent' Club is restricted for membership to those disasters that have lost 90 per cent of their launch valuation. A simple checklist shows what went wrong and could so easily have been avoided.

✓ Watch your gross margins – losing money on every transaction is a flawed business strategy to say the least.

✓ Do not overspend on customer acquisition – advertising is expensive, use it frugally and be sure that it includes the simple thought of why people should come to you. Use the search engines and PR (public relations) intelligently.

✓ Plan your site for high conversion rates – you must ensure that people come to your site, stay to buy and keep coming back. Many online businesses suffer because they lose money on the first sale and fail to attract profitable repeat business. Only by giving superior service can you hope to exploit the lifetime value of the customer.

✓ Offer a superior value proposition – people still need a good reason to buy online anything that they can get elsewhere. Too many dot coms have assumed wrongly that people will buy online just for the novelty. Even if they were right about the initial sale, where is the novelty when making repeat purchases?

✓ Make sure that your site is customer friendly – people have little time to waste in navigating an all-singing all-dancing plethora of irrelevance. If the serious buyer cannot find what they want quickly they will leave in droves. Above all make it easy to buy online.

✓ Ensure that your order fulfilment system works – find creative ways to keep costs down and quality up when it comes to getting the goods to the customer. Where possible deliver online for maximum profit.

*See also*:   The BIG question: why have so many dot coms failed so dramatically?

## WE NEED MONEY TO SUCCEED

### How does a new e-commerce initiative raise capital?

Thanks in part at least to the gross stupidity of some dot com initiatives and the questionable sense of those who threw money at them, raising investment capital for a pure online activity is now tough and getting tougher by the day. A report issued in May 2001 suggests that about 80 000 people have lost millionaire status in the past year. My heart bleeds for them a little less than it does for the homeless or hungry. They took a risk that has yet to pay off. But the practical outcome is that in the short term at least it is difficult to come by a capital injection for any online enterprise and Warren Buffet is suddenly popular again. The following notes are the minimum that ought to be borne most carefully in mind when looking for investment.

*Key points summary*

✓ It is inappropriate to use consultants if the need is for less than £3 million.

✓ Alternatives to venture capitalists such as Venture Capital Report (www.vcr.co.uk) should be explored. (Currently the Venture Capital Report charges £495 to put a professional summary of the business plan on line and distribute it to their subscribers in the paper newsletter.) In the USA and globally, companies should consider online investors including Yazam (www.yazam.com) who will, once their ownership discussions are sorted, provide seed capital from their own resources while they put together a suitable group of independent angels to provide more comprehensive funding.

✓ Consultants such as Regent of Windsor (UK) will provide advice and training to companies seeking investment, but their preferred client is looking for sums in excess of £3 million ($5 million). Typical charges of the industry are around 5 per cent of capital raised plus 2 per cent of the equity.

✓ Venture Capital Report currently charges the £495 for summarizing the plan and 4–5 per cent of capital raised.

✓ There are also various government and EU (European Union) schemes for hi-tech and other businesses that have difficulty raising capital by other means. (Examples: the Phoenix Fund, UK; the Small Business Funding Initiative, The Small Business Administration, USA, as well as the occasional EU schemes.)

✓ Average time to find funding is between four and six months, and is generally nearer to six. So, plan for it to take six months.

✓ Never underestimate your funding requirement. If you believe that you need funding for the whole of year one before you expect positive cash flow, bear in mind that if your timing proves to be wrong you will need a probable six months to attract any top-up investment to see you through.

✓ The amount sought should be enough to cover fully 18 months of operation even if profitability could/will be achieved earlier. Always assume the worst scenario in terms of profit and build in six months' breathing space in which additional investment can be sought should things take longer than expected.

✓ The business plan narrative needs to clearly state how the money is to be used.

✓ Pricing policy should be clear and backed by research/market testing where possible.

✓ The business plan should indicate a robust flexible marketing strategy and should specify how barriers to entry, including initial customer reluctance or inertia, have been overcome.

✓ Intention to move towards an IPO should be indicated if such a move is planned.

✓ If an IPO is planned, the narrative should indicate a market value to assets ratio that is high for any 'knowledge company'.

✓ The directors should be shown to be committed 100 per cent to the business. (For example, it is wise to show that if Tom Lambert is listed as a director he is putting his consultancy business on hold as well as stressing his global reputation.)

✓ The listing of directors should include a credible finance director who can be relied on to protect the investor's money.

✓ The business plan should show the company as being independent of any other and should not give the impression that revenues or profits can be moved out of A into B within a group of companies.

✓ A new dot com should show a clear pathway to profit within two years.

✓ Venture capitalists and incubator funders are unlikely to fund any Internet activity that cannot deliver a profit within two years.

✓ A robust and credible real-world strategy is essential to success. The strategy should be concisely but clearly summarized as part of the business plan narrative.

✓ Demonstrate in the business plan narrative that you know your market and your competition in detail, and that you have a clear view of how you will exploit that knowledge.

Newspapers and other parts of the media have been shedding tears, crocodile or otherwise, over the woes of investors during the last year (2000) and certainly those who invested solely in dot coms have fared badly in the short term. The Nasdaq has fallen by 25.6 per cent overall and many investors must be licking their wounds and hoping for an upturn as forecast by most pundits during the second half of this year. To add a little drama, the investment and incubator company CMGI is reported today to have lost no less than $2.6 billion during the year. But things are not always as bad as they are painted.

Although the small and institutional investor may have done badly in respect of dot coms, the old-fashioned venture capitalists are keeping their heads above water, albeit with some difficulty at times. They saw reducing returns during last year compared to the heady days of 'silly' IPOs, but came out of it with a 37.6 per cent return on investment which many businesspeople would consider healthy enough were it not for the relatively high risk factor. The venture capital firms will continue to invest. That is what they do, but they will increasingly be looking for experienced and proven management, probably either a mixed 'bricks and clicks' strategy or for firms that, rather than being pure dot coms, offer products or services that keep dot coms from going to the bad, and they will certainly want to see a robust and flexible business plan with strong financial controls. If you have all of the above the money is still out there. It is simply more difficult to get – thank goodness.

There have been recent reports that some private investors and venture capital companies have invented a new 'game' at the expense of cash strapped dot coms. Called 'cramming down', the idea is simple. The investors look for desperate companies and put in a very small amount of money for a considerable share of the equity. Having effectively reduced the market value of the company without giving any real financial foundation for success they are able to acquire the remainder of the equity at a rock bottom price and either fire the management to start again or retain the one-time owners as employees in what was once their own company. The more reputable venture capitalists look with scorn on such manoeuvres. They believe that:

✓ Either a firm has a chance of success or it does not.

✓ If it can succeed within a reasonable time then a normal capital injection is justified.

✓ If it is certain to fail it is better to leave bad enough alone.

If you have a serious cash problem and objectives are not being achieved, it may seem like a gift from heaven that someone, however niggardly, is prepared to give you a little cash and a little breathing space, but always bear in mind the effect that transferring a lot of equity for a little cash may have. If going belly up is a certainty there is little point in delaying the inevitable. If you can make it work you should be able to demonstrate the probability of success through a realistic business plan and persuade a reputable venture capital company to support you until revenues and profits roll in.

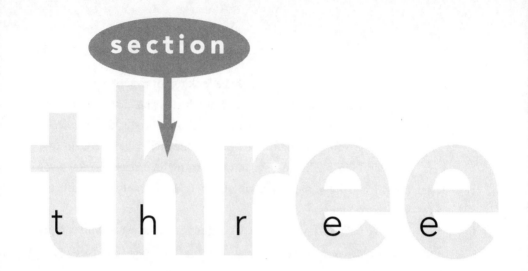

section

three

three

questions that only YOU can (and must) answer to optimize results

This section is vital to building and sustaining an e-market dominance strategy. The strategic thinker will want to revisit it again and again in order to ensure that the strategy continues to evolve and that the firm stays ahead of the game.

## How can we optimize the return on our web presence investment?

In order to optimize the return on your investment in developing and maintaining a web presence you must be ruthless. You need consistently to be ready to analyze and, where necessary, change your ideas in the light of customer experience and competitor activity. To retain focus in a volatile business environment you must approach your best ideas from the perspective of the customer all the time, but only after being absolutely clear as to what you intend to achieve through your online activities.

Being online offers many more opportunities than most people realize. The tools that follow will help you to begin the process of thinking about strategic and tactical matters. It is a process that never ends. You should be careful never to become, in Howard Shenson's phrase 'fat, dumb and happy'. Part of the new economy is the acceleration of the business cycle. Opportunity and crisis each now hit you more quickly than ever before. Eternal vigilance now really makes the difference between prosperity or disaster.

## What are the key things that we need to consider concerning our web-based business?

*E-business corporate analysis*

> *The Internet is not about technology. It is about sales and marketing. Those who insist otherwise really piss me off.*
> *(Marcus Bicknell, Chairman and owner of more than 60 web businesses, including Alta Vista)*

The following brief, but detailed, survey is designed to enable you to take a fresh look at your e-business strategy as you consider the degree to which you have established and are meeting optimal objectives for your firm. The survey is not exhaustive, but it is sufficiently comprehensive to enable at least one or two 'eureka!' thought breakthroughs for most businesses and professional practices.

What are the key strategic or tactical benefits that you are seeking from your e-business initiative? Why have you chosen to go to the expense and trouble of having a website? Please tick each item that you are seeking from an online presence and give the others some thought. Should you widen your thinking about what the Internet might deliver for you? Have you set your sights on the right outcomes for today and, more importantly, tomorrow?

Sale of online advertising      ___

Building brands – existing products/services      ___

Opt-in e-mail marketing ____

Customer/market information ____

Access to world markets ____

Affinity (host/beneficiary) marketing ____

Direct B2B sales ____

Direct B2C sales ____

Global presence/visibility ____

Knowledge-sharing ____

Online training and development ____

Sale of lists to e-mailers ____

Cost reductions ____

New advertising channel ____

Attracting new customers ____

Improved buying terms ____

Recruitment and retention of staff ____

Shorten supply chain (reduce intermediaries) ____

Personalized customer service ____

Reduced time-to-market ____

24x7 availability to customers ____

Global business platform ____

Identify new suppliers ____

Enhanced responsiveness to market ____

Online distribution ____

Faster decision-making ____

Low-cost entry into new markets ____

To what degree have you been successful in enjoying the benefits of your e-business strategy? How well is it working for you? Has the web delivered what you planned for? Has it delivered the unexpected? Do you need to revisit your strategy and beef it up a little – or a lot? Please circle the appropriate number using the following guidelines:

0 = No success as yet

1 = First glimmerings of results

2 = Some clear early benefits experienced

3 = Considerable benefits

4 = A major success

| | | | | | |
|---|---|---|---|---|---|
| Access to world markets | 0 | 1 | 2 | 3 | 4 |
| Sale of online advertising | 0 | 1 | 2 | 3 | 4 |
| Building brands – existing products/services | 0 | 1 | 2 | 3 | 4 |
| Opt-in e-mail marketing | 0 | 1 | 2 | 3 | 4 |
| Customer/market information | 0 | 1 | 2 | 3 | 4 |
| Customer retention | 0 | 1 | 2 | 3 | 4 |
| Affinity (host/beneficiary) marketing | 0 | 1 | 2 | 3 | 4 |
| Direct B2B sales | 0 | 1 | 2 | 3 | 4 |
| Direct B2C sales | 0 | 1 | 2 | 3 | 4 |
| Global presence/visibility | 0 | 1 | 2 | 3 | 4 |
| Knowledge-sharing | 0 | 1 | 2 | 3 | 4 |
| Online training and development | 0 | 1 | 2 | 3 | 4 |
| Sale of lists to e-mailers | 0 | 1 | 2 | 3 | 4 |
| Cost reductions | 0 | 1 | 2 | 3 | 4 |
| New advertising channel | 0 | 1 | 2 | 3 | 4 |

| | | | | | |
|---|---|---|---|---|---|
| Attracting new customers | 0 | 1 | 2 | 3 | 4 |
| Improved buying terms | 0 | 1 | 2 | 3 | 4 |
| Recruitment and retention of staff | 0 | 1 | 2 | 3 | 4 |
| Shorten supply chain (reduce intermediaries) | 0 | 1 | 2 | 3 | 4 |
| Personalized customer service | 0 | 1 | 2 | 3 | 4 |
| Reduced time-to-market | 0 | 1 | 2 | 3 | 4 |
| 24/7 availability to customers | 0 | 1 | 2 | 3 | 4 |
| Global business platform | 0 | 1 | 2 | 3 | 4 |
| Identify new suppliers | 0 | 1 | 2 | 3 | 4 |
| Enhanced responsiveness to market | 0 | 1 | 2 | 3 | 4 |
| Online distribution | 0 | 1 | 2 | 3 | 4 |
| Faster decision-making | 0 | 1 | 2 | 3 | 4 |
| Low cost entry into new markets | 0 | 1 | 2 | 3 | 4 |

What are the key performance indicators of your e-business? Please tick the appropriate items. What are the signposts which will tell you that it is working for you? What are the warning signs that should scream at you: 'do something different and do it now'?

| | |
|---|---|
| Increased sales revenues in existing markets | ___ |
| Increased share of revenues from new markets | ___ |
| Increased profitability | ___ |
| Enhanced return on capital employed | ___ |
| Investment funds attracted | ___ |
| Enhanced market value of company | ___ |
| Competencies developed | ___ |

Information flow ___

Cost per transaction ___

Information distribution cost ___

Increased stock turnover ___

Customer retention ___

Customer satisfaction ___

Market share ___

Share of customer ___

Overall cost reduction ___

Staff reductions ___

Sales per staff member ___

Overall productivity ___

Speed to market ___

Number of customers ___

Just-in-time deliveries ___

Number of website visits ___

Number of website transactions ___

Trends recognized ___

Sales per website visitor ___

Number of customer opt-ins ___

Speed of response ___

Service quality ___

Staff retention ___

Customer 'churn' ___

Staff 'churn' ___

Website downtime        ___

Brand recognition        ___

Transaction security failures    ___

## How does our web presence 'stack up'?

Having assessed your objectives, the status of your business to date and the key indicators of your online business success, you may well want to reassess or reconsider your initial strategic and tactical considerations. If this small survey has helped you to think again it has achieved its purpose.

Typical thoughts might include:

*The customer*

- Are we attracting enough visitors to our site?
- Are they the people that we need to attract?
- Do they stay and seek information?
- Do they welcome the offer of further information?
- Are we using technology creatively to treat our customers as individuals with different needs and desires?
- Do visitors buy online?
- Do they come back to visit and buy again?
- What does each visitor cost us in terms of promotion?
- What is the value of the initial order?
- How much, if any, profit are we making from the first order?
- How much more do we make from repeat business?

- What can we do to increase repeat business?
- Do we know with certainty what the emerging needs of our customers are?

*The competition*

- How do we compare against our competition when it comes to delighting the customer?
- Do we know who are our online competition by name and understand each one's unique marketing proposition?

*The website*

- Does our site add transactional value for buyers?
- Does it give us added value as sellers?
- Does it make it easier than ever to do business with us?
- Is our unique selling proposition emphasized effectively?
- Could we use online activities to sell and make rather than to make and sell?
- Is our site properly integrated with the rest of the business?
- Is our site too clever to be useful to visitors?
- Does our site help build our service standards?
- Are we attracting enough prospects of the right kind to our site?

*The strategy*

- Have we entered into the right online strategic alliances?
- Do we make it easy to do business online?

- Is our offline distribution up to the job?

- Should we find ways to enjoy the economies of delivering more online?

- Do we really understand how to keep in touch with the ever-changing search engine algorithms?

- Are we treating our site as a technology breakthrough rather than a marketing and sales operation?

- Have we been persuaded by those with an axe to grind that a website is merely an electronic brand-building exercise?

- Have we a comprehensive strategy in place or was our web presence cobbled together by junior 'techies' after the chairman returned from the golf course full of web enthusiasm?

- Does our offline marketing support success online?

- Has our web presence enabled us to cut costs?

- Have we passed some of the advantages we have gained to our customers in the exceptional value and quality of our offering?

- If our online business was based on bricks rather than clicks would it work? Is there a better way? Do we need to be online?

## What do (or should) the top consultants ask clients to think about?

It is at least as important to plan your success on the Internet as it is in the 'real world'. The cost of getting online may be modest, but the opportunities are not, so you owe it to yourself to think things through carefully. When I advise a corporation which is developing a new strategy these days the Internet is an important feature. I ensure that clients take it very seriously.

The following are some of the questions that I would typically ask to ensure that my clients were planning for online success and not assuming that a web presence is simply part of the old routine.

May I suggest that you carefully consider each question? The additional business and the profits that it will bring will make you glad that you took the time.

1. In an ideal world where anything is possible what would you choose to accomplish through your web presence?

2. What specific contribution to your strategy is your web presence designed to achieve?

3. What specifically in the design of your website shows that all your people know precisely what it is there for in purely business terms?

4. Your website, however modest, cost you both time and money so what is your objective for increased sales online in the first year?

5. How will a website support the achievement of this goal?

6. What are your specific cost-cutting goals?

7. How do you expect to measure the economies of being online?

8. How will your people become more productive as a result of having a website?

9. How will you enjoy low-cost/no-cost entry into new markets through your website?

10. How will you switch from make and sell to sell and make?

11. What products or services can be delivered online?

12. To which intermediaries can you stop paying commissions or margins as your website prospers?

13. Do all your people understand the enormously enhanced value of the 'customer for life'? (What are the three essential benefits of customer retention?)

14. Are they all fully committed to tying customers to you for life?

15. How does your website reflect this commitment from the customer's point of view?

16. What are you doing to make your best customers more loyal?

17. How do you reward the customer who gives you continued business?

18. What does your website contribute to encouraging your customers to buy more often and/or in greater quantities?

19. How does your website reduce or reverse the risk of buying from you?

20. How does your website encourage the placing of larger initial or trial orders?

21. Some experts believe that online business will take off and will grow at a cumulative rate of 30 per cent a year for the next five years. What are you doing to ensure that you can handle the distribution and customer service problems that could arise if your business grew that fast or faster? (At this stage clients grin and say: 'That's a problem I would like to have to deal with when it happens.' To which I rather bad temperedly reply: 'Never mind the problem. What's your solution?')

22. What are your goals for customer service improvements?

23. How will you measure your advances in customer service?

24. What motivates your best customers to buy?

25. What motivates them to buy from you?

26. What motivates others with the same or better potential to buy elsewhere?

27. Who do your best customers also do business with or get information from on the Internet?

28. What are your goals for doing joint ventures on the Internet?

29. Can you list the Internet chat rooms, publications, newsgroups that your best customers participate in?

30. What do your best customers say about you and your service online and off it?

31. How do your best customers perceive your business?

32. On any scale that you choose, what are the chances that you can use your online presence to turn delighted customers into advocates for your business?

33. What precisely are your competitors doing online and what are you doing to ensure that you gain and maintain a competitive edge?

34. As they change how will you stay ahead of the pack?

35. What is the profile of your best customers?

36. How specifically do your best, most profitable, customers differ from the others?

37. What future needs of your customers will your online presence enable you to identify and satisfy?

38. How do you plan to identify changing customer needs and expectations more quickly than does your competition?

39. How are you building right now the competencies that you will need in the most profitable markets of the future?

40. What is your online marketing budget?

41. What is your advertising policy?

42. What is the return on your advertising spend?

43. How many Internet PR pieces do you intend to have published each month?

44. Who will publish them?

45. Why will they publish your stuff?

46. What are your growth limitations?

47. What about order processing and fulfilment, e-mail capacity, credit card processing and security, distribution and delivery, customer service and customer delight?

48. What concrete steps have you put in place today to ensure your optimal future growth potential?

*Get an honest friend to assess your website*

1. Who, outside the company has checked your website for speed of loading and ease of use?

2. Do the headlines on each page sell to the customer as well as to the search engines?

3. What are the specific benefits that you use to attract business and encourage browsers (people, not systems) to become engaged with your site?

4. Can browsers easily give you leave to keep in touch?

5. Are all contact details on each page?

6. Do you give all potential customers clear and compelling reasons to give you their e-mail addresses for further information?

7. If I visited your page for — of your website, what specifically would make me want to permit you to keep in touch?

8. How do you measure website traffic?

9. How do you measure the sales per visitor?

10. What keywords do people use to get to your site?

11. What other sites, or newsrooms do they come from?

12. How often do you check the search engines to ensure that you are in the top ten places of the important ones that your customers use?

13. How do you make the required changes when you find that you are slipping?

14. Why do you choose not to use professional search engine positioning?

15. How many times each day do your people check e-mails?

16. How often do you check your auto-responder messages to customers to be certain that they are still relevant?

17. When was the product or service information that you are currently sending out last updated?

18. Where do you display customer testimonials?

*Down and dirty marketing*

1. How do you capture all customers, prospects, suppliers, distributors, affiliates, prospective affiliate promoters and joint venture partners' e-mail addresses?

2. Where would you find a list of, say, potential joint venture partners if you wanted to do it personally in a hurry?

3. What is the average purchase per visit?

4. What is the purchase lifetime of the average customer?

5. How frequently does the average customer buy?

6. What parts of your range are 'cash cows'?

7. How are they promoted?

8. What parts are 'stars'?

9. How are they promoted?

10. What items are 'question marks' at present?

11. How are you keeping the costs of market testing them within bounds?

12. How do you ensure that the 'market testing idiots' do not reject what can be shown to work in order to test something different and probably inferior? (There must be an end to market testing. There is an infinity of things that can be changed and there are always those who will continuously change them, but why not go with what works until you need to change, not because of stupid ideology, but because of results? What you are doing may not be optimal, but if it works … we live in a real world.)

13. What do you do to ensure that you can lose 'dogs' without losing customers? (Note: Cash cows are established product lines that generate high revenues without further investment. Stars are high-potential product lines that still require considerable investment of money and effort to market, but which are selling well. Question marks are possibly future stars which, at present, need thorough market testing to justify a high investment of time, creativity and money. Dogs are slow-moving low-value lines that probably cost more to supply than they generate in profit. It is probably a good exercise to look at clients and customers using the same definitions and the same nomenclature – but not in their hearing! No one wants to be referred to as a 'dog' or even a 'cow'.)

14. What specifically do you do to lengthen the product life cycle of cash cows and accelerate the wide acceptance of stars?

15. What is your policy for getting rid of customers who are and will remain more hassle than they are worth?

16. How often do you communicate with your customers?

17. How do you personalize communications?

18. What is in your signature file for e-mails? What does it do for the customer or you?

19. Which host/beneficiary deals are bringing in the most business?

20. Which are bringing in the most profitable business?

21. Which are competition's most profitable customers?

22. What is your strategy for capturing them?

23. What is your unique selling proposition online?

24. What is it in the dirt world?

25. Is your approach consistent?

26. What is your referral system?

27. How do you reward referrals?

28. If you could improve one key aspect of your marketing at a stroke what would it be?

I cannot pretend that this is an exhaustive list of questions that I ask in any specific situation. Good questions lead to supplementary questions and they only have relevance in the light of what has already been discussed. Similarly not all of the questions listed will be the key questions to which your specific situation and strategy demands full and careful answers. They should, however, be of considerable relevance and, at the very worst, they will remind you of the important questions that you ought to be asking yourself. From a marketer's viewpoint you must always keep in the forefront of your mind whether you market online or in the local flea market:

- Who is my best type of customer?

- What do they need?

- What do they want (WOMAN – wants overcome [lack of] money and needs)?

- What motivates them to buy?

- What motivates them to buy from a specific supplier?

- How can I give them more of what they like?

- How are their interests, needs and desires changing?

- If they want 'A' today could they be persuaded to want 'B' tomorrow?
- What is the lifetime value of a customer?
- How much can I spend to attract the right customer?
- How will I delight and go on delighting my customers?
- How can I dump those who are more trouble than they are worth without damaging my reputation, credibility and image?
- How can I make the best, most economical use of emerging technology to delight and go on delighting my customers?

## What are the 'tips' that current business research uncovers?

*Twelve tips for the small (and large) business website*

1. Identity – be clear about who you are and what you offer from the customer's viewpoint. Do whatever it takes to see yourself through the customer's eyes.

2. Take a pride in your expertise, but do not try to push what customers do not want. Marketing includes creating needs, but first satisfy those that exist in such a way that none can compete with you for quality of response.

3. Creativity – be creative, but never cloud the purpose of your business with cleverness for its own sake. Only a nerd enters a site and says 'love that technology'.

4. Constantly look at what works for others, adapt and adopt the best that your creativity and budget can manage. Then improve what you have adopted to make it your own.

5. Build customer loyalty with diligence and you will build employee loyalty without effort. Delighted customers develop committed employees.

6. Deliver more than you promise.

7. Remember customers online are short on time and attention, not money.

8. Make it easy for people to buy online.

9. Avoid pop-up advertising and 'get off my site' banners that distract customers from their purpose. Their purpose is to get the information that they want and do the business as easily as possible.

10. Be consistent – market consistently when you are fat, dumb and happy. Ensure that your messages consistently reflect the image that you want to build and maintain. Ensure that the customer is never confused by conflicting messages.

11. Make it easy to contact you and respond quickly. (Research suggests that a response that takes more than six hours is wasted effort. Get back to the customer at once, even if getting back is only to tell the customer when you will have the information that they seek.)

12. Really bust a gut to deliver more than you promise.

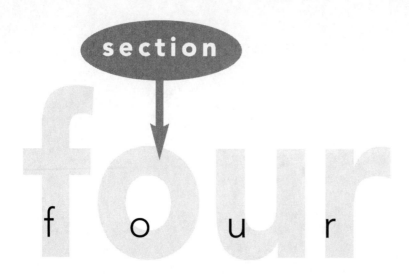

section

# four

f o u r

the big decision – why go online?

# IT ISN'T ALL PLAIN SAILING – BUT CAN IT BE?

## What are the potential or actual problems of using a commercial website?

There are still some, a reducing but significant number of, potential buyers who have serious concerns about security of transactions on the web. Ironically these same worriers will happily hand a credit card to a waiter in their local restaurant with absolutely no knowledge of what happens to it while it is both out of sight and out of mind.

Many senior directors of companies still dislike and fear computers that they continue to regard as being the tools normally used and therefore understood only by the lower orders. Computers remain, for too many executives, tools that are beneath their notice. Winning real top-level commitment to a web strategy can be tough and without commitment little that is worthwhile will happen. If Rupert Murdoch repeats again and again that the Internet serves no serious purpose and never will he can throw money and family members at a website, but it will never work because top management of his companies will conspire to prove him to be right even when they know he is wrong.

Those with an axe to grind, from 'techies' and web fanatics to advertising agencies, are trying to persuade the gullible that the Internet is either an all-singing, all-dancing exercise in technical ingenuity or a simple add-on to brand-building by traditional means.

The biggest single potential downside is that for success online all of the logistics of a business, quality, delivery and the rest need to be of the highest order. Recent research by Andersen Consulting suggests that up to 80 per cent of customers who buy online are dissatisfied by delivery times, stock shortages or other problems. This is worse for the business on the web than it is in the dirt world because online your competitor is only a click away.

*See also*:   How can we optimize the return on our web presence investment?

Isn't the competition tough online, possibly even tougher than in the real world?

Is going online workable without a solid distribution system where the customer lives in the real world?

## We have a prosperous business in the real world. Should we even be considering going online?

Forget the fancy technology, the Internet is a business and information medium second to none. Those who use it effectively will prosper. Those who try to ignore it will, in some cases at least, go under. Those who use it ineptly will, in all probability, go belly up even more quickly.

On the basis of the most conservative estimate that I can find online, revenues in Europe are expected to increase by 850 per cent by 2001.

This year (2001) Forrester Research estimate that those with web access will create a market of at least 52 million relatively articulate, relatively well educated, relatively choosy, relatively well-to-do consumers.

By 2002 Jupiter Communications expect 38 million households in the European Union to be looking to do at least part of their buying online.

In the very near future 25 per cent of all business-to-business transactions across the world are expected to take place on the Internet.

If you have analyzed why you are thinking of having a commercial website using the tools that precedes this section you are one massive step ahead of the herd when it comes to making an informed decision. Your prosperous business may or may not stay that way if you remain offline. Some offline businesses will prosper, some will fail. Some online businesses have already been shown to be badly conceived and badly run. One thing is certain. You will not build a profitable business online without careful and detailed planning.

General Motors, General Electric and other major corporations have clearly stated that if they cannot buy from you online then they will not buy from you at all. Where they lead most will follow when they see the reductions in costs of purchasing that are possible. If you sell to other businesses the time may come when you trade online or you do not trade at all. That being said, it is wise to ensure that what is done on the Internet is done at least as well as anything that is done in the 'dirt world'.

*See also*:   Why does online business seem to flourish when part of a 'bricks and clicks' enterprise?

## The BIG question: why have so many dot coms failed so dramatically?

This is really two questions in one. Dealing with the drama first, when there has been a craze there is almost always a dramatic reversal. From seventeenth-century Dutch tulip bulbs to the mania for throwing money at bad business ideas as long as they were online, the downturn when it comes is dramatic and because it is dramatic the media go to town on their unending quest to turn a problem into a crisis and a crisis into a drama. In short, the hype that created the problem is no less enthusiastic when the thing appears to go into reverse. You need to bear in mind that things are not necessarily what they seem. There is and always will be a shake out of bad sites and bad ideas, but businesses fail in the real world too. Had investment in untried people hopefully flaunting untried ideas not verged on the insane, the media would perhaps have turned its attentions to other matters, but as things stand billions of investors' money has been 'thrown away' by bright young things with nothing more than a newly minted MBA to keep them on track. No wonder some have gone off the rails. The miracle is that so many have been able to start the journey.

Of course the press tends to ignore simple economic realities. Unreasonable investment of necessity demands unreasonable expectation of returns, otherwise the system fails. The markets have given untried managers vast sums of money to play with on the back of simple and often simplistic ideas. The result is bound to appear to be far more than just tears before bedtime. An entrepreneur loses his home, his savings, his reputation and his marriage, and the press sighs, 'So what? It happens every day', and of course they are right. Some young enthusiast throws away millions of investors' money and that is news. If enough youthful hopefuls manage to do the same that is sheer theatre and the media worldwide do the job that they are paid to do and milk the situation for all that it can be magnified to appear to be worth.

The trouble is that not only does the media deal in simplification and multiplication, the dot coms are right there at their side. The management of Kozmo.com announced their cure for what ails the sector. They dropped the 'com' and will hereafter be known simply as Kozmo. If things were that straightforward business brains would be ten a penny, which is what, to all intents and purposes, the crazy investment in crazy schemes suggested that they are. So at the end of the day it is wrong to blame the press for manufacturing a crisis. The crisis has resulted from ignorance on the part of entrepreneurs, investors, managers and commentators. In other words the problem was created by me and thee, but mostly thee, as they say up home.

The knowledgeable executive, planning and controlling the development of e-commerce in their own operation will take heed of the lessons to be learned. They will use information to make mature judgements in the interest of the long-term prosperity of their companies. They will also be aware that for every dot com that fails with such drama there are hundreds of 'bricks and mortar' companies that sink with barely a ripple. That is the way of business and it is why risk must be rewarded. This time the investment community has cheerfully increased the risk to the point where for many there is no hope of adequate reward.

## Checklist Why dot coms fail

✓ They lack a meaningful business plan.

✓ They think that strategy is for wimps and those who ought to know better confirm to them that this is the case in the 'faster-moving new economy'.

✓ The members of the management team grossly overestimate their own intelligence and creativity and silly levels of investment substantiate their self-assessment.

✓ They lack experience of the market.

✓ Too frequently they lack experience of any market.

✓ What little they know has come mainly from case studies and textbooks discussed to destruction by 'third generation idiots'. (See Glossary.)

✓ In their enthusiasm they fail to develop an adequate infrastructure to deliver customer satisfaction and repeat buying.

✓ They allow themselves to be influenced by 'gurus' who insist that the world moves too fast for strategies and that 'seat of the pants' reactive tactics are all we have or need.

✓ They assume that a business idea that works in the real world will work online without understanding why it works anywhere. (Ideas such as 'people with feet like buying shoes' – which they do. But it gets stretched to 'people like to buy shoes without trying them on' – which they do not – yet.)

✓ The management team lack experience and have no one there to yell 'THINK' at appropriate moments.

✓ The management team has too much money to spend on too often meaningless advertising that is far too clever to include a message that has meaning to the serious customer.

✓ The company is given a whimsical name that has no meaning to anyone beyond the self-styled 'creatives' in the firm or among its advisers.

✓ The top team underestimates competition.

✓ Marketing costs outstrip revenues.

✓ They build all-singing and all-dancing sites where the serious buyer cannot discover how to place an order or make an enquiry.

✓ They believe that building a database is more important than building sales.

✓ They try to be 'all things to all men' and become nothing to most of us.

✓ They confuse what boy surfers want with what grown-ups in a hurry need and they pander to the boy surfers.

✓ They have no real understanding of how to generate site traffic economically.

✓ They believe that branding is all and then forget that branding must refer to a desired product or service if it is to have meaning for the buyer.

✓ Too often the management team lacks any sense of responsibility and loyalty to their investors and report that 'It was great fun spending so much of other people's money'.

✓ Resources are squandered on fancy offices, fancy cars and fancy lifestyles rather than on 'creating, identifying and satisfying customer desires at a profit'.

In short, thanks to stupid, overoptimistic investment by people who should have known better the management team frequently suffer from what my grandmother called MMTS disease (more money than sense). Unless they learn from the experience they are doomed to repeat their failures and sooner or later it will be with their own money. Paper fortunes of an estimated $4.6 trillion have disappeared without a trace or perhaps, given that they were never other than 'virtual', they did not exist in the first place. That might be a comforting thought but for one thing: paper profits for entrepreneurs only exist because investors put real money into their schemes.

Of course, there is fallout from this Gadarene swine approach to business. As I write perfectly sound start-ups run by experienced entrepreneurs are reporting that it grows harder by the day to find funding. The effect on economies of lost opportunities is literally incalculable.

*See also:* What is wrong with traditional marketing techniques?

## What is happening to the dot com casualties?

Some sink leaving no trace, but others are finding themselves in a rather odd position. As the market pendulums in the mad frenzy that one might expect of any organization that is made up in great part of third generation idiots (see Glossary), a number of dot coms are finding that their cash holdings, built in more optimistic times, considerably exceed their market value. In a phrase they are becoming 'cash shells'. If they can stem the haemorrhage of cash they are saleable, not as ongoing businesses but as potential subjects of 'cash stripping' (asset stripping of firms that have virtually no assets). Do not expect the most ambitious and silly to rise phoenix-like from the ashes of their own stupidity. Just because they have only thrown away the greater part of the cash that they attracted from 'growth funds' and the like no one believes that an unbusinesslike approach to business has suddenly become viable. Either they will continue to throw away their cash or they will conserve it only to be stripped of it by those who really do recognize an opportunity when they see it.

In spite of the doom and gloom that has dogged dot com results over the last few months there are some signs of a chink of light at the end of the tunnel – which reminds me of an unkind old joke: 'Why are New Yorkers so gloomy?' 'Because the light at the end of the tunnel is New Jersey.'

The light at the end of the dot com tunnel is not, however, generally credited with giving the USA 'flu as New Jersey is. Analysts are reporting on 23 April 2001 that the worst is over as far as dot com results are concerned. The nadir has been reached. The clearout is almost completed and the only way is up. Since the prognostications of those perceived to be in the know often prove to be self-fulfilling prophecies a touch of optimism is perhaps justified. Two more factors reported on the same day bolster the sense of relief. According to research by Jupiter Media Metrix the downturn in business activity in the USA has led to a major increase in purchases for some sectors online while in Europe there are emerging signs that companies are now rethinking their online strategies to learn better from others' past and expensive mistakes. For businesspeople the lesson to be learned is a clear one. In good times or in bad you need to have a clear strategy if you are to exploit opportunity or simply survive until things get better. To paraphrase President Lincoln, you can survive in all conditions without a strategy some of the time, but you can only prosper in all conditions if you have a strategy all of the time.

*See also*:    How do we avoid losing money online?

## EMPLOYEE BEHAVIOUR: TIME-WASTING HAS NEVER BEEN EASIER

### Does surfing the web take precedence with employees?

Research by Taylor Nelson Sofres published on 19 April 2001 suggests that this may well be the key. According to this research covering a random sample of 800 employees with access to the Internet:

✓ Fifty-two per cent choose and book their holidays online in the firm's time.

✓ Forty-one per cent surf websites that relate to their hobby.

✓ Twenty-seven per cent watch webcasts of sporting fixtures at work.

✓ Twenty-eight per cent are doing their shopping online from the office.

Note: that no significant number admits to looking at pornography. As Mandy Rice Davies would have said, 'they wouldn't would they?' But the question remains 'do they?' If they do, it suggests that the lost time is a considerable underestimate and the loss of time is substantial on the basis of the information that we have.

In total the average time admittedly spent online having fun rather than working came to three hours a week. Of course an average remains the 'best of the worst combined with the worst of the best' and is therefore not necessarily true of your firm. Yours may be much worse if you do not have it under control. A survey of a different sample in March 2001 suggested that employees may be spending an hour a day on surfing for pleasure rather than profit. If this pattern is repeated through the organization, that is a staggering 18 to 30 days a year of additional holiday being taken by each employee with web access. Are management doing anything about it? Some apparently are, but is it enough? In Great Britain 67 per cent of IT managers indicated that they had rules against misuse of the company's time and resources. Which means, of course, that one in three firms have a laissez-faire attitude to their employee's behaviour. Admirable if the employees are to be trusted, but on the basis of this research the question has to be, 'are they?'

For example the Gartner Group also issued some research findings in April 2001. They found that:

✓ Employees are spending an average of 49 minutes a day sorting e-mails.

✓ Twenty-five per cent are spending more than an hour a day.

✓ Thirty-four per cent of internal e-mails are 'unnecessary'.

Perhaps it is time to question intelligently the 'let my people go' school of empowerment, the myth that British workers actually work all the hours of attendance and to kick out some of the overpaid consultants who talk with tear-brimmed eyes of growing stress in the workplace and who offer cures and courses for 'information overload'. Above all, perhaps the time has come for managers to manage. The laws in the major countries allow management to monitor both web access and e-mails, and the interesting thing about e-mails, is that you can delete all you want, but they still can be retrieved. That is why George W. Bush has sworn off e-mails for the term of his presidency. He, wisely perhaps, has decided to leave no evidence that cannot be lost or 'inadvertently' shredded.

## How good are our potential online competitors?

Needless to say, standards vary, but overall things could yet be a very great deal better and those who really learn to look after their customers will have a massive advantage. In a way poor reports of customer service online help those who are truly customer-centric. They underline that there is a very real risk if you shop around for the cheapest price. Those who find a good supplier should realize that they have every incentive to be loyal because a large number of firms are delivering lousy service by any standard.

**Research Customer service, 19 April 2001, Atmyside 400 retailers, UK**

✓   British retailers give themselves a generous and unnecessary two days in theory to answer customers' requests for information.

✓   A frighteningly low 5 per cent actually monitor whether their people even meet response targets that would lose business anywhere that I have worked in the world.

✓   Marketing directors proved to be the worst of all with 90 per cent unable even to hazard an educated guess at how long it took to respond to a customer enquiry. Can they really be unaware that attracting customers is of no value if you then drive them away before they have a chance to buy?

If you run any kind of tight ship you should be rubbing your hands at the sheer incompetence of your competition. Sadly, the chances are, on the basis of this research that you believe that the customers that you are driving away in droves are unreasonable. Just as when we found business for British firms in the USA and asked for simple information that should have been at their fingertips we would be asked in return, 'Don't you know it's Friday? We cannot do anything on Friday.'

We can enjoy an expensive web presence with all the bells and whistles – the great good fortune of having it found by people who want to hand over their money and we are apparently incapable of managing things in a way that ensures that we get the business. I hope that God is anxious to help us for we have a strange disinclination to help ourselves. Research by Alta Vista a couple of years ago showed that 83 per cent of customers on average leave sites never to return because they cannot get the information that they want. Of those who persevere

✓ How many are driven away eventually by our failure to provide timely, accurate and full information?

✓ How many are driven away by ill-mannered, ill-trained customer-facing staff?

✓ How many are driven away by abjectly appalling fulfilment?

✓ How much did it cost to get them to come to you in the first place?

Why do our people take so long to respond to customers? Could it be that they are too busy attending to their personal business?

☞ *See also:*  How much time are people spending online?

Is surfing the web addictive?

## Isn't the competition tough online, possibly even tougher than in the real world?

The competition on the web is immense and growing daily. There are millions of companies vying for attention. A recent count suggested that there are more than 75 million websites, some of which run to up to half a million pages. Yes, the competition is tough and that underlines the fact that you need a comprehensive strategy aimed at attracting and retaining customers.

Those companies that have a web presence are by definition global. That means that somewhere in the world there is almost certainly a competitor that you have yet to hear of who is developing a strategy of cutting costs dramatically and attracting customers worldwide. Such a competitor may well be running a greedy eye over your customers right now. Drama aside, tough competition will become tougher as a direct result of the World Wide Web. If you are not part of the Internet you may find it difficult to fend off competitors that you never even knew existed.

*See also*:   How do we bring customers, old and new, to our site?

# FUTURE POSITIVE – FOR SOME

## What does the future hold?

Most major businesses are planning to do all their buying online in the relatively near future. If you supply a large corporation like General Motors you may have no choice but to develop a web presence. General Motors have already announced that where suppliers are unwilling or unable to provide online buying facilities they will simply change their suppliers. Few if any suppliers can dictate to General Motors or General Electrics or other large corporates, their power in the marketplace remains too great. Their suppliers, when told to jump can only ask, 'how high?'

The great businesses of the world foresee massive savings by buying exclusively online. Very soon much of the world's business-to-business sales will follow suit. So if you sell products or services to any other business you will need a user-friendly, interactive website, and it does not end there.

By the end of the year 2001 about half of American corporates will have 'private portals' in operation. A private portal is in effect a website that only those with a serious reason for going there can access where all the processes, information and resources that the firm and its strategic partners have are made available. Private portals have the ability to revolutionize the way in which information and resources that are critical to business to business and beyond are shared. Those who are not 'in' will face massive problems.

**Research US government agency, February 2001**

High-speed access to the Internet will be a major key to even faster growth of e-commerce and broadband facilities are the current key to high-speed access. The only trouble is that the relatively high cost of broadband is stifling growth in the short term. Half of web users in the USA currently have access to broadband technology, yet a current survey by the General Accounts Office shows that only 12 per cent of users are taking advantage of broadband, with the vast majority continuing to dial-up the web using the old-fashioned telephone networks. Of those who use the tried and tested modem and telephone line to reach the Internet, 47 per cent reported that it was simply because it was the 'cheapest option'. This will be good news for businesses eager to grow their e-commerce operation in the not too distant future. It is a truism that the cost of technology falls rapidly once usage reaches a 'critical mass'. The involvement of an American government department in publicizing the barrier to development of e-commerce that failure to use broadband represents, will help to accelerate the necessary price reductions because e-commerce is a cornerstone of American economic policy. As the cost falls broadband access will thrive and e-commerce growth will be given an ever-greater impetus.

Technical developments that are very close as I write could bring 10 million additional customers online in the USA, and many more in Europe and elsewhere. According to the National Bureau of Census there are currently that number of registered blind in the USA. Thanks to WebMaster, an organization that exists to provide technological support for the disabled, blind people will very soon be able to surf the net without the aid of sighted friends by using 'talking browsers'.

Some economists claim that we are now in an 'experience economy' (one in which entertainment takes on a new level of importance), and entertainment may see some major changes. Movie distribution is expected by some to become increasingly Internet based. The good old projection box, they say, will disappear forever as 'hit' movies are distributed increasingly by wireless DVD technology.

An interesting and challenging idea that has been announced in April 2001 could lead to the death of programming languages as we know them. Synapse Ltd of Cambridge has announced the development of plain language programming. A software system has been developed which, it is claimed, allows anyone, without any specialist knowledge, to program a computer. In theory this could lead to the demise not only of Java and C++, but also of the 'skills gap' since you or I would be able to indulge in 'do-it-yourself programming' with relative ease. The theory is fine, but the practice may be more difficult or more limited than is supposed by the optimists. The whole point about computer programming languages is that the most complex of them is simple. They avoid the subtleties and ambiguities of English or any other language in order to give simple instructions to simple machines. Contrary to what is occasionally still promoted by anthropologists, there is no such thing as a simple spoken language. Every language that has developed in any society must be capable of expressing any thought that any individual needs to express. Therefore, all real-world languages are subtle and complex. Whether any software can ever be developed that can respond accurately to spoken or written language remains very much an open question. If it cannot, then the Cambridge achievement may turn out to be more interesting than it is useful.

**Mini Case Study** The 'experience' economy – feel and try then buy!

Teesside University in England is putting the shopping experience back into web-based retailing by developing virtual reality programmes that enable the customer to 'touch' and 'feel' the product online. Others are producing scents – coffee, bread, perfumes and the rest – over your computer. All the concerns that bedevilled and sank boo.com, for example the simple fact that people did not want to buy shoes online, that they wanted to feel the softness of the leather and admire the shine, may very soon become a thing of the past. The technology exists in a rather crude form already.

It does not end there. Modern scientific research increasingly demands number-crunching on a hitherto undreamed-of scale. Even giant Cray SuperComputers can no longer cope as experiments require petabytes of computing power. (One petabyte is the total computing power of 100 000 40-gigabyte computers applied non-stop for a year.) So, under the management of CERN (European Laboratory for Particle Physics) and six major science partners in Europe, the scientific community in Europe is putting together a 'grid' to harness the computing power of millions of PCs when their rightful owners are not using them. What has this to do with the price of fish? Just this, the massive power of the grid, like the Internet itself, will start as a service to the scientific world, but as time goes on it will, like the World Wide Web, begin to serve a wider audience. In a few years' time every online shopper will be able to have his or her own avatar (a virtual model of the individual correct in every detail) that will be able to be directed to do any shopping that is required, visiting every virtual mall and, for example, trying on virtual clothes to check the fit and demonstrate how good they will look on the online shopper. Imagine how this will change things for shy men who attempt to buy lingerie for their wives with only the most tenuous idea of their size. They will be able to visit Victoria's Secret without embarrassment and have their partner's avatar try on all the sexiest undergarments that they stock. Their partners, in the mean time will be able to check for themselves before making an expensive mistake that the pants that looked so great on Mel Gibson or Brad Pitt will only serve to make their portly, ageing husband look ridiculous.

Some economists argue that the growth of e-commerce will be constrained by the user's desire for 'experience' shopping. Given the popularity of computer games, a passion that is by no means limited to the young, I suspect that the experience of sending a 'slave' to test and try before you buy will be, for some at least, irresistible.

Your website makes your business international. If you can ensure distribution and product support you have a low-cost/no-cost entry into overseas markets.

There may be numerous solid business reasons why you should be considering a web presence. If you need to have a web presence is it not simple business prudence to look at ways to leverage this resource? Be sure of one thing. People everywhere seem to want more 'stuff'. We want more goods and we want more choice concerning the goods that we buy. The Internet can give us that choice, but at a price. There is every reason to believe that it will continue to offer ever-greater choice. As a customer we enjoy greater choice – fine, but that means that as a worker we all, whatever our position in the firm, will increasingly need to work smarter to be the choice that the customer makes. Perhaps we should all think more seriously about the homily that airline captains deliver at the end of each flight: 'We know that you have a choice in air travel, thank you for flying . . .'

*See also*:   Is this the time to go online? What is the global business outlook?

Will new methods for accessing the Internet build business opportunities?

## Are companies really using the Internet more for business buying?

The speed of the Internet is increasing and access is becoming cheaper every year. Since convenience has for many years been the major determinant of buyer behaviour, progress in sales, like access to the web, may become faster than we dream possible.

Even lack of a computer will not be a bar to trading online. Within a few years access will be split between television, the personal computer and the mobile telephone.

At present, however, B2B (business to business) sales take the lion's share. In March 2001 the US Department of Commerce released detailed figures for 1999. Although things move quickly in the new economy the 1999 figures are all that we have for the moment so they are worth considering. Overall B2B accounted for 90 per cent of e-commerce. The main sectors were as follows:

| Sector | Sales ($US billions) |
| --- | --- |
| Manufacturing | 485 |
| Wholesales merchants (75% drugs and pharmaceuticals) | 134 |
| Automotive | 33 |
| Publishing | 25 |
| Electronics | 15 |

Ironically the most important factor in the development of B2B e-commerce may turn out to be the fact that it is deadly dull. In general B2B websites have been designed with a simple objective in mind they are there to facilitate buying. They are not sexy. They lack the whiz-bang wonders of the B2C (business to consumer) sites. They sit there on the World Wide Web, utilitarian and unglamorous, doing the job for which they were designed. Consumer sales can never afford to be that dull. Customers want a little entertainment with their information, but the e-tailer ('cute' term for 'online retailer') may wish to consider whether in the last resort it is better to have all the latest whistles and flutes on a site that is difficult to use, or whether the great thing is to first facilitate the process of ordering. When I want a flight back to my beloved Chicago I do not need to hear a jazz band or have a virtual tour of Grant Park. I want availability and price and I want both quickly. Are you any different?

# IT'S THE MONEY, STUPID

## Can we save money by being online?

Internet trading can reduce costs dramatically. Expensive offices could finally become a thing of the past. The automation and personalization of customer communication is already a fact. Firms can do more with less. Some can sell and make rather than make, stock and sell. Inventory costs could approach zero while the turnover of working capital could become almost infinite. Return on capital employed could reach unprecedented heights. Thoughtful use of the web could make the chief financial officer's dreams a reality and do so at extremely low initial cost. All of this is true and has been proved by some, but by no means all, online businesses. To put it very bluntly, customer care online stinks. Research by Jupiter Media Metrix published on 30 April 2001 repeats a sad story that anyone who is taking business seriously should never be tired of hearing: the shortcomings of others are our opportunities.

Middlemen and their frequently substantial share of the selling price will cease to play a role in many industries. Meanwhile, new types of intermediaries will see an opportunity and grasp it.

The simple virtually no-cost e-mail is increasingly replacing costly postal, telephone and fax. Entry into new markets at home and overseas can become relatively cost- and risk-free. Customer loyalty can be built through free information and entertainment, and companies can target a greater share of customer buying power. Affinity marketing can slash advertising budgets while massively increasing sales and customer delight.

There is economic evidence that market penetration follows a simple 'S' curve such that growth becomes increasingly rapid once a critical mass is achieved. In the USA that critical mass in the use of computers has recently been reached. Productivity has risen from a little less than 2 per cent to better than 4 per cent in the last five years. This is unprecedented growth, but it appears to be sustainable. Access to the Internet is still on the gentle lower slopes of acceptance, but it is growing fast. Productivity is the foundation of any economy. We are seven times as well off as our ancestors were at the beginning of the twentieth century. In simple terms this is because we are seven times more productive. Making more with less is the most sustainable way to save money in business or in the economy at large.

*See also*: The BIG question: why have so many dot coms failed so dramatically?

## How are so many online companies throwing money away?

### Research Jupiter Media Metrix, 30 April 2001

Only 38 per cent of firms respond to customer e-mail enquiries within six hours. Twenty-five per cent fail to respond at all.

Why is six hours an important deadline? Customers are surprisingly patient. On average they have been shown to wait six hours before they either pick up a telephone and try to speak 'to a human being' or give up and take their business elsewhere. Given the subtleties of auto-responders and the speed of transmission of information, this is not merely appalling, it is suicidal. A key factor in e-commerce is the ability to cut costs and enhance competitiveness. Companies that choose to force their customers to chase the response to their enquiries are presumably doubling up on staff to resource call centres that could well be smaller or unnecessary. So, on the one hand they throw away business, and on the other they double the cost of doing whatever business they manage to salvage. As W.S. Gilbert might have said: 'My dear boy, "smart" is simply not the word.'

For many companies the key saving of being in e-commerce is that the delivery of knowledge products can be achieved cost-free electronically. For others the ability to 'sell and make' rather than 'make, stock, market and sell' is crucial. Others are exploiting the ability that the Internet delivers to enter new markets both cost- and risk-free. Any combination of these is available to those who really think through their web and real-world strategies and the potential markets are growing as the world becomes richer.

World GDP (gross domestic product) per person has risen more than fourfold during the computer age. Current projections suggest that the curve is becoming almost vertical. We can make more with less and we can create an ever-growing customer base at the same time. The key question therefore is, 'can we enjoy the economies and the market opportunities best with or without a web presence?' This book will help you to make the business decision that is right for you, but if you are not prepared to look after your customers the decision is made for you. Having a web presence without real customer care only means that you will fall further, harder and sooner.

**Mini Case Study** **Online economy**

Cisco Systems went over to online ordering to solve the problem that around 25 per cent of their phone and fax orders had errors. Online ordering has cut the error rate by 95 per cent leading to a saving for a single corporation of $500 million a year.

British Telecom claims to have cut transaction costs by 90 per cent leading to a direct reduction in the overall cost of goods and services it buys of 11 per cent.

The Nissan Corporation estimates that shifting to electronic business will reduce the cost of building a car by 14 per cent, according to recent research.

## Are small companies at a big disadvantage?

You do not have to be a big corporation to look big on the Internet. Small can really be beautiful when the web creates an almost level playing field for the mighty corporation and the 'one person' band.

Small companies can become global overnight if they have a web presence combined with the capability to get the product or service to the customer efficiently and economically. Sun Tse argued 5000 years ago that the weak could combine to surround and destroy the strong. The web makes this a real possibility through carefully planned strategic alliances.

# THE ONLINE CUSTOMER

## Not everybody can access the Internet, surely?

Equipment to access the web will continue to become more ubiquitous, less expensive and more reliable. The experience of Argos who beat their customers rather than their competitors to the punch by setting up a website before their customers had computers, with the result that they had only 30 or so 'hits' in the first 18 months, is unlikely to be repeated.

Efforts by the computer giants and governments will ensure that some people in the developing world will access information, goods and services online even before they have made a simple telephone call. The numbers able to access the Internet are growing at unprecedented rates. What is most important for business, however, is that by the year 2002 virtually all relatively affluent buyers, business and retail, will be able to reach your website.

*See also*:    What does the future hold?

Will new methods for accessing the Internet build business opportunities?

## Is the online customer a different sort of animal?

Thinking about the Internet has routinely led too many into unproductive consideration of a menagerie of geeks and freaks. Who actually is using the Internet? Who are your customers online likely to be? Research suggests that they are people just like you and me. They are like you and me, that is if we class ourselves as being among the better educated, more affluent, more articulate, more inquisitive and possibly more acquisitive members of society. We are also likely, only just, to be male and American, although there are signs that both nationality and gender mix are changing.

Two years ago approximately half the people online were American, and almost 53 per cent were men. More recent figures suggest that, although the dominance of the USA continues, it will decline as the addition of people from other countries and cultures means that the world is truly moving into cyberspace.

Other demographics make it clear that contrary to myths that the Internet is populated largely by children, the largest single group is made up of 'thirty- and forty-somethings' with money to spend. Six out of ten web surfers are between the ages of 25 and 54 and six out of ten have disposable incomes of between $50000 and $1 million. The majority, in America at least, are college graduates with 17 in every 100 having postgraduate degrees – a far greater proportion than of the population at large. To repeat the hopefully by now obvious, your customers and mine are bright and have the money to satisfy their desires. As marketers, therefore, we need to consider carefully how we may win and retain a greater share of the lifetime business of people who are not in general prepared to play games.

Those who presumably do like to play games, the under-18s of limited means, constitute a little over 19 per cent of the population. A healthy proportion of people who are growing up regard the Internet and all that it offers as a normal part of life rather than as a technological or marketing miracle. Those who get their web strategy right and survive to prosper online have a rapidly growing and maturing market that will sustain their businesses in the not far distant future, as well as having an affluent mature market today.

### As of today (June 2001) the average Internet user is

- thirty-something
- married or in a stable relationship
- a college graduate
- in a non-technical occupation
- likely to have no better than average computer skills
- involved in sports, social or community activities
- concerned that he or she has less disposable time than disposable income
- likely to have close relationships beyond the family

- very articulate
- able to articulate needs
- not excessively religious
- mildly, but not excessively introverted
- relatively comfortable with his or her feelings.

To prosper in e-commerce you need to bear in mind that your potential customer is not a nerd nor a geek. He and, increasingly, she combine smartness and affluence with concern for the well-being of others.

### Research findings A cognitive map of customer decision-making – online or off

I am Important – will my needs be treated as imperative or will they attempt a 'snow job' on me? How will I be treated online and afterwards?

I have developed a point of view – will my opinion be respected, understood and will my valued experience be taken into account in all dealings with these people? Will the online experience attempt to 'dehumanize' me?

I'm a busy person – should I really attend to this or just think of ways to say 'no' quickly or leave? Are they making it easy for me to find what I want?

What is the idea? – what is the detail? How does it work? Would it work for me? Is it safe? Is it new? Is it attractive? Is it exciting? Is it fun? Will they continue to give me the support and information that I want? Will this save me precious time? Can I find ALL the information that I want? Are they willing to provide more information as things evolve?

Will this idea help me and give me what I want? – does this person understand what I want? Is success guaranteed? Is there a rational case to buy? What are the benefits to me of trading online?

Am I being unduly pressured? – am I genuinely free to make up my own mind or am I in danger of being pushed into something that I will regret?

OK – it will give me what I want with least effort on my part so let's do it.

*See also:*    How can I easily bring more customers to my site?

# THINGS THAT WORRY US

## Are we opening up our systems to hackers and other online 'terrorists' by being online?

Some people believe that games and the familiarity with computers that games have spawned leads directly to the development of hackers, viruses and computer fraudsters. The future of such people may be brief. The UK government is putting money behind an idea designed to bring such tricksters to their knees. The human body deals with antigens (chemicals, bacteria and viruses that should not be there) through its immune system. Kings College is building on an idea originally spawned in the USA to give computers their own immune system. In outline the computer builds a dossier of knowledge of what is normal and as soon as it recognizes the abnormal it responds by attacking and destroying the virus. Having built a defence it retains it for future rapid deployment. It does not take a genius to see the enormous potential value or dangers of such a system. Our own built-in immune responses save our lives more times than we can imagine. They also go wrong occasionally and so we experience debilitating problems such as arthritis or killer problems such as AIDs. Few businesspeople will not have experienced the frustration that builds when a computer system refuses to allow us to do what we want. As I write, the intention is to rely heavily on computers giving an 'early warning' allowing human beings to make decisions and initiate or override action. So, as computers increasingly ape human behaviour the need for human intervention grows rather than recedes.

Hackers are misguided, but clever people. As defences become more efficient they engage all their ingenuity to overcome them, but effective defences already exist and they will get better. In the mean while it would frankly help a great deal if in addition to updating and using the defences that are available, idiots in the workplace learn to desist from opening e-mails from sources unknown to them with the subject 'I Love You' or the promise of a nude photograph of a tennis star.

## Do we open up our systems to viruses when we go online?

The sad answer while we still have talented nutcases dedicated to creating chaos is 'yes, we all have to be aware of the danger of viruses'. This is an area in which your technical people really should be worth their weight in gold. The latest news is that whereas in the past viruses were 'polymorphic', that is, they were transferred unchanged from computer to computer, those of the future will be 'metamorphic', that is, they will mimic retroviruses, such as the AIDS virus in real life. They will change with each new infection. That means that they will always develop in ways that will make them practically impossible to detect as they spread and evolve. If I were a cynic I might suggest that when your techies hand back the business development aspects of the Internet to those who know about business they might apply their ingenuity to finding ways to address the problem of metamorphic viruses – because the signs are that your present anti-virus software will not be up to the job. Meanwhile there are software programs on sale over the Internet and elsewhere that mean that anyone can spread viruses. Without going into any detail for obvious reasons, these programs basically invite the demented to enter the kind of damage that would tickle their perverted fancy and, hey presto, the idiot has created a virus.

It is worth bearing in mind that the viruses that have hit the headlines recently have all tended to be of the old-fashioned 'polymorphic' variety that would have been stopped by a modicum of common sense and an up-to-date version of a reputable anti-virus software program.

Hackers would seem to be the key problem as far as British companies are concerned. Recent research by CMA (Communications Managers' Association, April 2001) suggests that as many as one-third of British firms have been the victims of hackers. As a result CMA have announced the formation of the Institute for Communications Arbitration and Forensics to help executives who are concerned about the security of their IT operations.

The 31 May 2001 may just see life being made more difficult for hackers and the weird individuals who get their kicks from spreading viruses. Microsoft's new product, Outlook 2002 will be launched that day. The irritating time wasters that are so frequently sent attached to business e-mails will fail to get through with the new software. No games and no 'fun items' will hopefully mean a good deal less time wasted in the workplace and one avenue for the proliferation of viruses will be closed. But managers need to remember that it is only one avenue. The nuisances will still be rampant and businesspeople will still need to be vigilant.

## They say that we are in the Information or Knowledge Age and we either take part or die like the dinosaurs. Is this anything more than hype?

The web is the cheapest publishing medium yet devised. In an age when information is perceived as being the key to prosperity it has never been more freely available.

The web abolishes distance. Data can race around the world as cheaply and speedily as from across the street. This delivers to the businessperson new and exciting ways to develop and share knowledge.

Experts like Nonaka and Takeuchi have been pointing out for years that just as we have turned data into information by showing how it can be applied, we have the ability to turn information into knowledge and knowledge into business wisdom. There is every reason to believe that the Internet will be crucial in achieving this, and those who are best placed to bring together explicit information (data) with tacit information (the thoughts, feelings, hunches and ideas of employees and customers) will be those who use technology most creatively. There can be little doubt that those who use technology most creatively to achieve clear business goals prosper.

*Some brief thoughts on recent work by Nonaka, Takeuchi, de Geus, Lambert, du Toit, Peters and Drucker.*

The reader may want to consider whether or not he or she agrees with the following statements taken from recent research and the conclusions drawn from it. This is not a mere philosophical exercise. If the majority of these statements are true then knowledge products and the tools, skills and capabilities that will enable companies to use them effectively will be the prime products in the markets of the future.

- The Knowledge Age is already past – knowledge is no longer enough.
- The sole lasting competitive edge is wisdom, knowledge is now a commodity to be bought and sold online or off.
- Data is raw information and has very limited usefulness unless it is turned into knowledge and, eventually, wisdom.
- Information is data considered in the context of a meaningful strategic plan that is consistent with the strengths, competencies and culture of the organization.
- Knowledge is explicit and implicit (hunches, ideas, beliefs and values) information applied to the achievement of the strategic plan.
- Wisdom is knowledge reconsidered and tested in a changing environment to instil appropriate flexibility into the strategic plan.

  (Perhaps true sagacity is the implementation of wisdom such that the organization is increasingly able to shape the future of the sector(s) in which it competes such that others have no choice other than to play by the new rules and lose profits or withdraw – dominance strategy.)

- Knowledge in an organization is of two types: *Explicit* knowledge which is the effective and efficient application of data-based knowledge – facts, measurements, observable behaviours, skills, shared, communicated values and norms – and *Tacit* or *Implicit* knowledge which consists of the hunches, creativity, ideas and beliefs of the committed and informed people who are employed in the business at every level.

- Wisdom can only come from the balanced, effective application of tacit and explicit knowledge. The firm can only access and exploit tacit knowledge if it takes specific steps to:

  ✓ demonstrate that people and their thoughts are respected

  ✓ build commitment around a meaningful vision

  ✓ develop a culture in which ideas and learning are daily realities at every level, and communication is genuinely two way.

  (Tom Peter's dictum: 'We must learn to manage the imagination of our people. That is the new challenge.' The coming of the Internet and e-commerce may well lead us to the necessity of understanding if not managing the imagination of our customers. Because there are signs that what they can only imagine today they are being taught to want tomorrow – and someone out there is planning to give it to them – it should be you.)

- The imagination of our people can be stimulated by the successes of others if, and only if, we develop a 'leapfrog mentality'. Benchmarking, as it is usually practised, leads only to a 'me too' attitude which can only succeed if the competition stands still and kindly waits for us to catch up.

- Rather than trying to identify best practice, managers should be designing better than best practice.

  ('Managers must not attempt to manage change, it is too late for that, they must strive to get ahead of change by initiating it' [Peter Drucker at a conference, 11 December 1998])

- The Strategic Knowledge Unit is analogous to putting strategic planning into the hands of specialists. It becomes worse than a dry, academic exercise; it becomes somebody's turf, because in an organizational setting 'power flows to he or she who knows'. Strategic knowledge, like marketing and strategic thinking is the responsibility of the top team and is the right of everyone.

- If reward, sanctions and legitimacy are decreasingly becoming the bases for organizational power, then expert power, status power (through experience and assumed knowledge) and referent power (the power that comes from being the chosen role model because of past success) will increasingly tempt those who wish to progress personally more than they want the firm to prosper. There must be no barrier to creating the learning organization. Learning must be shared to ensure success, and the Internet provides easier and cheaper ways of sharing.

- Team success depends increasingly on consensus, and consensus only works where change is so fast that the past is not a reliable guide to the future and where relevant knowledge is spread among the population in such a way that even the knowledge holders are unaware of the utility of what they know until other pieces of the jigsaw are available.

- In a changing world the tendency of a winning team to freeze is the biggest single danger facing successful corporations.

- De Geus argues that the learning organization must be more than a repository of knowledge. It must apply what is learned in order to be flexible in strategic thinking and action. More than this, it must practise frugality so that it always has adequate financial resources with which to meet an emergency or a strategic sea change.

- Established companies (those that had survived beyond five years from launch) only a decade ago had a life expectancy averaging 60 years. In today's fast-moving markets that average has fallen to 12 years and is still declining (Harvard Business School global research, 1999). Survival depends, as never before, on building and fostering an appropriate culture and doing it more quickly than ever before.

● International cultural differences are frequently emphasized. With the growth of the Internet, perhaps we should be considering those similarities that are true of all cultures the world over and look at differences only when necessary. William du Toit, the anthropologist, has an interesting view of the way that we see other people's cultures. He suggests that the further we are from another's culture the more different it looks. For a European or American looking at, for example, Japan, from a distance and with a lack of involvement, the country and its people may look very exotic, but get up close and consider the individuals who make up the society and things change. We find that the Japanese love their families and want to do their best for them, just as we do. They care about basically similar values to those that we cherish, like honesty, decency, kindness and professionalism. Certainly there are differences between cultures, but these are normally emphasized in times of national stress, such as war or intense economic competition. If I understand his teaching correctly, du Toit suggests that in a knowledge-based global village we should first explore what we have in common and emphasize those things that we find easiest to understand because we share them to a perhaps greater or lesser degree. Then, if we want to go further we can step back a little and sensitively take account of the differences between us. This is a sound marketing approach for those who seek to become truly global in an economy in which wisdom comes from a combination of knowledge and sensitivity. First, we build bridges. Then, if necessary, we remove barriers to understanding and alignment.

If you agree with any of the above statements we are truly in a new economy in which information, knowledge and wisdom are at the same time essential strategic tools and the products and services of low-cost, high-profit businesses. The Internet did not create the growing need for knowledge, but it will certainly be the means of developing it, and e-commerce will increasingly be the means of exploiting it commercially.

# TOMORROW THE WORLD

**If we are considering breaking into new markets using the Internet, are there any indicators of the countries that we might aim for first?**

The EIU (Economist Intelligence Unit), probably the number one organization for analyzing international markets, published in late 2000 a report that suggests that after the USA, the Scandinavian countries, including Finland, are best placed and most committed to rapidly increase their buying online. Since their knowledge of English is first rate, there is probably little urgency in translating websites into languages other than English.

*Latin America*

Latin America, which for various reasons including widespread poverty has limited numbers having Internet access, is approaching the problem with a strong degree of creativity. They are allying themselves with the most advanced countries – the USA and the Scandinavian countries – in order to accelerate progress and avoid reinventing any wheels. Like Germany and Korea, Brazil is experimenting with PLC web access. PLC enables transfer of information cheaply at a rate of two megabits a second, or faster. Latin America has massive potential for B2B (business to business sales). In 2000 B2B sales in the region were a meagre 1.4 per cent of the world total at $3 billion. One company, anxious to sell online, indicated in a May 2001 report that of 350 000 possible trade customers only 6100 had the basic necessities of a telephone and a computer. In the region, however, this lack of equipment is seen as being an opportunity to start from a 'clean sheet' by introducing state-of-the-art equipment without the cost of dumping expensive systems already in place. The biggest Spanish telecommunications company is investing heavily in the region where Argentina, Brazil and Chile enjoy between them a $85 billion B2C (business to consumer) marketplace.

*Asia and the Pacific Rim*

It has a long way to go but, with a rapidly growing economy, China will eventually become the world's biggest market online. Meanwhile Asia as a region is making speedy progress in B2B sales. A simple extrapolation of current business (April 2001) suggests that total B2B sales for the region will grow from $12.8 billion in 2000 to $61 billion in 2002. If, in the mean while, Japan and other troubled 'Asian tigers' are able to overcome their economic problems, growth may be considerably greater. There are signs that South Korea at least is moving fast. Research by the Yankee Group in April 2001 indicates that Korea is set to go for e-commerce in a big way, a point that is confirmed by the IDC. Forecasts based on current growth suggest that Korea and China combined will account for around half of the e-commerce of the Asian Pacific region by 2005.

Those anticipating doing business in South Korea will need to explore the differences that exist between, say, Korean and American uses of the Internet. According to Neilsen/Net Ratings, surfers in the two countries have distinctive approaches:

| Country | Pages/session | Seconds/page | Session duration |
| --- | --- | --- | --- |
| Korea | 92 | 28 | 43 minutes |
| USA | 35 | 54 | 31.5 minutes |

So what does the strategist make of such information? Not much in isolation but, given the growth of buying volume in South Korea and the fact that the Yankee research indicates that 43 per cent of customers in

Korea indicate that they are looking for 'convenience', website design for those who wish to exploit this rapidly recovering and growing market needs to virtually scream 'look how easy this is' to the potential Korean customer or they will be away to another site before you know it. Throw in the tendency that the Korean web user has to click onto online advertising and you have possibly a very different online business environment. One in which the attention span of the potential customer is very short and the desire for novelty is strong.

*Note*: In marketing terms 'convenience' has always been the top scorer in any survey of the motivation to buy. The difficulty offline is that convenience has so many very different meanings:

- ✓ I pass that shop on my way to work.
- ✓ They are open when I have the leisure to shop.
- ✓ They take the type of credit card I use.
- ✓ They are near to my home.
- ✓ They offer a replacement vehicle service while mine is in the shop.
- ✓ They deliver.

The list is almost endless and the desire for convenience is difficult to quantify. Online, however, things are simplified. Convenience online is a simple function of the ease with which a customer can find relevant information and make a purchase.

### Research Findings International Retail Opportunities, April 2001

A recent study by Zogby International–Techwatch confirms in part the EIU findings concerning the 'e-commerce readiness' of various countries. Zogby looked specifically at potential buyers capability of accessing the Internet from home and found that although three out of four US customers can reach suppliers online, Denmark has moved into first place for domestic access.

| Country | Percentage of homes online |
|---------|---------------------------|
| Denmark | 54% |
| USA | 50.9% |
| Singapore | 47.4% |
| Taiwan | 40% |
| South Korea | 37.3% |

Spain and China remain at the bottom of the league table for the moment in Europe and Asia.

*See also*:    Is this the time to go online? What is the global business outlook?

## Where is the growth likely to occur?

According to Gartner research the USA continued to dominate the global B2B (business to business) e-commerce trading during the year 2000. Unsurprisingly perhaps the USA was responsible for 59 per cent of the total worldwide business. But things are unlikely to stay that way. Other regions are expected to begin to catch up this year (2001).

In 2000 the Asian Pacific region continued to experience the economic doldrums that have followed the crisis to which business structures, government and national banks have been so slow to respond, but finally there are faint signs that things may be on the mend. Total B2B trade in Asia last year amounted to $96.8 billion. This is a considerable sum during an economic slow down, but it is nothing when compared with what the region is capable of achieving. There are already signs that B2B trade in Asia Pacific will more than double in 2001 to $220 billion, helping to reduce the US share of such trade to 52 per cent.

Another area with a massive growth potential is Europe where B2B trade last year was a fairly meagre $72.5 billion, or 17 per cent of the world total. For a region with a bigger population than the USA this is disappointing. The current trend, however, points to rapid growth in Europe where total B2B e-commerce is on course to reach $188 billion this year.

The year will not see the end of North American dominance of world B2B trade, corporations in the USA will continue to account for half of the world's business for years to come, in good times and in bad, but the strategist will be planning to identify those regions and countries offering the minimum risk and an established business infrastructure with the maximum growth potential and, in the short term at least, to use the unique opportunities that the Internet affords to exploit overseas markets at relatively low entry cost.

### Fact file USA

The USA has 23 million small businesses operating in 2001.

Small business accounts for 47 per cent of all sales made by US companies.

In a time of limited business growth the number of small businesses is estimated to be expanding at a rate of 850 000 a year.

Small business in North America is supported by Partner America, a public–private partnership that combines the US Conference of Mayors with American Management Services to provide training and advice. When appropriate, this body works in conjunction with corporate America. As an example, in April 2001 Microsoft allied itself to Partner America in order to provide small companies with low-cost access to e-commerce and free training to enable entrepreneurs to appreciate the online opportunities for small businesses.

## Is it essential to have multi-language facilities on your international website?

The short answer is that it all depends, as always, on the needs and expectations of your customers. If your customers would prefer to do business with you because you have the courtesy to address them in their own language the answer must be obvious.

English, however, remains the language of business across the globe. This does not mean that the majority of those who access the Internet have English as their first language.

Current research suggests that 192.1 million native English speakers (47.6 per cent representing $12 257 billion in GDP) access the facilities of the Internet. The rest of the world (211.3 million people or 52.4 per cent of the online population representing $28 843 billion in GDP) speak other languages. No businessperson will lose sight, however, of the fact that of 211 million non-native speakers of English a large number will speak, read and write it very well as a second language. The fact that 70 per cent of the world's wealth is in the hands of people for whom English is a foreign tongue ought to make you think and should send you back to your customers, wherever they may be in the world, to ask if they need or want you to provide information in their language. It is a pure business decision, but like all business decisions it needs to be based on thoughts including:

**Checklist**

✓ Will it help to differentiate us in the marketplace?

✓ Will it add to our revenues and profits?

✓ Will it bind our customers closer to us?

✓ Will it help to turn our customers into advocates for our business?

✓ Can we actually deliver what is wanted with high quality and reliability?

**And a slight variant on Lambert's Laws of Business**

✓ Is there a customer-driven reason for doing this?

✓ Will it pay for itself in a reasonable time?

✓ Is it consistent with our strategic goals?

✓ Will the need be fully understood by those who need to make it work?

✓ Do we have the understanding, skills, knowledge and capabilities to do it right first time – every time?

As access to the Internet grows, the ratio of those users with English as a first language will decline. Current projections (Global Reach) suggest that the major locus of growth will be in countries where English is not the native language. As early as 2003 it is estimated that 230 million native English speakers will be accessing the Internet. This will reduce the English-speaking share of the global online economy to a fraction under 30 per cent while, with 560 million (projected) non-English speakers with access, the non-English share of the global economy will rise to 70 per cent.

For detailed and up-to-date projections the strategist will want to keep a careful eye on www.glreach.com as well as constantly reassessing their customers' emerging needs and the activities of competition.

Research Languages online

| Language | Number (M) of native speakers 2001 | Number (M) of native speakers 2003 (projected) |
|----------|----------|----------|
| English | 192.10 | 230.00 |
| Czech | 0.35 | 3.00 |
| Dutch | 6.90 | 10.00 |

| | | |
|---|---|---|
| Finnish | 2.20 | 4.00 |
| French | 14.20 | 30.00 |
| German | 22.40 | 46.00 |
| Greek | 1.50 | 3.00 |
| Hungarian | 0.80 | 3.00 |
| Italian | 12.30 | 23.00 |
| Polish | 3.10 | 6.00 |
| Portuguese | 11.60 | 32.00 |
| Romanian | 0.60 | 1.00 |
| Russian | 9.30 | 15.00 |
| Danish and Icelandic | 2.70 | 5.30 |
| Norwegian | 2.20 | 4.50 |
| Swedish | 4.50 | 10.00 |
| Slovak | 0.70 | 5.40 |
| Slovenian | 0.46 | 5.40 |
| Spanish | 21.70 | 60.00 |
| Turkish | 2.20 | 2.00 |

## Asian languages

| | | |
|---|---|---|
| Arabic | 2.53 | 6.00 |
| Chinese | 29.00 | 160.00 |
| Hebrew | 1.00 | 6.00 |
| Japanese | 38.80 | 58.00 |
| Korean | 16.80 | 35.00 |

Notes: Native language rather than country of birth is used so that, for example, 'Portuguese' includes Portuguese speakers in Brazil. Native speakers of any language may be fluent in another – so that a large number of Scandinavians, Dutch, Belgians and Swiss are fluent in more than their native tongue.

As far as business e-mails, newsletters and the like are concerned there may be good news on the horizon. Wordlingo is offering software that is able to translate such documents into any of ten most 'popular' languages. Their Commercial E-mail Translator was announced in April 2001 and will be available by the time this book goes to print. I am always a little sceptical about translation software. Even with some linguistic knowledge and a commercial dictionary I remember that in my early days with General Motors I advised Spanish customers to fill their lavatory cisterns with only certain grades of petrol – and software is supposed to be stupid. But the question does arise as to whether even that software that is least capable of thought can do worse than we human beings. Independent research suggests that 91 per cent of *Fortune* 500 companies currently get it wrong when responding to foreign language enquiries. Add to that Globalsight research that concludes that 62 per cent of companies fail to grasp the full challenges of globalization and it seems that we may need all the help that we can get.

☞ *See also*:    Where is the growth likely to occur?

## Is this the time to go online? What is the global business outlook?

These days it is difficulty to decide whether the global economy is wildly volatile or whether it is the prognostications of the soothsayers that change with a speed to make simple souls such as me dizzy. I take some comfort from David Myddleton's dictum that a forecast is merely what might have happened if what actually happened had not happened. In October 2000 the IMF (International Monetary Fund) was unworried by the expected turndown in the US economy and was forecasting world growth in trade of 4.2 per cent – a very healthy rate of expansion. Within six months all is relative gloom and doom. Not only is the IMF slashing their forecast by a full 1 per cent, they are suggesting real problems in some of the strongest trading nations.

| Revised forecast | |
| --- | --- |
| Global growth | 3.2% |
| Euro zone | 2.4% |
| (Germany) | 1.9% |
| USA | 1.5% |
| Japan | 0.6% |

These are depressing figures after the euphoria of only half a year ago, but perhaps we should not get too despondent.

✓ Continued growth, albeit with a slowdown, is being forecast. No one is talking about a recession – yet. They are getting depressed because the bigger cake is not so big as they dreamed it might be. It is not quite true that no one is talking about a recession. The Economic Cycle Research Institute, basing their thinking on the indicators that they identified in 1989, believe that a real recession may be difficult if not impossible to avoid. I think it is fair to say that they are virtually a lone voice, but it is, as always, a voice of which businesspeople need to be aware.

✓ Greenspan is still tweaking the US economy. He is a conservative by nature and will not risk doing too much too soon, but he has made it clear that he is prepared to do what it takes to get the American economy back on a fast track. He is unlikely to end up doing too little too late.

✓ The US economy might not be in such dire straits. In my old business, automobiles, there is a tendency whenever things begin to look less than rosy to reduce inventories drastically. The American automotive industry has made a hasty reduction from 90 days' supply to 67 days' supply. This is a lot of metal in a 17 million a year car market. And the size of that market is the key point. Sales have remained on track for that 17 million annual figure in spite of the 'downturn' in the economy as a whole. This means that the industry needs to build inventories again or risk being unable to exploit the demand. When inventories were cut this took a full 1 per cent of economic growth out of the picture. The return to normality plus the need to build quickly is expected to add 1.5 per cent. So the total effect could be to add as much as 2.5 per cent to the economic growth of the USA in the second quarter. But there is more. The automotive industry consumes a considerable share of the output of other industries from steel to microprocessors. The effect on the US and, subsequently, on the global economy of a change of tactic in this industry could be considerable, fast and sustained.

✓ Figures get skewed in strange ways. Manufacturing which accounts for only 16 per cent of the US economy accounted for 60 per cent of the reduction of corporate profits overall in the last quarter of 2000. The National Association of Purchasing report (April 2001) suggests there is reasonable hope of recovery in the manufacturing sector. Ironically it is technology that appears to continue to be a drag on the US economy as the hi-tech corporates, like the automotive manufacturers, reduce inventories and workforces.

✓ The general opinion among specialists is that, due to the increased global reach offered in part by the web, even a severe downturn in the USA would not have the devastating effect on world trade of years gone by.

✓ Much of the problem in advanced countries relates to the communications industry and the high borrowing that results from the crazy prices paid to governments as a result of the auction of G3 licences. What the government takes away it spends and, as Keynes showed, all that a government needs to do to avoid recession is to print and spend money. (Possibly this is the only thing that governments are good at doing. Recessions result from governments getting cold feet and failing to exercise their single talent.)

✓ As I write, Japan has a new prime minister and, as Anatole Kaletski of *The Times* has so lucidly shown, Japan's problems are relatively easy to solve given a determination to solve them. Their problem has been one of political and institutional will. Perhaps a new broom will sweep clean. At least Japan has some good news to digest. In February 2001 the jobless rate fell from a record 4.9 per cent to 4.7 per cent. No less than 280000 people found jobs, and household spending rose by 3.1 per cent.

On the other hand, the IMF seems to have ignored the potential for a worsening economic situation in Latin America, particularly Argentina. So it looks like a matter of 'you pays your money and takes your pick'. The lesson for businesspeople, however, is clear. If business appears to be harder to come by then many companies will be looking to find economies. There are major economies to be had online which, unlike other cost-cutting exercises can often lead to more rather than less business. The Internet gives companies the opportunity to be as global as they choose as long as they have customer-delighting infrastructure in place. This means that an online presence can, with a little thought enable them to reach those markets least affected by any turndown. Problems in business always create opportunities for someone. Liquidators, wind-up merchants that they are, long for an occasional recession. Consultants know that they can profit as much from good times when companies seek to expand as much as from bad times when they need help to survive. E-commerce is here to stay. Used intelligently it may help to proof a business against the worst effects of boom and bust. When is the right time is a strategic decision, but like all strategic decisions it needs to be based on understanding that goes a little deeper than the newspaper headline of the day.

**Mini Case Study** **Opportunity knocks for Campal Electronics, April 2001**

Just as computer manufacturers are throwing up their hands and openly talking of overproduction, saturation, downturn and falling demand, Ray Chen, the boss of Campal Electronics Inc., sees an opportunity where others see a problem. He is more than doubling his workforce and gearing up production from the $2.2 billion achieved last year. He supplies the 'naysayers ' of the moment, Compaq, Toshiba, Dell and the like, with notebook computers. In spite of the high inventories that are worrying his customers at present, he argues that if profits are falling they will want to buy a greater share of their total product from efficient low-cost producers such as his company in order to rebuild profitability. He sees their perception of a problem as his opportunity and is gearing up to exploit it.

Of course he is taking a risk. Of course he might turn out to be embarrassingly wrong, but if he is right he might prove to be embarrassingly prosperous. We cannot all swim against the tide, but it is incumbent on us in business to look for opportunity all the time while being ever vigilant to risk and conscious of what we will do if our fears prove to be more accurate than our hopes.

If you decide that the time to go online is when others are shaking their heads sadly and looking for the safe exit, I suggest that you might want to keep the advice of Nordea, arguably the Internet's most successful online bank to date, in mind.

- ✓ Start early. Things are unlikely to deliver success from day one so give yourself some time to work out the bugs before they become major problems.

- ✓ Start simple. Avoid trying to be all things to all customers simply because an online presence gives you exciting new opportunities. Do what you know you can do well and build on that firm base. Make it easy to do business with you, even if that business is limited at first.

- ✓ Start frugally. Do not be tempted into spending so much on your online initiative that there is nothing left over for intelligent marketing. Do not reinvent any wheels. Use what is readily and cheaply available as long as it does the job well enough for you to be able to deliver superb customer service.

✓ Start by leveraging what you already have. It is easier and cheaper to test a new idea with existing customers than to spend a fortune trying to attract passing trade. When you are consistently delighting the people who trust you, you have an opportunity to attract others like them at minimum cost.

✓ Let your customers drive your products or services. Add new products or services when you are convinced that your customers are prepared to pay for them rather than when you believe that you have a good idea. Years ago, when I was a callow consultant to the automotive industry, a client manufacturer believed that extended hours of service opening by its dealers would lead to increased customer loyalty. They planned to survey customers to ask if they would welcome being able to have their cars serviced at night. I was discussing this with a canny Scottish dealer who told me: 'We never ask the questions sent out by the corporation. We ask directly if we offered the service when would you buy it. We get profitable business, not warm feelings that way.'

## Will new methods for accessing the Internet build business opportunities?

The use of television to access the Internet is rapidly becoming commonplace and is enabling a growing number of people to e-mail and buy online. According to Ovum Consulting projections the growth of this medium will be dramatic. They forecast that there will be at least 13 million households using interactive television this year (2001), growing to 226 million by 2006. Buying through interactive television will, if Ovum's projections are correct, grow faster with sales of $58 million this year growing to $44.8 billion in five years' time.

Technically the major shortcoming of interactive television at present is that while the flow of information to the subscriber is fast and compares with the speed of corporate systems, the flow back is the equivalent of a 28 kps modem. To be truly interactive the flow in both directions needs to appear to be immediate.

In December 2000 Hewlett-Packard and ATG published a major survey of mobile e-business (www.hp-atg.com). Some of the key findings were as follows.

Only 17 per cent of respondents were using the Internet to enable consumers to shop online and only 21 per cent were offering businesses the opportunity to trade through their websites. The vast majority (98 per cent), whether they sold to business or directly to the consumer, were still seeing the Internet primarily as a means of delivering content and information (this in spite of the massive growth in online sales, particularly in the USA and UK).

A mere 17 per cent of respondents thought themselves to be 'very good' at providing a personalized customer experience or delivering very good integration between online and offline business. Just 15 per cent offered very good targeted and regular e-mail contact with customers or were doing equally well with integrated multi-channel offerings (web and WAP, etc.). Up to a little over one-third of the respondents believed that their organizations were 'very poor' in these key online business activities.

Seventy-seven per cent of businesses believed that their most important priority was to generate more people to visit their websites, and 87 per cent believed that the key issue was to build stronger relationships with customers.

Boards of directors of companies surveyed are in no hurry, it seems, to grasp the emerging business opportunities. A total of 67 per cent had either no strategy in place or had a plan to 'wait and see' based on further technology developments.

In summary, if mobile access is typical, and I think that it is, the new ways to access the Internet are taken seriously by the majority of businesses only to the extent that they see it as a challenge. In spite of the massive global growth potential very few have a strategy in place to exploit the opportunities. Many, it seems will 'wait and see' until they see competition setting the rules by which they must play in the future. I am convinced that this is due at least in part to a misunderstanding of the role of strategic thinking. A strategy is a flexible plan to take you from where you are to where you want to be – the keyword being 'flexible'. No firm that takes its future seriously can afford to be without a strategy in any key market. Some new ways of accessing the web will, in due course, dominate the market and make the PC and laptop almost redundant. Nobody knows which for sure, but one thing is certain. You need a well-thought-out strategy that includes cool consideration of what is happening in allied fields. Already the boffins have developed the capability to produce mobile telephone displays that are bigger and clearer than their predecessors, and in full colour. Where is such a capability likely to take us?

One research and consultancy company expects it to take us into an era of virtually universal online access. Cahner's report (28 March 2001) that as sales of PCs reduce, sales of alternative equipment will more than make up any gap. They estimate that sales of wireless, televisual and other means of accessing the Internet will increase by at least 40 per cent a year for the next four years.

*See also*: What does the future hold?

## How will the growth of wireless Internet access compare with other media?

The usual problem arises. Too much hype in the early days has led to too much disappointment today. The growth of wireless Internet access will be patchy with some countries specifically placing their eggs mainly in that basket while others stick principally to the 'tried and true'. Also you need to differentiate those who use wireless methods as a fashion accessory, as opposed to serious users – surfers and dilettantes against business users and buyers. In spite of current economic difficulties Japan has taken to wireless communication in a big way. Other countries are taking more of a wait-and-see approach.

The potential, however, remains considerable.

| Internet-enabled mobile telephone use, 2005 (projections) | |
| --- | --- |
| Asia Pacific | 481 million |
| Western Europe | 246 million |
| USA | 238 million (including 24 million in Canada) |
| Latin America | 82 million |
| Eastern Europe | 69 million |
| Afro-Mid East | 59 million |

# PEOPLE AGAIN

Some years ago the great Peter Drucker was a speaker at a major international conference. One who shared the platform offered a vision of a glorious future for business, but without any obvious conviction. When he had finished speaking, Drucker asked a question which made it clear why message and delivery appeared to jar: 'Please tell me sir. Why is it that you always snarl when you mention people?' I guess that one way or another people will get in the way of your future, if you let them.

## Isn't there a problem getting qualified people?

There is, but paradoxically that may not be a major problem. Where there is an area of difficulty there emerges a novel way to deal with it. According to the silicon.com Skills Survey, approximately 44 per cent of European companies are finding it difficult to identify and recruit people with the right kinds of skills. The shortages range from 39 per cent of companies in the UK to over 50 per cent in Germany. So there can be no reasonable doubt that a skills shortage exists.

Whether such a shortage is serious or not depends on the ability and willingness of firms to pool skilled labour. According to silicon.com, over one-third of British techies earn more than £70 000 a year, which suggests that there has been something of an auction for services. If, however, you could use and pay for only that part of a skilled team's costs that you actually need when you need it, it could prove to be an economical as well as efficient use of the limited skill base. That is what ASP is about (see below).

Of course there are reasons why you might want to employ your own team. You may believe that employment gives greater control for example, but you might wish to consider whether, generally speaking, you get treated better as a customer or as an employer, or whether you actually need the services of some employees for all the hours for which you pay.

There is no doubt that, while only a few individuals have critical skills, the cost of employing them is high and the temptation for them to be available to a better offer is great. When loyalty comes with a high price tag it may be that alternatives are worth considering. After all, there is only one Faith Popcorn, Tom Peters or even Tom Lambert. We make the best that we can of that situation by making ourselves available at fees that some will find outrageous, but we can deliver masses of added value to a firm from one day's work. Truly skilled people in any field can do the same.

Meanwhile the highly skilled element in e-commerce is declining fast as the really clever individuals develop ways in which anyone with a touch of common sense and a degree of application can do the necessary. For example Coastal Sites (United Kingdom) Ltd and our American partners can deliver top search engine positioning at relatively low cost because we have the systems that no longer require the high levels of skill of yore.

See also:   Is the Internet likely to become a preferred medium for training?
            What do 'coal face' managers need to know about the Internet?

*Note:* April 2001

Such is the volatility of the IT world at present that a number of companies have announced layoffs of qualified people. It seems now that suddenly the shortage of skilled workers that led countries to change their immigration policy is to be followed by a glut of expertise. Perhaps the time has come where IT professionals will themselves be seeking to develop a capability to sell their abilities and market their skills.

## How much time are people spending online?

According to Jupiter research (April 2001) the average time spent online in the UK is currently seven hours a week and growing at a rate of 94 per cent a year. In Germany and France, however, growth is stronger and in France the rate is 225 per cent, with Germany growing marginally more quickly at a rate of 226 per cent. The difference is due to three major factors. One is cultural, German and French Internet users tend to use the web in different ways that tend to be more time-consuming. The other is a simple matter of cost. It is still more expensive on average to access the Internet from the UK. Expensively marketed 'Friaco' (unmetered access for a monthly fee) systems are prevalent in the UK, but these appeal in general only to those who are specifically heavy Internet users. In continental Europe, however, the tendency is towards 'Bundled' telecommunication services in which 'free' Internet access is included. This approach appeals to a wider range of users who seek value across the broad spectrum of telecommunications services. It is perhaps significant that 'free' trial offers preceding Friaco monthly payment services have from time to time been oversubscribed in Great Britain to the degree that potential customers have spent hours trying to get online rather than surfing the net, and have gone back to paying for each call. From a business viewpoint the important factor is that, whatever the local disadvantages or benefits may be, time spent online is growing at a fast rate and it is arguable that the much hyped difficulties facing dot coms in recent months have little or no effect on Internet usage.

**STOP PRESS 2 April 2001**

It is almost as if they read my mind. No sooner was the above written than British Telecom announced that they had cut the cost of their Friaco service by 40 per cent. Where BT goes other telecommunications providers have little choice but to follow. Perhaps we will now see a major growth in time spent online in the UK to put domestic business opportunities closer to those of mainland Europe. (Or perhaps the time will be devoted to games and pornography sites. We will be watching with interest.)

*See also*:     What are the business barriers to growth?

## Is surfing the web addictive?

The question may seem like an odd one, but research firm Websense asked just that question of employees in the UK, France and Germany in April 2001. No less than 90 per cent of employees expressed the belief that one can be hooked on surfing the web. Surfing 'during breaks' was approved by 73 per cent of workers, although only 41 per cent actually admitted that they used work facilities and working time for 'personal' use of the Internet. Seventy-one per cent thought that it is 'reasonable' for management to manage access to the Internet during working hours.

Obviously web-surfing is not strictly speaking addictive in the sense that tobacco, alcohol or cocaine are, but like use of those substances 'web abuse' can and will be 'justified' on the grounds that it is hard to give it up and that the responsibility to ensure a 'clean' workforce lies with management. Let us hope that in this case management will not be so naive as the mythical American boss who, on hearing that his highly paid executives were snorting coke, wondered aloud how they got the bottles up their noses.

*See also*:     Below.

## Will our employees waste time on pornography sites and the like if we encourage them to go online?

The Internet can be a wonderful excuse for bored employees to waste time and therefore your money. There is so much to see that playing about or if you prefer it, surfing the web can become a major activity at work as much as at home. On 12 April 2001 a report suggesting that the average employee with Internet access is currently wasting almost an hour every day looking at pornography, planning their holidays or whatever. This is currently costing business in Great Britain alone £500 million each year. Fortunately governments, researchers and the mighty Microsoft are all working on the problem.

Like aimless chat around the coffee machine or using work resources for home interests, the use of the web must be managed. As W.E. Deming said, you can only manage what you can measure and web visits have the very real advantage of being easily measured and controlled.

You can have 'net nannies' installed to protect your children. Similarly you can control what your employees can access at work. It is also becoming legal in a growing number of countries, in spite of the lunatic fringe of the personal liberty union, for employers to monitor both Internet surfing and e-mails.

# THE ENVIRONMENT AND OTHER VALID CONCERNS

## Will being online ease the burden of environmental reporting?

The short answer must be not if a well-funded collection of politicians, bureaucrats, economists and eco-warriors have their way. In the UK under the leadership of Michael Meacher, the Forum for the Future, the DTI (Department of Trade and Industry), the DETR (Department of the Environment, Transport and the Regions), the Cabinet Office and the Demos Think Tank are combining to require online companies to complete potentially mandatory reports concerning their effect on the environment. As usual when government seeks to impose itself on business, Meacher is presenting this new imposition as if it were a cost-reduction exercise. Jonathon Porritt offers it as 'wealth creation without social or environmental costs'. If today the UK, then will it be tomorrow the world? At the same time as Meacher issued his threat of mandatory reporting, Porritt was able to announce that his Forum for the Future had received EU funding to extend their 'studies' throughout the union.

It is unlikely that the Bush administration in the USA will attempt to impose a similar obligation on American business, but meanwhile one is bound to wonder in a whimsical way about the environmental cost of bringing together the DTI, the DETR, the Forum of the Future, the Cabinet Office and Demos. Given the fact that the British government spends more on conferences and hotels than it does on helping sub-Saharan Africa to fight the AIDS epidemic, I am not optimistic that any environmental reporting will lead to anything more than a lot of talk by politicians and the imposition of a meaningless burden on business. The hot air expended on worthy discussions may have a deleterious effect on global warming while bureaucrat's unrestrained joy in issuing reports suggests deforestation on a grand scale. If Mr Porritt wants 'wealth creation without social or environmental costs', he might consider how to reduce the number of bureaucrats that he invites to his publicly funded jamborees in future.

Meanwhile, far from creating wealth, he and his friends appear to be hell bent on giving our American competitors another advantage.

*See also*:   In an international e-commerce dispute, which country has jurisdiction?

## Is the Internet providing new opportunities for fraud?

Security systems for online transactions are getting better by the day and, in general, it is safer to use a credit card online than to hand it to a waiter in your favourite restaurant or to give your details over the telephone. The EU Commission, however, announced on 20 February 2001 a worrying increase in fraud using the Internet. In the year 2000 there was a 50 per cent increase in fraudulent misuse of credit cards online, at a cost of $553 million. In the interest of protecting your customers you are strongly advised to use the best security systems that you can afford and to keep abreast of developments in electronic signatures and the like.

### A new cold war?

The Federal Bureau of Investigation no less has recently issued warnings that hackers operating from the new badlands of Russia and the Ukraine are conducting blackmail activities by breaking into e-commerce sites and stealing customers' credit card information which they either sell to crooked third parties or publish on the Internet if their demands are not met. Such cases will cause some would-be buyers online to think twice. The fact remains, however, that credit card fraud continues to be a bigger problem offline than it is on. Few readers will not know someone whose statement suddenly showed, for example, someone else's mobile telephone account after using the card in a restaurant, shop or petrol station. They will also know that the credit card companies are efficient in cancelling the debt and tracing the crook.

Just to give an idea of how easy credit card fraud is offline consider this. A lifer in an American gaol a couple of years ago used his own credit card and phone card to take out an advertisement offering the kind of deal that nobody who failed to believe the old adage that 'if a deal looks too good to be true, it is' could refuse. Credit card details flooded to his prison cell. He then used the telephone to place orders for goods using others' card details and, just for the hell of it, had the goods delivered randomly to addresses all over the USA that he picked out of telephone directories. The fact is and will remain that no matter how smart the security becomes there will be someone, somewhere, spending their time finding a way to breach it. If business believed that the existence of smart criminals was a reason to cease trading we would have gone back to local barter years ago. As it is, companies owe it to their customers to do everything that they can to protect them, but if you wait for perfect security you will be like the businessperson who never makes assumptions – you will never make anything.

At least in the USA customers who believe that they have had a raw deal have somewhere to turn. The Internet Fraud Complaints Center (*sic*) handles complaints and works with authorities to bring the fraudsters to book. In the first six months of operation they dealt with 20 014 complaints ranging from serious fraud and money laundering to those who, having looked for pornography on the Internet, discovered that they did not like what they found. There is no similar organization in Europe or elsewhere at present, although one ought to be able to assume that if the American model is successful it will be copied elsewhere. The gross number of 20 014 complaints in one year seems huge, but the massive growth in online buying suggests that, in spite of the best efforts of the high-tech fraudsters and crooks, the vast majority of customers either feel that they have not been taken for a ride or they simply feel that it is not serious enough to complain.

### No rest for the wicked

As the USA increasingly establishes a tougher anti-fraud climate, users elsewhere need to be increasingly on their guard. The global scope of the Internet means that if the going gets tough in any country, fraudsters can readily turn their attentions elsewhere. As it becomes more difficult to get away with fraudulent activity in the USA more crooks will naturally seek to gravitate towards Europe. As Europe solves the problem they will follow the Bonnie and Clyde philosophy, 'we rob banks because that is where the money is'. Fraud is not limited to individuals being robbed by bogus auction sites and the like. Business is increasingly being subjected to invoices for services that were never carried out or goods that were neither ordered nor delivered. These are crude attempts to defraud business that should fail through normal checking of authorizations and bought ledgers, but they are indicative of the fact that somewhere out there, there will be more creative brains at work and the Internet provides new opportunities for them to cast their net worldwide.

In April 2001 silicon.com announced the first results of their ongoing investigation into Internet fraud and again it seems that people are too often failing to make matters public. The latest scam is one in which fraudsters are producing clones of major corporate websites that are accurate in virtually every detail. People rarely think twice, even online about giving their credit card or telephone account details to respected banks or telecommunications companies and it appears that there is a real risk that the crooks are in for something of a bonanza. It is alleged that problems seldom get reported because the major institutions have no wish to damage further the sometimes fragile reputation of online security. In these days when anyone in the world can, at relatively low cost, be their own ISP (Internet Service Provider) we cannot be sure that there is a firm out there ready and willing to pull the plug on the crooks. It is therefore incumbent on all of us to report all cases of fraud, no matter how apparently trivial. The online world is no more subject to criminal activity than any other, but unless we know accurately the size of the problem the motivation to introduce solutions is sometimes barely strong enough to lead to action.

Concerns are still being expressed concerning fraud online, especially after a dishwasher in the USA acquired details of the rich and famous and allegedly used free library online facilities to defraud them of millions. But keep it in perspective. Fraud online still accounts for only 2 per cent of total known business fraud.

*The business to business situation*

In spite of massive growth the full potential of B2B is still being constrained by concerns over security. In a recent research study by ICL of firms who have taken a 'wait and see' attitude to buying online, no less than 95 per cent indicated that they are not yet satisfied that financial transactions are secure. Forty-four per cent of respondents expressed concerns that commercially sensitive information might not be secure online and 50 per cent were worried about 'technology integration issues'. On the other hand, of those companies that had bought online, 85 per cent reported a reduction in order processing time and 61 per cent had won lower purchasing costs.

*It's all in the game*

Online security remains a major factor and a moving feast. On St George's Day 2001 it was announced that a $50 000 prize for hacking into a dummy website protected by all the bells and whistles of security had been won by a Polish team of hackers. This competition was both a promotional tactic for a security conference and a real-world test of security arrangements. The same challenge had been issued three times previously and all attempts to hack into the site had failed.

On the same day, however, it was announced that the Better Business Bureau in the USA is partnering with leading European bodies to support the development of better online security. The ongoing competition between hackers and business will continue, but life will also continue to get tougher for those who choose to fool around making a nuisance of themselves to no good purpose.

Security is by no means perfect. I suspect it never is, nor will it be, online or off, but good systems are in place and they are getting better all the time. Major corporations worldwide are not worried and are putting their buying policy where their trust is so confidence will grow with experience.

## What can a busy manager do about security?

### Security checklist

The executive needs to ensure that professional advice is taken where necessary and:

✓ Authentication: Your communications reach the intended recipient and nobody else.

✓ Non-repudiation: Your system shows that the communication was actually received.

✓ Integrity: What you sent was received unchanged and in its entirety.

✓ Confidentiality: Nobody other than the recipient is able to access confidential or sensitive information.

Various tried and trusted systems are now in place for ensuring the above. Your technical people should, in turn, be able to convince you that the systems that they have put in place work. Simply asking the right questions of those who supply and those who operate the systems is a major step in making sure that your transactions are as secure as is possible. Asking the right questions may also ensure that your people keep themselves appraised of developments as they arise and make sensible decisions as to which, if any, they employ in the future.

Research 'I'm not at home – please burgle me!'
Research by UPAQ (a firm specializing in online security) suggests that some of us are not exactly doing our bit when it comes to tackling fraud on the Internet. According to UPAQ's latest survey:

Ninety-five per cent of users expect to be the victims of some form of online fraud.

Ninety-six per cent send sensitive information by e-mail in spite of their fears.

Sixty-eight per cent understand that e-mail is not normally secure.

Fifty-seven per cent are nonetheless happy to send, for example, their bank details.

With intelligent and committed crooks around nothing is entirely secure and although we know that handing a credit card to a waiter is fraught with danger, is it not reasonable to expect that those who recognize the danger should avoid inviting trouble. Encryption and other security techniques need to be explored, but the question arises 'what do we do about laziness and stupidity?' Regularly I read or hear of senior businesspeople that receive by e-mail confidential and sensitive information from employees of competitors who seem to be either too stupid or too lazy to check their address books before squirting secret information around the Internet. As an example, one leading businessman was surprised to find that during a delicate negotiation with another company he was sent details of that company's negotiating stance and fallback position. This did not turn out to be a double bluff. It was sheer carelessness.

As a purveyor of a possible solution UPAQ may have an axe to grind, but any businessperson should be sensitive to a timely warning and consider all the actions open to them.

## Can we trust the predictions of the so-called gurus – like you?

David Myddleton pointed out that a forecast is 'what might have happened if what did happen didn't'. Forecasters of any kind can get it embarrassingly wrong at times. But before you throw the baby out with the bath water consider this: contrary to idiocy on the part of the trainer who used to write 'never assume, because you make an "ass" out of "u" and "me"' the predictions of the online gurus are based on extrapolating facts, not inventing fictions. Certainly there will be times when they get things wrong, but trend analysis is now closer to a science than it is to an art form. You can if you wish ignore the best available information, but where does that leave you? You will be facing the ultimate assumption – that total ignorance is a meaningful tool.

I can only suggest that you take the best information available and make an executive decision that it does or does not seem convincing to you, and then act, because if you wait for perfect information before you act, I predict that you will wait an eternity, and then some.

## What are the effects on business of the assumption that the Internet is best left to technical people?

Research by Alta Vista shows that as many as 83 per cent of potential buyers visit a website once and, finding that they cannot easily buy online, they leave never to return. Technical people like technical solutions. This means that far too often they develop beautiful and impressive websites that distract the buyer from their main purposes of getting information or making a purchase. The University of Wisconsin at Madison has conducted a four-year study that shows that serious users of the Internet prefer dark writing on a white background and easy navigation through the site. They find the bells and whistles beloved of technical people to be an irritating distraction that tends to make them leave the site and make their purchases elsewhere.

There is also the question of technology for its own sake. Not only do technical people want to use technology to the extreme, they often want the extremes of technology to use. This can be a massive cost for a company as technical wizards pursue one technology after another in the hunt for the Holy Grail of perfection. On the other hand the purchase of the wrong technology can be an even greater cost. So what is the non-technical executive to do?

Forrester, one of the leading names in web research, has a belief that it can help the executive to, at the very least, continue to play a part in the decision-making process where technology is concerned. It has for much of the year 2000 conducted e-business techrankings where if laboratory tests and surveys technical products giving each a ranking based on 100 key points of utility and effectiveness. Forrester has announced that this service is soon (March 2001) to be available in Europe. Armed with this information the executive and the technical team should be in an enhanced position to cut costs and improve performance. Take a look at www.forrester.com and keep your eye on it for future developments.

## Are there market sectors that are having greater than normal difficulties online?

In spite of the apparently growing confidence of Tesco's online operation in the UK, North American grocers are continuing to experience real difficulties. As of late February 2001 Priceline.com has withdrawn from the online grocery business as has Streamline.com, while Webvan.com has been forced to shelve its expansion plans and has cut 220 jobs.

The following mini case study is an example of what can happen to the online grocer as success creates record levels of losses.

### Mini Case Study   It's been a great quarter, but!

Peapod.com the Chicago based online grocer serves the US customer from coast to coast, and that seems to be part of the problem. In the last quarter of 2000 Peapod attracted cohorts of new customers and produced record sales of $23.7 million. Does this success give cause for celebration? Apparently not. In the same financial period the company recorded record losses of $23.8 million, just $100 000 more than their total sales revenues.

With 124 000 active customers Peapod have done well building the business, but at a cost. They now have only an estimated $44.7 million in the kitty ($14.7 million in cash and $30 million in committed loan capital) with a minimum cash requirement of $50 million to keep them in business this year up to the point where they anticipate turning a profit (2001).

There are a number of problems that the online grocery business needs to overcome. They need to have and maintain a delivery infrastructure from day one in each market that they cover, regardless of how long it takes to get the customers to begin to buy in significant and profitable volumes. They need major investment in warehouse facilities, vehicles and people. Unless they have a substantial bricks and mortar operation that is turning in high profits and attracting large numbers of customers, they have a branding and advertising problem that must be solved quickly and as economically as possible. They need suppliers that can and will offer a 'just-in-time' delivery that is state of the art or they must have other outlets that can be turned on immediately, particularly for perishables. Unless this and more has been carefully and comprehensively built into the strategic plan the online grocery sector will continue to be beset by problems.

Tesco have the advantage of a reasonably compact, but highly populous market in the UK, along with a national identity as the leading supermarket in the country, yet they found online trading tough at first. American grocers are tempted to attack well-populated conurbations that can be 1000 miles or more away from even the most centrally placed base. Perhaps their current difficulties will see the return of your friendly neighbourhood corner shop – only online.

The BCG (Boston Consulting Group) published a report at the end of February 2001 that offers a solution to the problems being faced by e-tailers. 'Winning the Online Consumer 2.0' concludes that what ails the B2C Internet business is that companies have not planned their infrastructure in such a way as to be able to 'respond effectively to customer demands'. This is borne out by research findings that indicate that the best of the web e-tailing activities (books and health products) manage to satisfy only 31 per cent of their customers, while four out of five customers of travel and computer hardware were dissatisfied with the service given. A more detailed look at the BCG report shows that more than one in ten buyers paid their money and received no goods in return. All this dissatisfaction did not stop 68 million customers in the USA from spending $28 billion online in the year 2000, according to the US Census Bureau. But if something is not done to improve matters, one can only assume that it soon will. Thus, having read this book, the pessimist will be thinking that 'this online business is too tough to work', the realist will see a superb business opportunity based on nothing more than doing what any business should be doing every day of every week. To underline the opportunity the average spend by the satisfied customer in this fast-growing marketplace was $673 last year.

The Boston Consulting Group five-point plan is aimed at benchmarking and they make it clear that doing one or two rather than doing all five will not cut it. They suggest that you measure and improve the following:

✓ Visitor to buyer conversion rates. Remember that one research project by Alta Vista showed that 83 per cent of potential buyers leave a website 'never to return' because buying or getting the information that would lead to an informed buying decision was simply too difficult.

✓ Traffic in terms of the number of unique visitors. Traffic-building is important, but it is not enough. Millions of adolescents of all ages visited the Victoria's Secret (a leading lingerie company) website, but only a small minority were buyers. Design your website to attract customers (and worthwhile customers at that) first and foremost, and then ensure that you are listed high on the major search engines.

✓ The proportion of repeat customers. Many customers make their first purchase online with their hearts in their mouths. Give them the service and the sense of security that they crave and they will come back for more.

✓ Orders per customer. There are only three economic ways to increase revenues: sell bigger initial orders, sell bigger repeat orders, or attract customers to buy more frequently. Make sure that you are doing what is right for your customers and your business.

✓ Ratio of repeat order revenue to first-time order revenue. If you build customer satisfaction and it fails to translate into bigger orders then you have failed to build satisfaction high enough. Research by the US Census Bureau shows that the level of satisfaction can make almost a 40 per cent difference to the level of buying.

And you back all this by 'tailoring your offering for the high-value customer segment and cement loyalty by offering flawless service'.

Whether you serve a retail or a business market, whether you sell products or services, or whether you are online or only trading from bricks and mortar premises, the Internet has opened the way to a new level of international competition. To survive and prosper every firm now needs to think about how it can achieve and sustain being a world-class company.

### Research Achieving world class

Recent work at the London Business School has led to the development of a ten-point agenda for achieving world class:

1. Think before using the next faddish idea.

2. Copying what others are rushing to do is inadequate, the aim is to find new ways of gaining an edge on competitors, not aping them.

3. Success comes from incorporating the best ideas into distinctly local solutions.

4. The role of the CEO in pushing forward change remains crucial. (But one person cannot often do it alone. The CEO needs to galvanize his or her direct reports so that consistent leadership comes from the whole team.)

5. Financial measures are a misleading guide to the corporation's long-term health.

6. Non-financial measures – customer satisfaction, retention and advocacy, employee morale, quality, productivity growth or decline – are vital warning or encouraging signs for the three or four years ahead.

7. Set ambitious goals.

8. Survival is never enough. (Either you know what others are doing worldwide and strive with passion to be the best or you will not survive.)

9. Combine efficiency with effectiveness. (Constantly improve skills and competencies in advance of competitors and in line with the most worthwhile customer's expectations.)

10. Strategic innovation is vital. (The only sustainable competitive advantage is a company's ability to achieve continuous improvement. This means freeing up creativity and innovation, which in turn calls for state-of-the-art facilitation and group dynamics skills within the company.)

## How do we become a world-class business?

*Lambert's Laws*

*Nothing should be done in a business, unless:*

- There is a clear business reason for doing it.
- It will pay for itself in a reasonable time.
- It can be explained in simple language to all those who will play a part in making it work.

*The effort to become world class is justified if:*

- Doing so meets a specific business objective and provides a sustainable competitive edge in a worthwhile marketplace.

- The timing and value of the return on the investment of effort and money can be forecast with confidence.

- The initiative can be presented in a way that ensures that everyone involved in the business is committed to success and competent to achieve it.

*Becoming world class demands continuous building of capabilities*

1. Develop long-, medium- and short-term objectives, identify the capabilities needed to reach them and determine strategies to acquire or develop them.

2. Balance the dilemmas. (World-class business leaders, and those whom they manage and develop, become adept at balancing the strategic and practical goals of the corporation they are also skilled at balancing the needs of efficiency vs effectiveness, differentiation vs low cost, current financial goals vs long-term vision, consistency vs flexibility, centralization vs local autonomy.)

3. Look outward. The international dimension is increasingly important even for companies that choose not to strive to be global. Nothing less than being at the forefront of the highest international standards is sufficient to ensure success, even in the domestic market. The more sophisticated the domestic market is, the more there is a need to be able to compete, head on, with the world's best, especially online.

4. Maintain a bias for action. World-class businesses (large or small) must foster risk-taking, but must do so only as part of a well-established process of learning from triumphs as well as mistakes and speedy and effective problem-solving without blame-fixing.

In addition the global company must:

✓ Bridge the paradox of using standardized products to meet customized needs.

✓ Be responsive and flexible, but at the lowest possible cost.

✓ Have a physical presence in key markets that it wants to dominate even if that presence is limited to having the right strategic partner. Few things will give a new customer greater confidence than knowing that your partner in their locality is someone that they already have reason to trust.

✓ Constantly monitor the emerging needs of even apparently homogenous markets. Needs, wants and desires change and with their change the opportunities for giving superior service, often at lower cost, grow.

✓ Utilize global cost efficiencies flexibly in a constantly changing economic and political environment. Customer and employee loyalty can each be vital to delivering cost reductions, so foster both.

✓ Avoid duplication of data acquisition etc.

✓ Share information skills and knowledge speedily within the business and with your strategic partners.

✓ Have an excellent system of communications backed by a willingness to communicate. Learn to use electronic means to keep every stakeholder appraised of what is happening and why they should be happy and proud to be with you.

## In an international e-commerce dispute, which country has jurisdiction?

**Mini Case Study** **Who decides?**

You are a customer in Great Britain and you are less than satisfied with the service of an e-tailer in the USA. Where do you go for a legal remedy? The short answer is that at present nobody is sure and it seems that the situation is unlikely to change in the immediate future.

THE BIG BOOK OF E—COMMERCE ANSWERS

The Hague Convention on Jurisdiction decides international jurisdiction. They have a scheduled meeting in Ottawa on 28 February 2001 to discuss the matter, but as I write a mere four days before that meeting it is destined to reach no very satisfactory conclusion. The idea is that the Ottawa shindig should explore the situation and make recommendations that will be ratified in June. Unfortunately the new Bush administration appears to be using this opportunity to flex its muscles. The Americans are making it clear that unless they get their way there will be no agreement. Worse, they are suggesting that if there can be no agreement there is little point in holding the meeting. The USA still dominates much of e-commerce so they want legal wrangles to be in the jurisdiction of the seller's country. From the international customer's point of view this would mean the expense of going to law would, in most cases, be automatically prohibitive unless they reside in the USA, in which case questions of international jurisdiction would not apply.

We have a stalemate that may appear to be in the interest of suppliers and therefore business, but I have my doubts. E-commerce is still relatively new, but it is, in theory at least, the ideal low-cost way to penetrate new foreign markets. What stands in the way of the even more rapid growth of e-commerce worldwide is the suspicion that some buyers have that they may be badly served, and even cheated, and have no redress. An approach by politicians that leads those whose interests are in the rapid growth of e-commerce to appear to be adversaries rather than collaborators is in no one's interest.

This series of books is intended to be supported by up-to-the-minute online information. You need to know what is going on and we intend to keep you abreast of developments. In the mean while as chaos invites the world to claim jurisdiction the wise international e-tailer will ensure exemplary service, creating happy customers for life, and will stay well clear of the courts.

On an apparently happier note the UK and Canadian governments digitally signed an agreement to work together to promote and support the development of international e-commerce (23 February 2001). The word 'apparently' is there because those who know, for example Forrester Research, are suggesting that the British government's lack of real understanding and support is costing the UK almost $6 billion a year in potential cost savings alone.

Commit a minor crime, however, and you will soon be able to avoid the embarrassment and inconvenience of appearing in court – at least until you are convicted. The British Lord Chancellor's Office has announced plans to speed the legal process by allowing the accused to enter a plea by e-mail. Those found guilty will initially need to make a personal appearance for sentencing, but it is envisaged that the future will include sentencing by e-mail. In a country where many believe that the prison population is continuing to grow beyond reason can we anticipate that our 'with it' Lord Chancellor will soon announce the alternative of virtual imprisonment?

## Will I be able to cope with the jargon?

Jargon proliferates on and around the Internet, and where jargon is rife it is used to create a mystique. Where there is mystery there are invariably those who seek to mislead the unwary. But take heart. The Glossary at the end of this book will put all the useful terms at your fingertips.

*See also:* The Glossary – *when you have a moment to sit and reflect you will find some thought starters there as well as simple definitions.*

*A bluffers timetable of Internet facts*

When I became a consultant my son David, cheeky pup, bought me a copy of that excellent book, *Bluff Your Way in Consultancy*. The following time-line of e-commerce should enable you to impress all with your knowledge of arcane online names and dates. It may, more seriously help to put the business of e-business into a historical perspective.

| Event | Date |
|---|---|
| Charles Babbage designs, but is unable to build his 'analytical engine' (due to withdrawal of government backing). | 1833 |
| Hermann Hollerith designs a computer using punched cards and reduces the analysis of the US census data by two-thirds. | 1890 |
| Alan Turing builds the first totally electronic computer, 'Collosus'. | 1943 |
| John Mauchly and Presper Eckert Jr build the first general purpose computer, 'ENIAC' (Electronic Numerical Integrator and Calculator). | 1946 |
| Engineering Research Associates of Minneapolis build the first commercially produced computer. | 1950 |
| Lyons Tea Rooms develop and produce the first British business computer LEO (Lyons Electronic Office). | 1951 |
| IBM sells 450 of its new model the IBM 650 in one year. | 1954 |
| IBM produces its first transistor model (IBM 7000). | 1959 |
| IBM dominates the world market with an 81 per cent market share. | 1961 |
| JCR Licklider of MIT proposes a 'Galactic Network' of interlinked computers. | 1962 |
| Leonard Kleinrock designs packet switching that is the basis of Internet connection today. | 1962 |
| IBM introduces the 'System 360' and computer sales climb to 1000 a month within two years. | 1964 |
| Digital Equipment introduce the PDP-8, the first commercially successful minicomputer, at only 20 per cent of the price of a mainframe. | 1965 |
| Lawrence Roberts connects a computer in Massachusetts with one in California over a dial-up line. | 1965 |

Hewlett-Packard build their first general purpose computer (HP-2115). 1966

Data General produce the 'Nova' selling for a mere $8000. 1968

Apollo 11 reaches the moon guided by the Apollo Guidance Computer. 1969

David Lambert born. 1969

Charley Kline of UCLA uses the ARPNET for the first time to connect to Stanford Research. 1969

ARPNET (granddaddy of the Internet) adopted by the US Department of Defence. 1972

Intel develops the 8008 microprocessor. 1972

The first e-mail sent and received. 1972

Robert Metcalfe at the Xerox Palo Alto Centre devises the Ethernet. 1973

The French company, R2E, builds the first non-kit PC. 1973

Carole Lambert born. 1973

ftp protocol developed allowing file transfer between Internet sites. 1973

Robert Metcalfe publishes his concept of the Ethernet. 1974

Seagate Technology develop the first hard disk drive for microcomputers. 1980

IBM introduces the first commercial PC using MS-DOS. 1981

National Science Foundation funds NFSNet, a backbone for the Internet. 1986

Peter Deutsch of McGill develops the first archive of Internet sites (Archie). 1989

Tim Berners-Lee outlines the World Wide Web concept. 1989

| | |
|---|---|
| The University of Minnesota introduces the first 'user-friendly' interface to the Internet (Gopher). | 1991 |
| Marc Andreeson at the National Center for Supercomputing Applications develops a graphical browser that becomes Netscape Navigator. | 1991 |
| Delphi offers the first commercial Internet service. | 1992 |
| AOL, Prodigy and Compuserve come online. | 1995 |
| Amazon.com created by Jeff Bezos. | 1995 |
| Yahoo! incorporated. | 1995 |
| Yahoo! floated. | 1996 |
| Dot com stupidity reaches its climax. | 1999–2000 |
| Common sense about e-commerce begins to emerge. | 2000–2001 |

To anybody who is even approaching my age, the growth of e-commerce has been at a breakneck pace. To the young techie the 1990s seem to be ancient history. Here is a rich potential for a complete mismatch in terms of interpreting the world of e-business. I have even stuck in here the most important two events of my life to create a real perspective of the speed with which the new economy has emerged, flourished insanely and found a small degree of sanity again.

E-commerce and everything about it is still experiencing birth pangs. The entrepreneur and the executive need to take a long hard look at the business implications of the contracted time frame before their views, positive or negative, become too entrenched. Getting it wrong is expensive and the days when bright young things could get it wrong at other's expense are largely behind us.

**Mini Case Study**  **Babies and bath water**

Research by the Conference Board (April 2001) suggests that e-commerce euphoria is changing to e-commerce phobia for managers and directors of many small to medium companies. Only 10 per cent of those questioned now see the Internet as the key to future sales growth. They indicate a number of reasons, some of which make absolute sense – or do they?

> *'We are a local company serving local needs.*
> *We are not set up to do business outside our own backyard.'*
> *'We have only one or two major customers.*
> *They don't want us to be online.'*

Both reasons may be fine for the business right now. But the question that is not being asked is, 'Have these managers thought through the strategic and tactical implications of either be reliant on a very small customer base or of being unwilling and therefore unable to enter new markets?' Too often businesspeople do not ask such questions. Dangerously often they convince themselves that the way things have been is the way that they will remain. Meanwhile, careful follow-up within some of the companies surveyed suggests that there is a growing number of younger managers who are increasingly frustrated by the firm's inability to move forward and recognize opportunities for growth. Unless strategic issues are really thought through openly an 'us and them' situation can grow until, in the words of Bob Mager: 'The brightest brains fire the company.' E-commerce phobia may be a symptom of something far more dangerous even than being late into the game shouting 'me too!'.

It might be wise for executives to remind themselves and others from time to time of Peter Drucker's objectives for a business:

✓  To create and keep customers.

✓  To perpetuate itself.

✓  To grow.

Above all, perhaps some of us might be well advised that growth does not necessarily mean just getting bigger. It often means doing things better, learning and applying what we learn or simply following Jack Welch's idea of 'picking low-hanging fruit in order to continuously do more with less'.

section

five

five

marketing your website

The average consumer sees around 1 million messages a year, or 2739 each day, or up to 171 in an average hour. You may see as many as 10 000 in a single trip to the shopping mall. Television programme segments that fill the spaces between the advertisements are shorter and the advertising slot is getting longer. There can be up to 300 advertisements in a single newspaper. To cut through that background noise and make your voice heard you really need to do it right and, since it is expensive, you need to do it right first time. What is more, advertising is almost certainly not 'it' for your online business.

Times have changed. Not long ago there was a degree of novelty that ensured that your fax number featured strongly on all your business stationery. Now it is your e-mail address and website URL that are important. Be absolutely certain that no communication ever leaves your firm that does not have your web address clearly shown.

# KILLING THE INFOCLUTTERBUG

## How do we bring customers, old and new, to our site?

✓ Never forget that customers exist in a real world and you must contact them there before they are likely to visit your site.

✓ Ensure that your website address features prominently in and on every communication that you send into that real world.

✓ If you decide that you must advertise your site don't allow the self-styled 'creatives' to con you into being too clever. Decide on the message and make it very clear.

✓ Select your medium with care. Ensure that it reaches not merely those who will buy your product or service, but those who will want to buy it now if given the chance.

✓ Check your copy with intense care.

1. Does the communication demand immediate, favourable attention?
2. Is the headline powerful enough to dominate the infoclutter (excessive 'information' to which we are subjected every day of our lives) that surrounds it?
3. Am I offering real benefits that are clear and desirable to my carefully chosen audience?
4. Is the message concise, but unambiguous? Does it address a known need or desire?
5. Is the layout clear and easy to read without wasting too much money on 'white space'? (Black print on a white background remains the easiest to read, reverse printing takes time and people are no longer generous with their time. Colour is fine, though expensive, for pictures. It is less good for the text.)
6. Is the image of the firm that is conveyed appropriate and positive?

7. Would the stimulus to action NOW work even on those with only a lukewarm interest in my offering? (Am I appealing to people's self-interest? Will they be eager to find my site, get information and buy?)

8. Is it absolutely clear how to respond?

9. Are the simple things like terrestrial address, website address, telephone number, e-mail address and fax number accurate and easy to find?

10. Does any advertisement show why you should consider what I have to offer or buy from me rather than from my competitors?

11. Would I spend my own time or money on what is offered in this advertisement?

12. How would I rate the overall impression created? What will be the 'gut' response of the people I want to reach?

✓ Remember that every piece of paper that you place before a current or potential customer is a marketing communication – an 'advertisement' if you will. So make it work for you. Be sure that it contains your web address and a reason for going there – very soon.

✓ Internet fortunes have been made without recourse to 'dirt world' advertising.

✓ Companies that have failed and folded have spent laughable sums on risible advertising, but whether you choose to use advertising or not there is one thing that you will have no chance of avoiding. You will need to communicate with potential and existing customers. Your site, if you choose to have one, must sell for you. Your e-mails must bring in business. You must understand the secrets of direct mail.

See also: *Please read everything on SEARCH ENGINES, they are important and too often underestimated.*

## What is 'infoclutter'?

'Infoclutter' is a word coined by Seth Godin to describe the proliferation of advertising in the real world – advertising that is forced to scream for attention often by being so clever that the message, if there is one, is lost. Infoclutter forces us to surf television channels to escape from advertisements; it forces would-be buyers to leave 'creative' websites without spending their money.

The successful business must find ways to cut through the infoclutter and get its message to those who may buy. The Internet provides tools to do this at virtually no cost.

## How can we cut through 'infloclutter' online or off?

As the infoclutter of paid advertising increases, more and more businesses in the real world are turning to direct mail. Some are even becoming pretty good at it.

Whether you use the old pen and paper routines or electronic communication, most of the secrets of good copy-writing remain the same. The key difference is that the culture of e-mail is informal. Clarity is more important than style or layout.

For all marketing communication it is the message that counts and that message tells you one thing above all others – the offer.

In a world that is overwhelmed with advertising the key secret is not to be cleverer or more entertaining than the others. It is to be more, as the politicians have it, 'on message'.

*See also:* Why do I need to use an opt-in e-mail facility for my customers?

## Should we use purchased e-mail mailing lists?

When using direct mail, whether on the Internet or on the doormat, there is another key factor – the mailing list.

Drayton Bird, the world's leading direct mail guru has studied what counts when it comes to getting the punter to take action.

- The mailing list (factor × 6).

- The offer (factor × 3).

- The timing (factor × 2).

- Creativity (factor × 1.35).

- Response mechanism (factor × 1.2).

If you get it all right you can improve your success rate by a factor of $6 \times 3 \times 2 \times 1.35 \times 1.2 = 58$.

The beauty of Internet marketing includes the fact that no medium has ever given so much control over the quality of lists, or the success of advertising for that matter.

The only mailing lists that work online are opt-in lists where people have expressed an interest in receiving information on one or more topics. These neither attract the anger of recipients nor of Internet Service Providers. They are an invitation to send information and, although they are by no means unique to online marketing, the Internet greatly simplifies their collection and proper use.

*See also:* What is 'spam'?

Avoiding spam: a self-assessment

## Is direct mail, online or off, a pure numbers game?

Sadly it has been treated that way offline. That is why we call such a major part of our daily mail delivery 'junk mail' and why so many forests are felled in vain. Those with an interest in the Internet believe strongly that junk mail has no place in modern communications. The Internet Service Providers all have a policy of suspending service to those who abuse the system by making a nuisance of themselves.

It is possible to buy online 'opt-in e-mail' addresses, but please consider whether there is any point in writing to people who have opted to receive any and all communications. Some e-mail lists contain as many as a million addresses and are sold with the suggestion that 'even a 1 per cent response offers great business'. True perhaps, except that a 1 per cent response is little short of a miracle if the list is not focused on those who have expressed real interest in your product or service. So the answer is 'no', mailing online or off is not a pure numbers game. It is a matter of finding and using lists of people who have asked to receive relevant and timely information about offers such as yours.

# SPAM MAY NOT BE GOOD FOR YOU

## What is 'spam'?

'Spam' is unsolicited e-mails sent in large numbers to unwilling recipients. All ISPs respond to complaints by customers concerning spam by the simple expedient of removing the offending sender's e-mail address and website.

## Avoiding spam: a self-assessment

E-mail marketing can be both useful and effective, but only if it provides timely desired information. Anything else is spam. Your product or service may be the greatest thing that you ever conceived. You may genuinely think that you are doing me a great service by buying my e-mail address from a vendor, who may have got it by dubious means, and sending me unasked for information telling me what you think you can do for me. Forgive me if I fail to agree with you. In a world of 'infoclutter' my e-mail facility enables me to get information that I want from people from whom I want to hear. Frankly, the number of electronic communications that come from friends, readers and suppliers of goods and services that I have expressed an interest in keeps me busy enough. I do not want to receive unasked for 'junk mail', no matter how well intentioned the sender.

If you want my business attract me to your site, hold me there by actively engaging my interest and give me the opportunity to request further information. That way we will build a relationship and you will gain a customer for life. There are ways to have customers 'beat a path to your site', stay there, buy and come back to buy again from you. This book (and *e-Market Dominance* by Tom Lambert and Brian Ash) will tell you how.

By the very nature of things, if you attempt to play the mailing numbers game online you will attract some business – fine. You will cause no great upset to the majority of recipients who will simply delete your missive. You will irritate a minority among whom there just may be a small number who will be annoyed enough to:

- flame you in return
- complain to your ISP.

Either of the above could put you out of business, at least in the short term. Is it worth the risk? Is your business really about annoying the many in order to win business from the few? Can you afford the real costs of untargeted marketing? If the answer to any of these questions is 'no', please take our little spam test before you consider an e-mailing campaign.

*Spam test*

Instructions: Please answer every question. Total your scores and check your readiness to build friendships and influence customers online.

How familiar is the recipient with my business before I mail?

| | | |
|---|---|---|
| Not at all | Score 0 | \_\_\_\_\_ |
| Somewhat | Score 2 | \_\_\_\_\_ |
| Very | Score 5 | \_\_\_\_\_ |

Has this prospect ever indicated that they have a real interest in my product or service before I mailed?

| | | |
|---|---|---|
| None at all | Score 0 | \_\_\_\_\_ |
| A little (we know for certain that they buy similar products or services elsewhere) | Score 2 | \_\_\_\_\_ |
| Directly to us | Score 5 | \_\_\_\_\_ |

Has this prospect confirmed their wish to be contacted by me?

| | | |
|---|---|---|
| No | Score 0 | \_\_\_\_\_ |
| Yes | Score 5 | \_\_\_\_\_ |

Have I given recipients an easy way to opt out of future mailings?

| | | |
|---|---|---|
| No | Score 0 | \_\_\_\_\_ |
| I offer a simple one step process to opt out | Score 5 | \_\_\_\_\_ |

Is my message of real value to the recipient?

| | | |
|---|---|---|
| None whatever | Score 0 | \_\_\_\_\_ |
| Some (it's a good product/service) | Score 2 | \_\_\_\_\_ |
| They say that it's of real value | Score 5 | \_\_\_\_\_ |

Am I ready to handle all enquiries in a timely manner?

| | | |
|---|---|---|
| Not yet | Score 0 | \_\_\_\_\_ |
| Pretty well | Score 2 | \_\_\_\_\_ |
| Yes | Score 5 | \_\_\_\_\_ |

## Am I ready to get purchases to the customer in a timely manner?

| | | |
|---|---|---|
| No | Score 0 | _____ |
| If there is not too heavy a response | Score 1 | _____ |
| Absolutely | Score 5 | _____ |

## Have I got everything in place to ensure customer delight at the end of every transaction?

| | | |
|---|---|---|
| Be realistic! | Score 0 | _____ |
| Yes | Score 5 | _____ |

## Was my list totally generated in house?

| | | |
|---|---|---|
| I bought it in | Score 0 | _____ |
| A list broker found it for me | Score 1 | _____ |
| I combined what I have in-house with a bought-in list | Score 1 | _____ |
| My list is totally in-house captured from visitors to my site | Score 3 | _____ |
| People on my list specifically opted in for this information | Score 5 | _____ |

*Scoring*: If you have scored 45 you are doing a wonderful customer-centred job of e-mail marketing. You will prosper, as you deserve to prosper. If you have scored anything less you have a potential problem. You may have been conned into believing that marketing is a numbers game in which reach is everything. You may have failed to understand the simple, but unique, fact that only online can breaking the rules leave you without a business.

I live in the real world. I know that the proliferation of ISPs is such that you may be ejected from one if you spam to re-emerge on another *tout de suite*. But neither the opportunity nor the benefits will last much longer.

Very soon ISPs will advise their peers or competitors of those that are breaking the rules. Very soon, the freedoms of the Internet notwithstanding, those who are trawling for suckers will have no access to the fishing grounds.

In a way I have misled you. I have presented this little questionnaire as if it were a definitive exercise that would provide easy answers. It cannot be so. In marketing there are no easy answers. Some will thrive (at least in the short term) as a result of using very questionable means. Others will act with complete probity and will remain poor until they find that magic formula that turns worth into gold. What is different with the Internet is that the crooks, the scam merchants and the smoke-and-mirrors conjurors can easily be dealt with when they are identified. If you step out of line online, the risk is greater not less. With this in mind my concern was not to provide easy answers; it was to get you to think in detail about the questions. Let me come clean, and in so doing let me try to make amends by reviewing some of the key thoughts question by question.

*Some thoughts on your answers*

### How familiar is the recipient with my business before I mail?

If the recipient is unfamiliar with your business, how familiar are you with theirs or their needs? What makes you think that you have anything to offer them? If they are not familiar with your business, what makes you think that they will take even 8 seconds (that is what research suggests is the time taken to scrutinize unrequested mail to assess whether it should be read) to consider your message? At least if you have created awareness of the name of your company readers might ask themselves, 'what do they want?'

If your answers to the above are negative or doubtful you may wish to consider trying to get some press coverage in advance of any direct mail, electronic or otherwise. If you cannot do that you need to write an eye-catching headline followed by an eye-popping offer at the very least. (At the last resort, if I like what you have to say and think it helpful I will not think it is spam.)

### Has this prospect ever indicated that they have a real interest in my product or service before I mailed?

Like it or not we all tend to believe these days that we are overwhelmed by infoclutter. We like anything that we have requested to save us time and there is an excellent chance that we will hate anything else. If I have expressed a desire to have you contact me with further information good, if not, consider the question above again.

Opt-in e-mail is useful to recipient and sender. Anything else may be seen as an intrusion on limited time.

### Has this prospect confirmed their wish to be contacted by me?

Opt-in e-mail is an effective way of building a relationship with the customer that can lead to a business lifelong 'affair'. It is one of the tools that will enable you to dominate your e-market. Take a look at Ash and Lambert's book, *e-Market Dominance* (McGraw-Hill) for the rest.

### Have I given recipients an easy way to opt out of future mailings?

If you are providing the reader with anticipated, relevant and desired information as requested by them, you have no need to fear offering them an easy 'one click' means of opting out. If you are not doing the above you are doing yourself no good and simply delivering spam that is more likely to harm your business than otherwise, so an easy opt-out is as much in your interest as anybody's. In a growing number of countries ISPs and the law require an opt-out mechanism, so why not make it easy for the customer to exercise choice? They may even like you the more for it and someday opt back in.

### Is my message of real value to the recipient?

Always write or speak from the 'listener's/reader's point of view'. My book, *The Power of Influence* (Nicholas Brealey Publishing), details a total of more than 120 years' research into the psychology of putting yourself into the other person's shoes. In summary you need to structure your communication as follows:

✓ What the reader is trying to achieve that you can help with.

✓ What they are up against. Barriers to achievement in the real world.

✓ What they will gain be reading your communication.

✓ What is your offer –the key features that deliver relevant benefits; why will it work for them; who else has tried it; what they say about it; what guarantees you offer.

✓ The benefits that they will experience on their way to achieving their objective listed in logical sequence and finishing by proving that they will achieve their goal by using your product, service or idea.

If you write this way at least the reader will feel that they are the centre of attention rather than an audience for your cleverness.

### Am I ready to handle all enquiries in a timely manner?

The vast majority of complaints from those who buy online refer to the failure of the supplier to live up to their promise of speedy handling. If you do not have the infrastructure in place to give efficient, speedy and accurate service you are doing your business harm by soliciting orders. Internet Service Providers are under pressure to dispense with the third-rate wannabes, and at least 1000 new sites are placed on the web every day. You need the goodwill of ISPs and customers; frankly, neither need you so you are not only in danger of driving away customers, you are in danger of putting yourself out of business.

### Am I ready to get purchases to the customer in a timely manner?

What is true of enquiries is doubled when it comes to customers who have parted with cash.

### Have I got everything in place to ensure customer delight at the end of every transaction?

Call it 'total quality' if you must. Call it intelligent business practice if you will. Delighting the customer is as much an essential prerequisite of staying in business today as is making a profit. Customers can painlessly find your competition. They can, if you annoy them enough, communicate with your potential customers. Finally the old saw that claims that 'the customer is king' is beginning to mean something. Soon it will mean the demise of crappy businesses.

### Was my list totally generated in-house?

The average customer is bombarded with up to 10000 'messages' a day, each attempting to scream 'look at me' louder than the others. We have limited time and limited attention. We want to make the best use of both. Only lists of real prospects generated by the seller from those who have asked to be informed are likely to lead to economic business and an ongoing relationship that leads to customers for life. Buy in lists if you must, but don't expect the game to be worth the cost of playing.

## How do you get your message across by e-mail?

*To write letters or e-mails that sell on or off the web*

✓ Plan. The great copy-writers say that they spend 90 per cent of their time planning and 10 per cent writing. Those who do the most effective writing and therefore plan best can charge up to $50 000 for a single letter. If an e-mail is worth a multiple of $50 000 to a hard-headed business person it is worth thinking about.

✓ Personalize your letter. Build a personal relationship with your customer from the first moment. You need to become the friend that they rely on. (Most of us regard letters that are sent without the courtesy of addressing us by name as the worst of junk mail. To recover from a start like that demands a wonderful offer and a truly creative letter. Worst of all is 'Dear Sir or Madam', if you cannot even get the reader's sex right, what chance do you have in accurately predicting his or her needs?)

✓ Write your letter from the recipient's point of view. If you can offer the solution to an important problem which you and I both know that I face, I might bite your hand off. (Frankly, the wonderful technology or what have you that your firm has does not interest me. I want to know what your superior widgets will do for me, not how clever you think you are.)

✓ Customers buy benefits. Your biggest benefit is your offer. Tell the reader early and powerfully what your offer is, then build your case until the reader cannot wait to buy. (Remember you only have, on average, 8 seconds to grab your reader's attention.)

✓ If your product is new to your reader, explain it to the reader in detail and hammer home what it will do for him or her. If it has been around for some time tell the reader what makes it different and better than competitive widgets, and emphasize what that difference does for them. The more ferocious competition is, the more you must convince the reader that you are offering them better value.

✓ Prove that you can deliver all that you promise, and more. Include quotes from delighted customers or authorities. If you use 'authorities' make sure that they are truly authorities to your readers. 'Tom Lambert says . . .' does not mean a row of beans to those benighted millions who have yet to hear of Tom Lambert.

✓ Most firms spend most of their time and efforts on trying to attract new customers – don't. Delighted existing customers are six to eight times easier to sell. That means that you can get six to eight times the sales by simply keeping in touch. (You might even consider saying 'thank you' now and again without pushing for a sale. Happy customers who have a need will come to you to fulfil it.)

✓ We all make rational decisions that would delight the economist. Others use emotions when they decide to buy. Mix emotions and logic in your correspondence. (Logic implies that the reader is logical and that appeals to their emotions.)

✓ Move the reader to buy now and make buying easy.

✓ <u>Underline and emphasize what you want the reader to notice</u>. (But remember that if you emphasize everything, you emphasize nothing.)

✓ If your product or service is expensive, your letter needs to be longer. Long copy sells, and there is a proven relationship between the cost of the offer and the length of the letter.

✓ Sign letters. It may be a chore, but people like to buy from people that they like and we do not like impersonal facsimile signatures. E-mail relieves you of this chore. Electronic signatures are acceptable and can even be fun.

✓ Never forget the old dictum that a letter needs to be 'a salesperson in an envelope'. To which we may now add that e-mail must be an electronic salesperson needing neither envelope nor stamp nor days to arrive.

## What is the best opening for an e-mail?

Research into unsolicited direct mail response consistently shows that you have a little less than 8 seconds to catch and keep your reader's attention. Copy-writing gurus have tested opening sentences of letters and have suggested a number that have been proven to work in a range of circumstances for a range of products and services. The first few words of a letter determine whether your reader will read greedily and sell himself or herself on the offer or will consign your work of literature to the bin. Why not try the appropriate openings from ideas listed here:

✓ Ask a provocative question. I sometimes ask prospective clients, 'How much have you wasted on training in the last few years?' Most tell me in great detail and with not a little chagrin. Then I tell them how they need never waste another cent. Provocative questions take a little by way of guts, but they arouse, sometimes passionate, interest in what you have to say.

✓ Suggest a vital decision. 'The decision that you will make after reading this letter may make the difference between disaster today and lifelong prosperity.' Your offer, of course, must be sufficiently important to the customer to justify such an approach.

✓ 'As you know . . . ' People love to be told how knowledgeable they are, that is why those who most enjoy training courses are those who did not really need the training in the first place. They had it confirmed for them that they were right all along and now they think that the trainer is a genius and they commend the training to all their colleagues.

✓ 'If you're anything like me . . . ' People like to buy from people that they like and we like best people who are most like us.

✓ What if . . . 'If you could wave a magic marketing wand right now, what would you wish for?' You make an informed guess and show them that they will get it from you. (More profit, higher sales, happier customers, less customer hassle or making that elusive fortune on the Internet.)

✓ Congratulations. 'Your position as an industry opinion leader entitles you to . . . ' Only the other person likes flattery. You and I are immune, but it is amazing how much everyone else loves it.

✓ Invitation. 'You are invited to a secret preview of . . .'

✓ Free gift. Preferably with no strings attached.

✓ Narrative. 'A funny thing happened when I took up my pen to write this letter . . .'

✓ Introduction. 'We don't know each other, but we should because you and I share . . .' A literary agent once told me that to get his attention a letter should start with the words, 'Your mother asked me to write to you.' I think he was joking, but only because I do not know his mother or need an agent.

✓ You did that, so we're doing this. 'Your generous action has not gone unnoticed . . .'

✓ You're a rare bird. 'The American Express Gold Card is not for everyone.'

✓ 'The experts say . . .' Respect for expert authority is a hardwired part of the human psyche.

✓ 'Are you paying too much . . .'

✓ 'Why are we doing this?' (Your good reason for doing it must be good for the customer, not you.)

✓ Give good news after bad. 'Competition gets tougher every day, but you have the answer in your hands right now.'

✓ 'Have you ever wished . . .'

✓ 'Why don't (do) *they* . . .' (It helps when we all hate 'them'.) The great W.E. Deming was talking to an audience of HR (human resource) specialists and, to their obvious disgust, was demonstrating that job performance appraisal, at best encouraged mediocrity. One personnel director tolerated this onslaught on his core passion as long as he could.

Finally he could stand no more. Trembling with rage he rose to his feet, his face as red as the sky that delights shepherds. 'If I can't appraise people, what can I do?' It was less a question than a scream of pain. Deming looked at him above his rimless half-spectacles. 'Forgive me sir if I check that I understand your question. You are asking; "What else can I humiliate people with?"' I suspect that it was in that moment that my lifetime adoration of Deming and hatred of HR was formed. (Be contentious when you dare to. People will love you or hate you, but they will not ignore you.)

✓ 'I've missed you so I . . .' (A bit 'Readers Digest' perhaps, but Readers Digest does pretty well out of direct mail.)

✓ 'I've enclosed . . .' Make sure that the enclosure is interesting, valuable or useful to the recipient.

✓ Solve a problem. 'You don't need to lose sleep over rising interest rates . . .' As a business consultant I have found that asking the client when face to face, 'What keeps you awake nights?', pays rich dividends because most have problems and I peddle solutions.

✓ 'I'll get straight to the point.' (If you try this you must be brief, even terse, so be sure that you can get your offer across in very few words.)

✓ Because you're an 'A' you must be a 'B'. 'Cat lovers like you and me all love . . .'

✓ 'You are important to me so I want you to be the first to know . . .'

✓ Others cannot, we can. 'No one dare promise to get your website consistently in the top ten. No one but us . . .'

✓ 'When was the last time that you . . .' The way that our minds respond to such a question is interesting to all who dabble in psychology. During the research for the Kinsey Report many years ago they found that if they were to ask, for example: 'Have you ever masturbated?' they got a speedy and indignant denial. If they asked, 'When did you last masturbate?' they got a detailed response from male and female alike. Or to be more accurate they got graphic details from almost 100 per cent of the men and around 60 per cent of women.

✓ 'Less than an hour ago I realized . . .' (The shorter the period of time the more compelling – within reason.)

✓ 'I love to share great ideas with people like you who . . .'

✓ 'I'm surprised that we haven't heard from you because you . . .'

✓ 'In the less than two minutes that it will take you to read this letter you . . .'

✓ Notice, if you will, the number of times that the words 'you' and 'yours' appear near the start of good sales communications. Far ahead of 'new' and 'secret' and the other magic words of the marketing lexicon, 'you' will get attention. (For details on the key power words see *The Power of Influence* (Nicholas Brealey Publishing).)

✓ After you get attention you must sustain it. With a website it is the same. First you must get people to visit. Then you must get them to want to stay. Next they must buy. Finally, they must keep coming back to buy again and again.

Almost everything that we read has a psychological effect and you want that effect to be invariably positive. Research (Suler et al., 1999) indicates that the way that we address the recipient of an e-mail may prove to be crucial in his or her decision whether to read on or simply hit the delete button.

Although the days of 'TO: Mr George Smith, Esteemed Sir' are happily now two centuries behind us, it is arguable that few of us think enough about what is acceptable to the recipient of our communications. Suler's research should help us to get it right and, in so doing, help us to surmount that infamous 8-second barrier.

# How informal should my e-mails be?

### Research  The salutation of e-mails

Dear Mr Lambert – formal, polite and something of a nod back towards letter writing. Ardent believers in the e-mail culture find the use of the word 'dear' too old-fashioned and frown upon its use in any circumstances. Such fanatics tend to look down upon the sender as being naive when it comes to the social dynamics of e-mail.

Dear Tom – since book covers always carry given names and the e-mail is a relatively informal medium, the use of the first name seems appropriate to most people. The e-mail nut, however, would still respond to the use of 'dear' with a sigh of sorrow or mild contempt.

Hello Tom – an approach that is used to set a tone of friendliness among peers that usually waits until at least the second communication in polite society.

Hi Tom! – e-mailers seem to enjoy using punctuation marks that are rarely seen beyond the second grade schoolroom. In part this is to make up for the lack of vocal and behavioural cues as mentioned above, but in the main it is simply a sign of exuberance and enthusiasm. The combination of informality and enthusiasm is the equivalent of indicating with a broad smile and hand rubbing for instance, 'have I got news for you'. If an e-mailer wants to turn up the volume of enthusiasm and add a dash of urgency they are likely to drop the 'Hi' and multiply the number of exclamation points (Tom!!!!).

Tom – this is the e-mail equivalent of 'we are both busy people so let's cut to the chase' in conversation. The use of the given name retains a degree of friendliness, but there will be no wasting of words on niceties if the e-mail is consistent with the greeting.

Hey there! – very informal and generally restricted to correspondents whose friendship has blossomed to the point where names are no longer thought to be necessary.

Yo Dude!!! – this can only have come from a friend in the USA and since it comes from a friend, and only because it comes from a friend, I shall read it.

Greetings! – this is seen by the initiated as a sure sign of spam. To make matters worse it is the most unacceptable form of junk mail where the sender knows nothing about me. They have not taken the trouble to know my gender, my name or my wants. Like the wonderful Manuel in *Fawlty Towers* – 'they know nothings'. Such e-mails are deservedly deleted unread. The same fate awaits 'Dear Friend', 'Dear Colleague', 'Dear Fellow Professional' and other clear warnings of junk to come.

Real professionals construct the body of the message with the reader firmly in mind. They use the whole of the keyboard to make their message visually interesting and easy to read. I have e-mail friends who use the ability of today's software to add attractive stationery creatively and thoughtfully. It takes a little longer to send and receive mail with a pretty background, but the effect can be enough to brighten a dull day.

Jab Creative ([www.jabcreative.com](www.jabcreative.com)) go further, they create all-singing and all-dancing e-mails for major corporate clients that they claim are one-tenth the cost of normal direct mail, but that can attract ten times the response.

Psychological research shows that apparent spontaneity is valued in e-mails and some people plan in depth to make their messages look and feel absolutely spontaneous. (It is a little like a conversation in play that I saw recently where a couple are discussing their sex life.)

> *He: Why can't we be more spontaneous?*

> *She: We didn't plan it that way.*

Spelling errors can be perceived as a sign of friendship and spur-of-the-moment eagerness to get in touch for purely social exchanges, but the businessperson needs to balance a desire for friendliness with professionalism.

Typed text obviously must work very hard if it wants to convey feelings, as would a smile, an eager or a downcast look. E-mailers have developed the sometimes engaging, sometimes irritating habit of writing feelings in parentheses.

I wanted to tell you (feeling a little insecure here) that I . . .

I completely forgot (slapping self on the forehead).

I know exactly what I am talking about (looking hopefully

heavenward).

Psychologically these comments in parentheses combine the roles of body language and subvocal talking to one's self, but they can be easily overdone and become trite and less than businesslike. The businessperson must be unceasingly aware that what is cute in intimate correspondence is probably inappropriate when attempting to build a business relationship. At the same time it is important to realize that you are building a relationship, if for no better reason than that 'people like to buy from people that they like' and a little unveiling of feelings may be constructive from time to time. The use of 'smiley faces' ☺ and the like has probably been so overdone that it is more likely to irritate than to charm. I would question whether 'emoticons' have any place in business correspondence not because of any intrinsic shortcoming, but because they have been overdone. ☹ In fact, they have been so overused in the past that I only now discover that this software automatically turns the sideways-on emoticon into an upright face. Time to be moving on from the smiley, the frown and the winky I think. The same is probably true of the ubiquitous use of abbreviations. You may think it is smart to inform a correspondent that you 'LMAO' (laughed my ass off) at something that they said, but in the world of business it is passé as well as frequently not understood. The purpose of business communication is clarity so do not be tempted.

## What do the Internet Service Providers do about spam?

As a generalization the answer is very simple. All ISPs have an anti-spam policy and if they receive validated complaints they pull the plug on the website that is indiscriminately sending out unwanted e-mailings. That is the theory, but please read on for a major, but hopefully temporary caveat.

## How does spam continue to exist?

New ISPs are emerging daily and have yet to establish a fully effective communication system between them. So offenders can, in the short term, move from ISP to ISP. This is why some recipients take the law into their own hands and use technology to give the offending firms a taste of their own medicine. Senders of spam can be 'flamed' by angry recipients.

## What is 'flaming'?

Tens even hundreds of thousands of 'replies' can easily be sent to those companies or individuals that send out mass unsolicited e-mailings. The indiscriminate mailer's business grinds to a halt under the weight of so much electronic mail.

# THE SERIOUS BUSINESS OF MARKETING A WEBSITE

## Will customers and prospects be able to find our site?

People are inherently lazy. If your site is not among the first 20 or so that are listed by the search engine that any potential customer uses they are unlikely to continue looking for it. You must ensure that you are easy to find as well as easy to use. This means that either you become expert in presenting your site to the search engines or you need to buy in the expertise, either through employing a specialist or by using consultants. Contact the author at info@tom-lambert.com if you want a no-obligation exploratory discussion. I am the chairman of the European end of a consortium of the world's leading web positioning advisers and may be able to point you in the right direction for your firm.

*See also*:　What is the most effective way to market a website?

　　　　　　Does online advertising work?

## Can I advertise on other people's websites?

You can buy advertising online and use the supplier to track its effectiveness for you. Take a look at these sites:

www.nielson-netratings.com

www.flycast.com

www.adknowledge.com

www.enliven.com

www.doubleclick.com

www.mediametrix.com

www.mediaplex.com

With direct mail things are even more simple, you get people to ask you to send them your sales information as I shall explain. Meanwhile why not take a few more tips from the masters of writing copy that sells?

## Does online advertising work?

Independent research suggests that it is not the best way to spend your advertising dollars or pounds. WebCMO completed a research programme when novelty made online advertising something of a necessity for many e-commerce sites. Their results (on a scale of 1, very little use, to 5, perfect) were as follows:

| | |
|---|---|
| Search engine submissions | 3.35 |
| Opt-in e-mail | 3.34 |
| Offline advertising | 3.04 |
| Press releases | 3.00 |
| Banner advertising (online) | 2.85 |
| Discussion forums | 2.83 |
| Sponsorship | 2.61 |
| Newsgroups | 2.46 |
| Strategic linking | 2.44 |
| Mass e-mail campaigns | 1.80 |

Online advertising worked, but less well than other media when it was a novelty. It is certain that nothing is more effective in bringing serious potential customers to your website than sustained search engine positioning, but online advertising may just be about to enjoy a new lease of creative life. Three of the world's greatest advertising groups have announced that they are banding together to exploit Internet technology to the full. The Interpublic Group, Omnicom Group and WPP Group (which includes J. Walter Thompson and Ogilvy and Mather Worldwide) are capable of bringing more talent to online advertising than ever before. At the same time, the ability of firms such as Coastal Sites Inc. and Coastal Sites (UK) Ltd to get their clients onto the front pages of the leading search engines and to keep them there starts at much better than 95 per cent and improves daily.

*Search engine positioning*

This works best at present because:

✓ Serious prospects generally start their search on one of the leading search engines.

✓ Serious buyers know what they are looking for and use the best defined keywords and key phrases.

✓ Having found an appropriate site serious buyers are unlikely to be seduced into going elsewhere on the basis of an advertisement until they have the information that they need.

And, most important:

✓ If your site delivers key information in a readily accessible form, offers the right quality of products or services at the right price, reduces the risk of making a purchase and makes buying easy, the serious buyer, who is usually short of time, will have made the decision, bought and only moved on to look for 'something completely different'.

But the big guns in advertising will not let it rest there. The gauntlet is thrown down. The challenge is issued and any resulting conflict can only be in the interest of the client because measurable results are what count in marketing (the number of new and worthwhile buyers who beat a path to your door, not the number of 'hits' or the number who saw your advertisement), and the quality of marketing will improve from more intelligent competition.

I still advise clients to allow no advertisements on their sites and to consider the following question if they feel tempted by the apparent lure of easy money:

✓ <u>Having spent good money to bring serious prospects to my site why on earth should I now encourage them to go away before they have time to make a purchase?</u>

Unless you have an answer to that question that escapes me you may choose to buy online advertising, but you will never allow it to sully your site or distract your customers.

## What is the most effective way to market a website?

There is no doubt in my mind that the most effective way to bring customers to your site is through sustained search engine positioning carefully tailored to your specific needs and that of your customers. Independent research shows this to be the case, as does the experience of visitor growth enjoyed by the sites that have chosen this to be the vanguard of their marketing strategy. In addition to the American research quoted in response to the question 'Does online advertising work?'

✓ Eighty-two per cent of European businesses identified search engine positioning as being more effective than advertising (online or off), press releases, links from other websites or affiliate marketing programmes.

✓ Seventy-nine per cent of British firms believed that search engine positioning maintained by a specialist company 'provided a global solution' to the problem of being noticed online.

The problem for most businesses is not that they cannot see the solution, but that the search engine positioning companies that exist have been lax in their own communications with the market. Recent research showed that 70 per cent of IT managers in the UK could not name a single company that could provide the service that they recognize that they need. With that in mind I unblushingly suggest that you might like to take a look at the following websites:

www.coastalsitesuk.co.uk

www.tom-lambert.com

www.coastalsites.com

If I may be permitted a prediction, search engine positioning companies will proliferate over the next couple of years and their services will be highly variable. There is a huge market out there. This year (2001) it is estimated that 80 per cent of businesses worldwide will have some sort of web presence. By 2002 there is forecast to be no less than 8 billion web pages online, all jockeying to be visited. Only dedicated surfers go beyond page three of the search engine listings. The process of getting onto the first two pages of all the major search engines is massively time-consuming and complex, staying there is worse. The demand for this service will rocket. As demand grows the cowboys will emerge. I can only suggest that businesspeople exercise due diligence in discovering suppliers that have the skills and experience to deliver.

*See also*:    Does online advertising work?

## Can we get high on the search engines without heavy advertising?

Yes, but you must work at it or have others work at it on your behalf. The rules that govern the behaviour of search engines are a moving feast and it takes constant assessment and response to keep up with the game. If you choose a do-it-yourself strategy you will not be the first to succeed. If you prefer to put onerous tasks out to others we will make some reliable suggestions.

You need not just expertise, but constantly updated expertise to get and keep your site up among the vital top 20 or so. Fortunately businesses exist that do the work for you. So please turn to page 187 for detailed information.

The web is a complex medium and the speed of change is dazzling. Keeping abreast of change is difficult in an area where keeping ahead of change is essential.

# WHAT'S IN A NAME? A ROSE BY ANY OTHER NAME WOULD NOT SMELL AS SWEET

One of the idiocies spawned by the inventiveness of many of the dot com entrepreneurs is the use of crazy names that mean nothing to the potential customer. Domain names are important. Please take a few minutes to quickly read the following section.

## Is what you call your website, your domain name, important?

*Domain names*

For reasons best known to their psyches or psychiatrists the early dot coms chose names that seemed to vie with each other for sheer daftness. They gave no indication of what the companies were about and, although they doubtless gave great pleasure to those who spawned them, they were a major factor in forcing companies to spend many millions on frequently inane advertising in the hope that sheer curiosity would drive us to the site.

Your domain name must play a role in bringing people to your site.

## How do domain names and keywords work together to bring traffic to my website?

If you have a well-known company name, that will work for you. People visit Disney or Coca-Cola directly without recourse to keywords. If you are new to business or to the web you need to try to get a name that will incorporate a keyword or words that will help people to find you when they need what you have to sell.

### How do I find out what domain names are available?

Once you have selected a number of suitable domain names you need to check if they are available. You can do this through www.networksolutions.com or www.nameboy.com amongst many others.

### How do I register my domain name?

Once you know that your chosen name is available get your webmaster to register it on your behalf. Make certain that you are registered as 'administrative and billing contact' if you may need to prove ownership at some future date.

### What domain names can I register?

You can register any available name. There is a new scam in which the unscrupulous are registering famous names in order to sell them back to their rightful owners at a massive profit when the rightful owners want to go online. Famous authors are currently being held to ransom as they pay to regain their kidnapped names.

You may be wise to register all that are relevant and available to you in one go. You may soon want to have a number of domains up and running, with each promoting and linked to the others.

You can register available domestic names yourself online, www.nominet.org.uk on a site that also gives useful information about ISPs.

## KEYWORDS HOLD A KEY

### How can I easily bring more customers to my site?

There have been two forms of cheating which have been successful in the past. One is to initially fill your home page with a gobbledegook minestrone of keywords having no sense or meaning. These are of little help to any human being, but old, unsophisticated search engines loved them and they would emerge high in the top 20. Search engines have moved on and it is unlikely that more than a few dinosaurs are now benefiting from this approach, and they tend to be found mainly among pornography sites where, for obvious reasons, a few simple Anglo-Saxon words say it all.

A truly wicked trick (interpret 'wicked' as you will) practised by a few is to resubmit a competitor's pages to a search engine in the hope that recent sifters, filters and processes will downgrade it. This is sometimes justified because some pages which for purely historic reasons appear high on the listings have disappeared and only their title and blurb continues to pop up to annoy the surfer. The resubmission at least clears out the 'no longer there'.

*See also:*   What is the most effective way to market a website?

## Where can I get free information to help me?

Keep your eyes firmly on some of the excellent newsletters that the web provides. A number of these are devoted to e-commerce. Try www.trendscape.com for excellent free strategic information. You may want to subscribe to www.net-profit.com. This is a subscriber service that requires a password, but the investment is worth considering.

Never overlook the potential value of the normal sources of information. *The Economist* delivers the business and political news to my computer every Friday free of charge (www.economist.com) and I can, and do, use the *Financial Times* archives to check business news past and present (www.ft.com).

All of this may seem a lot of work, but the rewards are immense, and do not undervalue Michael Gerber's advice that you should spend your time working on your business, not in it, if you want to prosper.

While you are about it, why not let others work on your business on your behalf.

For current information on the use by customers of keywords you cannot do better than look at www.WebpositionGold.com or www.iprospect.com websites.

# HAVING OTHERS SELL FOR YOU
## Can I find others who will bring business to my site?

You can through host/beneficiary or affinity marketing.

*See also:*   Below.


## What is host/beneficiary or affinity marketing?

It is an intelligent florist who works with a bridal gown shop and it is a smart hairdresser who works with both. Everywhere in business there are independent operators who are selling different products or services to the same customers. Accountants are seldom in direct competition with lawyers, but they serve the same clients. Most of us buy new shoes with each new suit, but seldom from the same shop. It makes sense to look for strategic allies.

The web provides incomparable opportunities for trustworthy people to scratch each other's backs. And it does not stop with promotion. For many years, corporations like IBM and Du Pont have shared information so that one does not repeat the other's expensive mistakes, and the plethora of partners attracted to Microsoft are not only in it for the odd extra sale. Looking for and working with strategic partners makes absolute sense, and it is easy online.


## How do I find and select strategic allies?

You need to select your allies with some care. You would not wish to be associated with some fly-by-nights who treat their customers as 'marks' and who are there for a quick buck and a speedy exit. You do not want to attract customers who are more hassle to serve than they are worth. Above all, if you are wise you want to be associated exclusively with those who will add to your status and reputation as the association brings you additional business.

On the web nothing could be easier.

## How should I use the facility of linking to other sites?

At the lowest level you may link to other sites. This in itself is a sort of endorsement. A link suggests that others think that what you offer is worth considering and that you are nice people to do business with, but there is more to affinity marketing than simple links.

Links boost your search engine positioning, but it is real affinity marketing that brings immediate sales and lifelong customers. Just as brides need gowns and flowers and a stunning new hairstyle all more or less at the same time, customers in one area are often potential buyers in another related area. So the first place to look for allies is in related industries that are not in direct competition with you.

*See also*:    What is the most effective way to market a website?

## How do I contact potential allies?

One advantage of the web is that it is an information channel second to none. There are ezines (online magazines) by the thousand offering masses of information to an ever-expanding readership. Look for those that serve readers with a profile similar to that of your best clients and customers, and invite them to test your products or services.

If they like it they are often happy to write a brief review that does not sound too much like a paid advertisement. 'Last week "her indoors" became sicker than usual of having me under her feet and booked me into one of Tom Lambert's seminars. I'm glad I went. I learned how to . . . '

Follow up with some thoughtful PR using the same ezines. Offer and deliver articles that you know will appeal to their readership and which keep your name constantly in front of their readers. When you write articles, whether for ezines or trade and professional journals in the dirt world, the rules are basically the same. You are out to promote your products or services but, more than that, you are committed to informing, entertaining and in the final analysis delighting the reader. Responsibility goes with the benefits of access. Your primary responsibility is to provide copy that the editor knows will enhance the loyalty of the publication's readership. You must find out by careful reading what is likely to appeal and then use your creativity to craft pieces that promote your credibility and status in the eyes of the readership and the editorial staff. Use your expertise to give the readers what they want and you will be a welcome contributor. Make a brash attempt to push your offering down their throats and the publishers will rightly ban you from their pages or ask you to pay for your advertisements.

It is tempting, but it is not a good idea to take paid advertising in an ezine that has promoted your products or services. Above all, you need to maintain the belief that the editor who praised your goods is an honest broker. If, subsequently, buyers see paid advertising appearing, some will begin to wonder.

This does not mean that you should not or cannot do a deal to get your offering a mention. Some editors will not accept payment and stick rigidly to their editorial freedom, others are happy to accept payment for what they see as a commercial service. Like them you should let your own values guide your actions, but if you pay for extra business you can afford to be very generous and you would be wise to do so.

Sponsorship does not only bring in immediate visitors, it brings you customers. If you look after those customers as you should, you will have them for life. Your lifetime return is presumably far greater than the value of the initial, often minimal, sale. You could well afford to give all of the profits from that first sale to win a customer for life.

## How do I find more strategic partners?

*Newsletter publishers*

Visit http://www.mediafinder.com/ today. With almost 100 000 newsletters listed, there will be a number that appeal to people to whom your products and services would be a welcome addition. Click on to a few newsletters.

Read them and identify those who could help you to become the web millionaire about whom we are always reading. With a first-rate product or service, great information or entertainment and lifelong relationships with delighted customers you deserve everything that is coming to you. If you prosper the ethical way you will continue to prosper.

### Mailing lists

I am never truly happy with mailing lists. Too often they are cobbled together by means of which I disapprove. They require the addressee to opt out rather than opt in. They are often far from well maintained and their sale on the Internet far too often leads to unrestrained spamming. In the world of stamps and envelopes I recommend that you always use a reputable professional list broker who knows how to navigate through the minefield, or the list that you use will have only one response: 'Please take my name off your list.' If, however, you know better, mediafinder.com lists owners of lists as well and good luck to you.

### Business directories

If a firm is likely to have a sizeable customer base which shares the interests of your customers you can find them in the various directories online from Thompson or Yellow Pages upwards. Before you approach any as a strategic ally try being a customer. Check out their website, opt in to any e-mail contact or newsletter and see for yourself whether their communications are of a type with which you want to be associated.

### Ezine directories

Many ezines have thousands of subscribers who, in general, share interests. They could, therefore, endorse your products or services to great effect. Subscribe to those that appear interesting for an issue or two before approaching as a potential strategic ally. The directories are many. Try some of the following for information and ideas:

- Our List of Hundreds of Ezines
- eZines Database
- John Labovitz's E-Zine List
- Electronic Journal Access
- Zine Rack.

*Website directories*

When it comes right down to it you cannot beat a strategic ally who is already doing something very similar to what you are doing, only possibly better at present. A list of web marketers, listed by category is worth more than gold dust. Try:

- Yahoo (probably the biggest and best directory of them all)
- Click Trade
- Web Side Story.

*Surfing the web*

The web often responds kindly to those who play with it. The right keywords and phrases open a treasure trove of information. If someone who looks appropriate comes close to the top of the list for a given keyword, that is a real treasure. Work with them and the world will come to know your name. I am told that the professionals use WebFerret to enable them to search seven search engines all at the same time. Wow! It sounds complicated to me, but look at http://www.webferret.com/. Not everyone is a technophobe like me.

*Bulletin boards, forums and discussion groups*

Most chat rooms and the like bring together like-minded people to share their interests and knowledge. Most fight shy of promoting products or services directly, but none stop you from asking, 'does anyone know a good source for . . .?' To find forums that are appropriate to you, you may wish to try:

- Yahoo message boards
- ForumOne
- Lycos Search: Message Boards.

Some forums exist solely to promote online business. Why not look at:

- Ezine Publishers Business Exchange
- LinkUp Discussion Group
- Expose

(in addition to the links given on page 196).

*Networking*

If you know people who know people they might very well be able to recommend a possible strategic ally. Internet discussion groups can help to quickly build the extent of your personal network. (Beware of multilevel marketers. Although I am sure that many are ethical and hard-working, I have personally met a sufficient number of those who are neither so be wary of the whole tribe. The desire to build 'downlines' makes these people ace networkers, but I suspect that few benefit from the relationship, not even those who build it.)

*Frequently seen banner advertisements*

If you see an advertisement over and over again it is probably doing some good. If it is appropriate, take a closer look, as above – you have nothing to lose from intelligent checking.

*Authors and other strange people*

People who write about the field in which you operate almost certainly have websites these days and those websites are there for a commercial purpose. With the exception of rare business bodice-rippers, royalty payments would seldom keep a very small monkey in peanuts, so many distinguished writers need other sources of income. Conversely, any human that writes about anything has a sort of specious authority that makes any endorsement that they make powerful, at least to their readers. Add to this the fact that they almost certainly keep in touch with their readers though a newsletter or something similar and you may have a prime case for a strategic alliance.

*Summary strategic plan*

- ✓ Find suppliers of non-competing products that appeal to customers with the same wants and needs as yours.
- ✓ Show them that your product or service is something that will genuinely benefit and delight many of their customers.
- ✓ Offer them a deal whereby they endorse your products or services. (The deal can be one of mutual endorsements or commission on sales according to circumstances.)
- ✓ Monitor sales and track orders.
- ✓ Build an e-market dominance (see below) relationship with each of your new customers.

✓ Develop a new group of loyal customers for life.

✓ Delight these new customers with your communications, products and service.

✓ Create many more advocates for your business.

✓ Watch your business flourish.

E-market dominance is the first truly comprehensive approach to building and sustaining an Internet business and is the title of Brian Ash and Tom Lambert's new book, published by McGraw-Hill.

## How does affinity marketing work?

### No cash outlay

If you pay anything at all you only pay commission on sales. If you can honestly endorse and promote your partners' offerings to your loyal customers you pay nothing more than a little of your time saying something nice about someone else to your customers and, if you do it honestly, you delight your customers further in the process – the only really proper use of your time as a clear-thinking business person.

### The response rate is up to four times that of 'permission' marketing alone

Tests show that those who promote their own products, in a permission marketing role, can often get an even better response rate through honest third-party endorsement of another firm's products or services.

### The approach combines and creates a synergy between your e-market dominance and that of similar, responsible others

Nowhere does synergy mean that two plus two equals a great deal more than five than when used as part of an e-market dominance strategy.

*Costs are low and controllable*

You buy no mailing list. You pay for neither printing nor stamps. You provide a communicator with something more (and new) to communicate to people who want to read about it. Even at that level it is a win-win situation, as any busy journalist will tell you. All that you must be sure to do is to back up your strategic partner by offering a superior product and top-quality service to his or her customers. Their customers become your customers, but no one loses out. You both benefit at virtually zero cost.

*There are no better ways to target buyers*

By definition these prospects are interested in the products, services and information that you can deliver. They want a relationship with you. The only problem is that, up to now, they probably did not know that you existed.

*It is a genuine third party endorsement*

You and your partners must only endorse offerings which will genuinely satisfy the customer's need in such a way as to delight, and go on delighting them. If an editor endorses anything and everything for a price they are not suitable partners for you, so check out at least one or two endorsements that they have made before you get in too deep.

*Your 'sponsor' delights his or her customers further through providing easy access your ability to serve*

Surfing the net can be a laborious kind of fun. Many keywords lead to literally millions of sites. If you have what it takes to delight another firm's customers, those customers will be eternally grateful that their time has been saved. In the affluent world of the northern hemisphere most of us are fortunate enough to have money to spend. The two things that we lack above all else are time and attention. Anyone who can save us time or make our meagre expenditure of attention worthwhile has, and deserves, a little of our money and our thanks.

### Neither loses customers, but you both gain

As long as one offering does not replace the other and you both play straight down the line, you each gain new, profitable customers for life. If either partner tries to be oversmart you may be sure that he or she will be seen for what he or she is, and the web has ways of dealing with scam artists.

### These are customers for life

These customers have chosen to opt in. Times may change. Their needs and wants may change, but if you stay in touch, you will change your offering to meet their emergent desires. They will be with you for life and they will become advocates for your business.

### The Internet is all about information

People love news and newsletters. They always have. My one-time personal guru, Howard Shenson, attracted around a quarter of a million people worldwide to subscribe to a 'post and paper' newsletter many years ago. The appearance of the publication was far from artistic, the style of writing was idiosyncratic, but Howard gave people what they wanted, information and ideas that they could use to build their businesses. He and they prospered together.

The Internet has made it easy to provide information and entertainment related directly to the reader's interests. What people want to read they read avidly. There are no gatekeepers to stop your information reaching the decision maker as there is with direct mail.

## What should I offer strategic partners?

*Step One: Get your offering right*

If you expect someone to recommend your product or service to their valued and valuable customers you have to be offering something which will enhance, not threaten, the relationship that they may well have built up over years. You must, therefore, ensure that your offer and the service that backs it is capable of consistently delivering delight.

## How do I contact strategic partners?

*Step Two: Find the right partners*

The vital word here is 'right'. Your prospective partners must:

✓ Have built a strong relationship with their customers built on trust. These customers must have similar interests to your own.

✓ Contact their customers regularly delivering information or entertainment that is desired, personal, timely and relevant.

✓ Have a large enough database of prospects to make the partnership worthwhile for you both.

*Step Three: Making contact*

Most websites offer a range of ways to make contact. Identify the most personal and use that, after all, this relationship is among the most important that you will make. Where it is possible, a telephone call is good; so is a fax or a letter. The thing to avoid is a bulk e-mail squirted out to hundreds of potential partners. Whatever you call it, spam remains spam and people who trade online are probably more sensitive to it than most.

## How do I influence others to want to partner with me?

*The initial contact*

An outline of the kind of things that you might say:

- I loved your website.

- Your customers and mine have much in common.

- Could we help each other?

- I can see how you treat your customers. I treat mine in the same caring way.

- An alliance with me could enhance your relationship with your customers and make you money.

- May I send you a sample of my product (description of my service – with testimonials) for you to consider?

- If you are happy to recommend my product/service I would be delighted to offer a special deal to your customers. (Be careful here that the deal that you offer is not one that would upset your current customers. Where possible make your own loyal customers a good deal at the same time. Some will be on both your database as well as that of your prospective partner.)

- Since my customers tend to become customers for life I would be glad to pay you most of the profit on the initial deals I make with your customers. I will make my money from the recurrent repeat sales ... or ...

- I will happily do a similar endorsement for your products.

- I believe absolutely that for both of us our relationships with our customers can be enhanced if we work together.

## Why is risk reversal important?

*Risk reversal*

Risk reversal is a useful marketing technique designed to encourage customers to place initial orders with confidence. It is equally useful when used to ensure that a strategic partner is happy to promote your goods or services. You cannot expect anyone to put their hard-won customer confidence and trust at risk on your behalf. If you have belief in your products or services you will have no qualms about assuming the risk of doing business. A no-questions-asked cashback policy for those who are less than totally satisfied is only the beginning.

Offer credible and worthwhile guarantees for your partner and the new customers. Make sure that your 'host' has the choice of selling direct if preferred. You have no wish to take customers or business away from him or her. If he or she wants to, agree to the endorsement being tested with a small subset of his or her customers. Write the endorsement yourself if you can, but make it clear that nothing goes out to the customers unless the host feels totally comfortable with it.

## How do I develop an agreement with potential strategic allies?

*Step Four: The agreement*

No one but lawyers like lengthy and legalistic contracts, but in business clear agreements, in writing, are essential. This is not an invitation to an open season on distributing writs. A contract is simply a clear, unambiguous statement of what has been agreed between you and another businessperson. The contract is for clarity and to avoid misunderstandings.

I have spent far too much of my business life assuming that nice people are honest and decent. As a result I have all too often helped others without a contract. Let me admit it. I am a fool. When the chips are down I find that

I have met and worked with more crooks than honest people. Make sure that you have a clear, simple written agreement that will stand up to the worst that a crooked partner's lawyer can throw at it.

Going to law is a distraction that most reputable businesspeople avoid, but which some very disreputable people use as a smoke screen. Whenever the late and unlamented Robert Maxwell was up to something crooked he threatened those who might challenge him with the law.

In most countries today the simplest of contracts is thought of as binding on both parties, so a clear letter stating what you agree to do, what your strategic partner will do, who will pay how much to whom and when is about all that you are likely to need. It is pleasant if you each sign two copies. That shows a degree of commitment and even enthusiasm for the deal, but in many countries this is unnecessary. As long as one party sends a copy to the other and can show that it was received and not amended, it normally stands as a contract that is binding on both.

See also: In an international e-commerce dispute, which country has jurisdiction?

## I AM A SUPERIOR SALESPERSON

### Can I make money selling other people's products and services from my website?

It is possible that you are interested neither in finding strategic partners to promote your products or services nor in a two-way reciprocal arrangement. You may prefer the simple idea of making more money from your database of customers. In that case you may want to consider a simple hosting arrangement where you promote others' goods or services online for a substantial commission.

You must, of course already have a sufficiently large and affluent database of existing customers or clients to whom to promote products or services that they would wish to buy and an established medium of communication. If you have both there is nothing to stop you from identifying suppliers and offerings that are relevant to your customers.

*See also:    How does affinity marketing work?*

## How can I find partners that I can host on my website?

*Action plan for prospective hosts*

✓ Contact the owner of the business whose products or services you believe that you can ethically and effectively endorse.

✓ Explain how your customer base could provide profitable extra sales.

✓ Outline your terms of business, especially your expectations in terms of sales commissions. (Perhaps 55–65 per cent of initial sales and 10 per cent of repeat business.)

✓ Suggest a clear and concise contract that gives you your fair share of repeat sales.

✓ Indicate how you expect orders to be tracked.

✓ Point out that the real money is in back-end sales and that you are only prepared to do business with those who treat their customers in such a way as to generate such sales.

✓ Remind them that they have no advertising or marketing costs for this additional, lifelong business, if they work with you . . . and . . .

✓ If they reject your offer simply move on, it is their loss and you have plenty of other fish to fry.

section

# six

the market in brief

# A REMINDER OF IMPORTANT MATTERS

## What are the demographics of the Internet customer?

Although the situation will change, the most recent available figures show that the web is still mainly a male domain with 85 per cent of users in Britain, and 91 per cent in France and Germany being males. In the USA things are more equal with only 53 per cent of users being male.

Recent research in the USA suggests that the web customer as opposed to 'surfer' is likely to be:

- thirty-something
- articulate
- a relatively high earner
- well educated
- short of time
- short of patience.

*See also:*   How much time are people spending online?

## Is lifetime customer value still important or does the web encourage disloyalty?

✓  The customer is likely to be young enough to make their lifetime purchases well worth having and, more importantly, well worth striving to keep.

✓  They will be clear about what they want and will actively seek out those sites that provide the information that they want in a form that suits their needs.

✓  They can pay for what they want, and one thing that they want is to save time.

✓  They are well educated so they can absorb and use a great deal of information. When they want to know, they want to know as much as possible as long as it is relevant to their needs.

✓  If you can make life easy for them without patronizing them they will be yours for life.

✓  Time is more important than money to website buyers. They want to be able to make an informed decision with the minimum hassle. They do not want to spend unnecessary time looking to save pennies, but they do expect value and that includes understanding and responding to their personal needs.

✓  These are people who understand enough of the technology to know that auto-responders are more likely to generate communication than real people. They also know that, as long as they get the information that they want when they want it, it is an intelligent use of technology that causes them no concerns. It is the information that counts. Whether that comes from other human beings directly or is mediated by technology is immaterial.

For detail on the research by Bains and Company into the effects of customer loyalty on employee retention and satisfaction as well as profit see *The Loyal Customer* by Frederick Reichheld, or for a brief summary see *E-Market Dominance* by Brian Ash and Tom Lambert.

## Will commerce on the Internet follow a predestined path?

Most experts would agree that the Internet is less easy to make a fortune on than much of the hype would suggest. It still needs to discover the so-called 'killer application' that will make it the only way to do business. Until then you need a strategy as robust and as flexible as that which, hopefully, you have in place for your more terrestrial business activities.

Only two things are certain: e-commerce will grow in importance in spite of any early difficulty and we are in for some exciting surprises.

*See also:* What are the business barriers to growth?

## What do the forecasters say?

- By 2005 e-mail marketing alone will have increased in value to $7.3 billion (4000 per cent growth in just five years).

- In the USA in 1999 each e-mail subscriber received on average 40 business e-mails. By 2005 they will receive 1600.

- The attention deficit that now strangles at birth so many direct mail and advertising campaigns will hit the web within five years.

- Current research shows that customers are 49 per cent more likely to buy if the marketing effort is synergistic. (E-market dominance is the only truly synergistic approach that is relevant to present and future circumstances.)

● By 2003 US business intends to spend almost half of its total advertising budget on the web, not necessarily on online advertising.

● Opt-in e-mail (the provision of a mandate to provide information) is increasing at a rate of:

| Year | Growth |
| --- | --- |
| 2000 | 52% |
| 2001 | 66% |
| 2002 | 70% |

While total e-mail is growing at a rate of:

| Year | Growth |
| --- | --- |
| 2000 | 29% |
| 2001 | 33% |
| 2002 | 34% |

*Sources*: Jupiter Research, eMarketer Report.

*See also*:   Can we trust the predictions of the so-called gurus – like you?

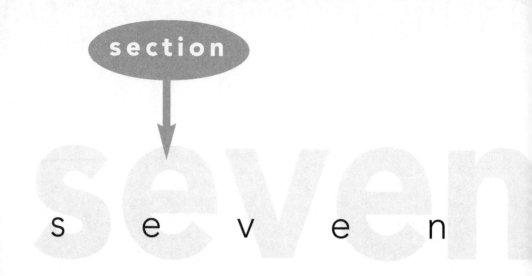

# planning your Internet strategy and tactics

If you are in business your online presence is an investment that ought to deliver a better than usual return. If you are not enjoying such a return you need to revisit your strategy, your tactics or both.

# THE BASICS OF ONLINE MARKETING AND SELLING

## The chairman wants a website. What do we need to think about?

There are more than 70 million sites on the web today. It would take me 21 months to visit each for one second if I surfed the web day and night without ceasing for rest or repast. There will be a great many more tomorrow. So why should I want to visit yours among so many?

If you want to make money you do not want to attract any old (or young) surfer. You want to attract those who want to buy the kind of thing that you offer, have the money and the desire to buy it now and who will come back again and again to buy more.

The first crucial step is to build a site that is worth visiting. This does not mean that it must be adorned with every irrelevant bell and whistle that a creative 'techie' believes is a technological possibility. It means developing a site that delivers useful, relevant, easy-to-find information that people want. It means that those who want to buy can do so without hassle and, since the majority of worthwhile customers put convenience above price, it means creating a site to which they will return again and again, prepared to pay premium prices because they get what they want.

If you build and launch such a site you can, in theory, sit back and wait for customers to arrive. The web is the ultimate in gossip and newsgroups, and online magazines (ezines) make a wondrous grapevine. If they like what they stumble on, they are happy to tell the world.

The process, however, has two drawbacks. The people who are involved in the newsgroups or who read the ezines may not be those whom you wish to attract and the process takes time.

Some will wish to speed the process by bringing in expert help. There are literally thousands of consultants out there in the dirt world. All willing for more or less (usually less) modest fees to do all that you desire.

☞ *See also*:  The BIG question – why have so many dot coms failed so dramatically?

## Is there a single key to online success?

Yes. The question that you should continuously be asking yourself is, 'how can I use the Internet to improve the profitability of my business?'

Ask that question every day, not just of yourself, but ask every champion of having a web presence. The purpose of asking the question is not to find a reason to reject online marketing. It is to ensure that you exploit the opportunities to the full. If you ask yourself and others that question and develop relevant, flexible, customer-centred strategies you will succeed.

*See also*:   What is the most effective way to market a website?

Can we get high on the search engines without heavy advertising?

## Is a website simply another way to build the brand?

Some advertising agencies have been seeking an easy way of breaking into the new economy. Not surprisingly they highlight what they know best – brand-building – and use their 'creatives' extensively. The problems experienced by Disney and NewsCorp, two global brands, show the dangers of this approach. The businessperson also needs to bear in mind that if an advertising agency, or anyone else, is feeling its way in a new medium it is an attractive prospect to be able to make all the mistakes of learning at the client's expense.

It would not be unreasonable to suggest that your web presence can be so important to the future of your business that it deserves to have its own brand based on ease of use, reliability of information and quality of customer care. Many large corporations are thinking very seriously of the interplay between branding and the Internet so that each product or product range is allocated its own website with its own unique features. They are moving away from corporate branding as such and defining brands in a customer-centred rather than product-centred way.

*See also*:   Why is market dominance essential?

## Should we consider using consultants or our advertising agency for advice?

Some consultants are good, some are bad and many might be cowboys if they rode horses rather than bandwagons. Some charge fees that are a fair reflection of the services that they provide. Some charge peanut-size fees and deliver monkey-quality services. The majority charge whatever they believe that the market will bear. Some of these do a good job and many do not.

If you already employ the services of an advertising agency it is a racing certainty that they will offer their services to continue to build your brand online. They will have the advantage that they understand the brand strategy. They may lack skills in a different medium and may be looking for opportunities to experiment and build experience.

You need to understand that this is a new area of expertise where many are seeking to find their way, preferably at your expense.

*See also*:    What is the most effective way to market a website?

## Can I save money if I do it myself?

You can do it yourself. Others have started from scratch with excellent results. Take a look at http://www.botham.co.uk/ – this successful site was built as a spare-time activity by the managing director of this Yorkshire bakery. I hesitate to call him an amateur since he now runs his own web design agency.

Many of you will want to control your own destiny and will need to know how to:

✓  Build a website in-house.

✓  Manage search engines.

✓  Make the most of directories.

✓  Use online advertising.

✓  Create host/beneficiary relationships.

✓  Solicit opt-in e-mail.

✓  Use non-Internet marketing techniques.

✓  Exploit public/press relations opportunities.

✓  Develop a comprehensive web strategy.

This book will help you, as will a number of others, but be warned you are taking on a tough and time-consuming activity. Unless you are able to commit a good deal of time to maintaining your online success you may be well advised to seek professional help sooner rather than later.

*See also:* How do we avoid losing money online?

## How do I develop a website from the ground up?

There was a time when the secret of effective business was said to be 'location, location, location'. When designing a website the old saw could be changed to 'content, content, content'. It is vital that website design should begin and end with content, the rest is merely technology. The purpose of a commercial website is to encourage people to visit and revisit, make it worth their while to spend some time at your site and make it easy to do business with you. The content of your website will play a major part in doing these things, and content goes far beyond the promotional puff of an online advertisement.

*A simple checklist for website design*

*The dos*

✓ Think first, last and foremost about the kind of customer that you want to attract. Your website needs to speak directly to that customer and provide the information that the customer wants in a form that saves them time and tedium. (Attention spans online are short.)

✓ Design the informational content so that it is easy to navigate the site and get at those pieces of information that are most desired by the customer.

✓ Enable the customer to invite you to send by e-mail new and relevant information on a regular basis.

✓ Avoid asking the customer for any information that you do not immediately need. Too many websites are becoming tedious collectors of information that cause the customer to believe that the information that they will receive is not worth the trouble of completing impertinent (in the true sense of the word) forms.

✓ Prove your worth by providing timely, relevant, desired information before you begin to seek more data on your customers. Once you are seen as their 'friend' customers will be delighted to invite you to build your customer information a little at a time.

✓ Make sure that your site can use auto-responders intelligently to take the grind out of communication without making it seem impersonal.

✓ Use the best of modern technology to protect your customer transactions and tell the customer how it works in their interest.

✓ Make ordering easy and tracing the status of an order easier if possible.

✓ Ensure that your distribution system in the real world has no flaws.

✓ Make sure that there is enough in the budget to place your site high on the search engines and to market it in the real world. To spend your all on a website and hope for the best is just like buying a superb car, but leaving nothing with which to buy the petrol.

✓ Have real experts identify keywords, key phrases and metatags that will enable search engines to find your site. Scattering a generic term here and there, will not serve you well in a competition with 70 million plus sites on the web.

✓ Choose your domain name with care.

### The don'ts

✓ Do not clutter your site with singing and dancing technological marvels that serve no purpose. A four-year longitudinal study of serious Internet users by the University of Wisconsin showed that serious users see much of the all action stuff that merely decorates websites as an irritating distraction from the important business of finding information quickly and it inclines them to look elsewhere.

✓ Do not use frames that look pretty, but do not work with some browsers.

✓ Beware of the siren charms that Java has for technical people, some browsers have difficulty with it.

✓ Never lose sight of the business purpose of your site or the needs of the customers who will use it.

## If I decide to 'do it myself', what then?

There is a rule of marketing that you neglect at your peril. It demands that everything that you do to market and sell your products services and ideas should be three times consistent.

You should market consistently. To put that another way, you should work just as hard at marketing when you are tempted by success to become fat, dumb and happy as you do when you are not sure how you are going to put the next meal on the table.

✓ Everything that you do in marketing, including your website should be consistent with the image and status of your business that you want to promote.

✓ Your site and your promotion strategy must be consistent with your purpose. If you want to sell online you must make it easy and attractive to buy.

✓ As the cost of designing and setting up websites becomes more reasonable, you may decide to have a second site to promote the really important one where you plan to do most of your business. Be careful though not to have it perceived as a 'doorway' site or the search engines may reject it. The Internet is about information and search engines can be programmed to assess the information content of a web page.

✓ Some companies with a wide range of products and services or a number of brands like to have a site for each in order to make the most of a consistent approach on each site. Similarly multidivision operations may choose to have semi-autonomous sites for each.

✓ Avoid slickness for its own sake. You can lose a great deal of message in a little too much cleverness.

✓ Do not be seduced by technical wizardry unless you are appealing to the youth market, and even then use it with discretion. If potential customers find that your site takes too long to load they will go elsewhere and never see your expensive gimmicks.

✓ Decide on the level of sophistication that you need by considering only the needs of your customers and once you have decided what is right for your buyers do not be tempted to stray until they tell you that they want something smarter.

✓ Make sure that your home page, other people's first impression of your site and of your business, loads quickly and is striking. Include clear links to other parts of the site with everything within one screen's view. If you take a look at my little site http://www.tom-lambert.com/ you will notice that the designer put every link at the top of the home page. Visitors can go where they please without unnecessary scrolling.

✓ Err on other pages on too much rather than too little text. Those who are really interested are eager to get as much information as they can about their prospective purchase. They can always print a hard copy or be selective in what they read if they are pressed for time.

✓ Since people will generally want to exercise a degree of selection make sure that it is easy to navigate around the site. The experts say that you should never need to make more than three clicks to get to where you want to be.

✓ Have an easy link back to the home page on every page.

✓ Avoid splendidly elaborate graphics unless they serve a proper business purpose. They are another excellent way of driving off people with a limited amount of time. Most of us, even the keenest potential customers, are short of time and there are more than 70 million other sites where they can get rapid opportunities to spend their cash.

✓ Good examples of the latest software enable brilliant effects without the excessive use of bytes. Simple tricks such as quick graphics that can be overlaid with something more elaborate are child's play for the technologically gifted.

> Think carefully about the use of frames. They can give a nice professional appearance but some old browsers cannot handle them and some printers cannot cope either, so the potential customer's desire to keep a copy to study at leisure is thwarted.

✓ Above all make sure that those who wish to buy online can do so. Those who want to and find that they cannot, go away and stay away in droves.

✓ Necessary or highly desirable special effects can be limited to 'plug ins'. These are fancy add-ons that can be downloaded by the visitor. They put the choice back into the hands of the customer who can download or not, according to their interest and the time available. To get useful introduction to these take a look at:

> www.realaudio.com
> www.macromedia.com
> www.sseyo.com
> www.futurewave.com
> www.intervista.com

## How do I find the technical and strategic help that I might need?

- ✓ Talk to other business people who have an online, marketing and sales operation up and running and get their advice.

- ✓ Attend a seminar or two, having made sure that they are about business and not about technology. Learn at least the right questions to ask by listening to and talking with your peers.

- ✓ Go to meetings run by your professional or trade associations and judge whether the speaker is talking sense. If he or she is, ask his or her advice.

- ✓ Look at websites like www.net-profit.com. Sites that specialize in building web business offer a deal of sound advice and have a contacts section from which you can solicit proposals.

- ✓ Visit a few commercial websites. When you find one that seems to fit in with your needs make a note of the builder's contact details and check them out by e-mail or with a telephone call.

- ✓ Look for referrals. My website, http://www.tom-lambert.com/ is created and maintained by Gerald Allen's people who can be contacted at http://www.quadrantinternet.com/. Jeff Allen will probably be happy to talk to you and direct you to look at other sites that they have developed as well as introducing you to other clients with whom you can talk web business.

- ✓ When you talk to individual consultants ask them for a little about their background and experience. Check their technical skills as best you can, but remember that an understanding of business is a rarer and more essential commodity. Make sure that they demonstrate some signs of business understanding. Have them show you sites that they have built. Many years ago when I was with General Motors and was faced with the need to buy in expertise that I lacked I would have a more expert technically literate colleague with me. If he or she had any doubts they would say something that sounded impressive, but which was utter nonsense. If the would-be supplier agreed with what was said we had been warned.

✓ Talk to the owners of those sites that impress you to be sure that they work as well as they appear to and build business rather than mere admiration. If you believe that you need an artistic and graphically eye-catching website, bear in mind that it is easier to learn about computers than to develop visual flair so find a really good graphic designer before you go too far. The website www.sagittarius.com is that of a company that in my experience puts design and usability before technical tricks and tarradiddles.

✓ To save time and money choose those who have skills, knowledge and experience that complements your own, and do what you can yourself as a fast-track learning experience.

✓ When you buy-in expertise of any kind use it as a learning activity. Always try to learn enough so that you have the option of doing it yourself the next time that the need arises.

*See also:* What is the most effective way to market a website?

## Should I 'do it all myself' or use an ASP?

An ASP (Application Service Provider) is in principle pleasingly straightforward. It turns a product (software) into a service because the user pays only for what is used as applications are remotely managed and delivered to end-users by way of a network.

The advantages claimed are also refreshingly simple.

✓ You only pay for what you get and you do not need to make an investment in software that may soon be superseded as technology gallops ahead.

✓ The skills needed to make it work for you are with the vendor, so the use of ASP could ease the skills shortage for non-specialist companies.

✓ Growth of the business requires less investment and becomes only a matter using working capital.

The vendors claim that it is outsourcing perfected, that it enables users to exploit the full potential of the World Wide Web at a cost that starts and remains strictly in line with their individual circumstances irrespective of technological development. In short, it is claimed that by using ASP the business can concentrate on the business rather than the technology.

With basic applications outsourced, the firm can concentrate its expert resources on those activities and issues that really add value to the business – growth, e-business and planning.

So what is the downside? The principle is simple, but reality is more complex. Is the Internet reliable or secure enough to ensure that the firm has the information that it needs as it needs it? Some experts say, 'not yet'. If you believe that you need to rent a leased line to be able to take part, the costs can escalate without any discernible business advantages. Another problem is that, as with all software, an ASP can only deliver the applications that the software permits and, although these may appear to be impressive, your specific and detailed needs may not be fully met until some 'techie' tweaks the code because enough people have expressed the wish to have in the future what you need right now.

So the only sensible advice is to become familiar with what is available. Make a judgement based on the current and predicted needs of your business. Beware of too low a price of entry since suppliers may be scrimping on service to meet a price requirement, but even if now is not the time to go so far as to dip a toe in the water, keep an eye on developments. The idea is in its infancy, but the experts are indicating massive growth. Industry gurus at IDC, Gartner-Group Dataquest and Ovum all share the view that the proof of the pudding will be in the eating and that the taste will be good enough to sustain a business that will grow from an estimated $3.6 billion a year in 2001 to a projected $136 billion in 2006. Anticipated growth of that magnitude and speed suggests great value to business, but with the possibility of considerable growing pains.

The biggest ASPs are at present all situated in the USA, but big is not necessarily beautiful and in most countries there will be a growing number of providers. One minor word of warning concerning size may be appropriate, however. Big may not always be best, but ASPs are proliferating at a great rate and there will be some degree of 'shake out' if there is not enough business to go round. The weak go to the wall. When someone else is in effect handling all your online business you need to convince yourself that they can give you not only reliability, but also continuity.

To keep in touch with developments in this important area take an occasional look at: www.aspindustry.org.

### Research review  Outsourcing

Research by Logical suggests that outsourcing will be the principle strategy of at least UK SMEs by 2004. At the end of March 2001 52 per cent of small and medium enterprises are already outsourcing part or all of their IT requirements rather than attempting to manage them in-house. In a rapidly evolving field outsourcing is seen by most as preferable to attempting to keep up.

Similar research by the European Yankee Group identifies three further reasons why SMEs are choosing to outsource.

- ✓ Outsourcing reduces the problems of finding and employing qualified IT staff.
- ✓ It reduces up-front costs.
- ✓ It allows faster implementation of key IT strategies.

Finally, Ovum Research reported in March 2001 that for the first time the percentage of British firms with a web presence overtook companies from the USA. Their research suggests that whereas 57 per cent of American businesses have a commercial website, 58 per cent of British enterprises are online. Globally and in the UK it is anticipated that 80 per cent of firms will be online to some degree this year (2001). This results, the report claims, from the fact that British firms are more willing to outsource this part of their business as growth accelerates beyond the easy acquisition of skills and knowledge.

# SEARCH ENGINES AND DIRECTORIES

## I'm not a technician. What do I need to know about directories and search engines?

It is worth remembering that directories and search engines help to take us where we want to be, but they do it in very different ways. You need initially to make an educated guess about how customers will choose to find your site.

✓ Directories, such as Yahoo.com list sites by category. Search engines send spiders to crawl across the home page or in some cases every page, looking for keywords that denote content.

✓ On an average sort of day search engines complete more than 75 million searches, that is, 900 every second.

✓ In spite of the massive popularity of Yahoo, the leading directory, around 70 per cent of searchers use one of the most popular search engines to find the sites and the information that they need.

✓ Some of the best-known search engines include:

www.av.com
www.excite.com
www.google.com
www.goto.com
www.hotbot.com
www.infoseek.com

www.lycos.com
www.nlsearch.com
www.webcrawler.com

Leading directories are:

www.yahoo.com
www.looksmart.com
www.britannica.com

Some directories, including Yahoo, are hybrids that combine the attributes of a search engine with those of a carefully designed, interactive 'yellow pages'.

*See also*: Can we get high on the search engines without heavy advertising?

## What specifically do I need to know about search engines?

The secrets of search engines are difficult to unravel. There is an excellent reason why this is true. The very clever people who run them like it that way. They work according to sets of rules called 'algorithms' and to dazzle us simple businesspeople they change the rules a little (or a lot) when it takes their fancy. But you can bet that in this life ingenuity begets ingenuity. So some very clever tools exist to keep closely in touch with a moving feast.

**Mini Case Study** **Big can be beautiful**

It helps to be a big name online. In January 2001 the top 20 big name websites saw a 20 per cent increase in site traffic, while overall use of the web fell very slightly from that of the previous month.

Yahoo, for example, is credited with 13 billion page views in the month according to Jupiter Media Metrix. Unless the smaller online operations learn to fully exploit the search engines, the strong will get stronger simply because their names are known.

Of course, it is never sheer numbers that are important. It is the quality of the web traffic that comes to your site that counts. That is why all executives intending to drive forward a worthwhile and prosperous online business need to know a little about search engines and how to use the keywords and key phrases that will be effective in bringing the right customers who should be beating a path to your door.

Research by the Confederation of British Industry, the London Business School and KPMG Consulting in late February 2001 show that 93 per cent of companies expect e-commerce to be an important strand of their business and are forecasting that online revenues will at least double by 2003.

Meanwhile, profitability of British companies is slipping a little. In the year 2000 British companies slipped from number two position in the world profitability league to number five behind Finland, Israel, Norway and Singapore. It is probably no coincidence that the countries ahead of Britain in profitability include those that are snapping at the heels of the USA when it comes to e-commerce readiness according to the recent Economist Intelligence Unit report.

It is questionable whether a firm, as opposed to a country, can be seen as e-commerce ready unless the executives who are responsible for the strategy have some basic understanding of how customers will find their website.

*See also:* How do we bring in customers, old and new, to our site?

## Where might I get some reliable indication what is best done by experts and what can be done in-house?

If you choose to talk with the Allens (father or son) at www.coastalsitesuk.co.uk or their American partners at www.coastalsites.com they will doubtless tell you with unbounded enthusiasm of the tools that their company has tested and that they use on behalf of their clients. This is an area where it pays to talk to the practised experts. But, as always, there are strategic and tactical decisions that you need to make for yourself.

☞ *See also*:   Should we consider using consultants or our advertising agency for advice?

# MORE ABOUT KEYWORDS

## What are keywords and why are they important?

Search engines send little programs called 'spiders' to 'crawl' over sites and identify keywords. When a potential customer enters a word into the search box the engine lists those that offer the appropriate keywords in an order dictated by the algorithms that currently apply.

## Should I use 'safe' generic keywords?

The chances are that many sites are using the same keywords and so the position the site gets on the search engine is something of a lottery if you limit yourself to simple generic terms. It is often useful to link words into short phrases that surfers may use, but other sites will not. This enables you to score higher on the search engine.

## What happens when keywords are misspelled?

Many potential customers misspell words. Skilful web designers build the most popular misspellings into the website, hiding them carefully where only the spiders can find them. Your ISP may list the most regularly misspelled words or you can subscribe to a specialist service (see below), to be kept abreast of the latest vagaries and variations.

# MORE ABOUT SEARCH ENGINES AND DIRECTORIES

## How does a directory differ from a search engine?

A directory such as Yahoo lists sites according to submitted descriptions of the contents. They are a very sophisticated sort of online 'yellow pages'. A search engine is a program that analyzes a site strictly in accordance with a set of precisely defined rules. The fun starts when those rules are changed either for a very sound reason or just for the hell of it. Search engines use different algorithms from each other and directories use different criteria for listing so if you score high on one you may do very much less well on the other.

## If I do not score high on the search engines will customers find my site?

The really committed tracker may find you by working through a great many listings and a number of search engines and directories. Such committed people are rare. As a rule of thumb, if you cannot be found on the first three pages of listings (30 to 60 websites), you will not be found at all and the odds of you being visited if you are on page three are a very small fraction of those of the lucky – or clever – people who appear on page one.

The alternative is to advertise and advertise and advertise. That is why so many ill-conceived marketing approaches by dot coms are haemorrhaging cash through marketing efforts that cost around 25 per cent more than the revenues that they generate.

At the very least, however, you should ensure that every piece of paper, every advertisement and every letter that comes out of your office gives the reader your website address.

☞ *See also:*   How can we get high on the search engines without heavy advertising?
Does online advertising work?

## How do I score high on search engines?

You have three options:

1. You have a brand name so well known – Coca-Cola, Disney, Sony – that customers will find you no matter what.

2. You have a full-time expert prepared to spend many hours analyzing statistics and tweaking your website to meet the ever-changing demands of the search engines and criteria of directories.

3. You outsource the responsibility to those who make it all or a major part of their business to keep their clients on the first three pages.

Take a look at www.coastalsitesuk.co.uk to see the kind of service that is on offer.

There is another possibility. You may just be lucky. The odds against you are somewhat better than those of winning the lottery, but at the time of writing there are roughly 75 million times the average numbers of pages in each website being crawled over by search engine spiders, and one search engine recently reported that they add an average of 1500 sites a day to that total. (Some websites run to around half a million pages.)

## What are the tactical requirements to score high on search engines?

In designing your website you will have developed a list of keywords and key phrases, and you or your designer will have sorted them into some order of priority. It is essential that this is given the care that it deserves. Frankly, it is often far too important to be left to the technical wizards. The manager needs to be involved.

You will also have thought up some suitable titles for your site that will be likely to be used by those who seek your kind of service or product.

Some descriptions of your website for directories and search engines will have been developed that are meaningful to the searcher.

All of these, and more, are important. Remember always that the World Wide Web is not about technology. It is about sales, marketing and information. People who go online are looking for information and service.

# STRATEGY AND TACTICS IN GREATER DETAIL

## Where do I start?

Planning an Internet strategy is no different than planning any other strategy. You start by thinking deeply about what you are trying to achieve. That is the purpose of the E-Business Corporate Analysis starting on page 66. If you skipped over it before please go back now and carefully think through every question. Seldom has it been truer that those who fail to plan really do plan to fail.

Once you have a clear picture of where you want to be, encapsulate it in a few meaningful inspirational words that will ensure that others share your vision and help you to achieve it. Make sure that everybody understands what you are determined to achieve. Whatever else you do, be sure that the technical wizards who build and maintain your website are inspired to follow your dream, not theirs.

Write a real mission statement, not a pleasant sounding bundle of business-school speak, but a working document that guides action. A web mission that tells the world:

✓ What customer needs and desires your business exists to satisfy.

✓ What makes you and your enterprise different and the obvious first and last port of call for every worthwhile customer.

✓ Why and how you will consistently challenge yourself and your people to be better and better at everything that you do.

✓ How all stakeholders, customers, employees, suppliers, distributors and the community are to be treated by you and your enterprise.

✓ The principles and values on which you and all who are associated with you reach important business and ethical decisions.

Look with a critical, but wide-ranging eye at where you stand today.

What are strengths, competencies and resources that you can exploit to build your web business? What additional strengths will you need to develop to fully exploit current opportunities? What could you develop in order to dominate the most profitable markets of the future?

What are those weaknesses that clearly get in the way of attracting and delighting profitable customers right now? If you think of weaknesses that do not get in the way of attracting and retaining customers, forget them for the moment and concentrate on what is vital to build and sustain profitable business today. The rest can wait. Customers flock to buy from firms where they get satisfaction. You will make more sales at better profit by giving your customers more of what they like best about you than you will if you spend time and money trying to eradicate every tiny fault or shortcoming.

Specify in detail the opportunities which can be exploited, and record how your strengths, competencies and resources will enable you to be better than the best of your competition in taking full advantage of them.

Analyze the potential threats to your web business and divide those threats into two types. Take those that can be avoided by taking action now and write the appropriate action into your plan and make sure that you do what must be done before you can be caught out. For those threats that might take you by surprise specify the likely indicators of trouble and for each define the actions that you will take to minimize or obviate the threat.

Analyze customer needs, wants and expectations to the best of your current knowledge, and research your main competitors' capabilities in terms of satisfying those needs. Establish where you have a clear competitive advantage and specify how and when you will use that advantage to attract competitions' best, most profitable customers. (Take a look at 'Comparative Analysis' in my *Key Management Solutions* published by Pitman/FT.)

Consider the alternative strategies that are available to you and choose the most promising from among them on the basis of your analysis to date. Keep those that you reject today conveniently to hand. They may form the basis of a truly flexible approach if the environment in which you operate changes or if new and different customer needs emerge.

## What are the important strategic decisions?

✓ Will you be a low-cost supplier? Will you provide high-price items to a niche market? Where will your online activities fit into the overall picture of your total business? Should your online business be seamless with your terrestrial business or should it be a separate specialist enterprise appealing to new customers?

✓ Will you go for fast growth or steady consolidation? Will you attempt market dominance? Will you operate globally or remain a mainly domestic supplier? How will you attract more profitable customers and dump those that are more trouble than they are worth?

The list is potentially endless. The vital thing is that you know and can communicate what is right for your business and your desired customers.

✓ Write down strategic and tactical objectives that are in all cases specific, measurable, achievable with present or attainable resources, realistic in today's market and timed so that you know precisely when the benefits of your incursion into e-commerce will be experienced.

✓ Complete an action plan that specifies who is responsible for taking action, when it must be started, by when it must be finished and the maximum that any activity may cost. Where appropriate, indicate the limits of authority and who is to be informed of progress.

## How do we stop unknown global competitors attracting away our best customers?

You should constantly build into the strategic planning process the assurance that you can retain all that you wish to retain of your current customer base. Too many firms go happily out to conquer the world only to neglect the valuable but undervalued customers that they already have. Think carefully about those customers who cost least to service and provide your profits. Retaining them is your strategic priority.

### Self-assessment

Are you under threat? Could your most valued customers defect?
Any business manager should be looking to the future. This does not mean that they should fail to conduct an inventory of their present situation. It is suggested that you consider, and demand that others consider, the following before entering on an Internet strategy.

Do you know, with certainty, from where the major competitive threats to your revenues and profits will come in a global market? **Yes No**

Have you analyzed what your key customers want now and are likely to want in the future in sufficient detail to be able to write it down and get their unqualified agreement? **Yes No**

Have you clearly identified threats to your business which are avoidable and put in place strategies to ensure that you cannot be caught off guard?
**Yes No**

Have you specifically identified threats to your revenues and profits that cannot be avoided by any action that you take now and developed contingency plans based on key indicators that you are in actual or potential danger? **Yes No**

Do you know specifically – from your customers' point of view – where competition could offer satisfactions which you do not offer at present, or cannot offer in the near (very near) future? **Yes No**

Do you know precisely what your key customers most important needs are now? **Yes No**

Do you know what your key customers might like, but would not expect at present? **Yes No**

Can you satisfy the most important needs of worthwhile customers better than your competition can? **Yes No**

Have you planned how you might build on your present strengths to give your customers what they might dream about tomorrow – today? **Yes No**
Have you considered how you could make any competitor see the cost of entry into your chosen markets as too high? **Yes No**

Unless your answer to every question is an unqualified 'yes' you are vulnerable where you could be most easily hurt by global competition using technology to its utmost.

## What is Customer Relationship Management?

Customer Relationship Management systems (CRM) are software systems that allow you to build a relationship with your customers by automating your customer care communications. The wonder of the Internet is that increasingly it enables business to automate while still giving a convincing appearance of being personal and caring about each customer's needs and expectations. Systems are improving all the time and some are a great deal more creative than others. In a moving feast like this the strategist keeps abreast with what is emerging, but this is not an excuse for a 'wait and see' attitude. What can already be achieved is impressive and, although tomorrow will see the birth of even greater wonders, you need to have a programme in place right now.

*See also*:    What are the business barriers to growth?

## How can I use PR to bring business to my website?

You can and you should use PR. People give more credence to editorials than to any kind of direct promotion by the company, but bear the following points in mind.

✓ Free ink is not necessarily cheap. You will need either to brief a consultant or to be your own PR expert. The first costs you money, the second costs time.

✓ In order to make your investment work for you maximize your chances of getting printed by ensuring that it is of interest to editors and their readers. Anything seen to be pure promotional puff should never be printed. If it is, it is unlikely to do you any good.

✓ Make your story as 'newsy' as you can. Constantly ask yourself why the reader should spend time on this? Be contentious, follow-up discussion in the letters page often gets you more coverage with little effort as your views are reinforced or attacked.

✓ Ask other team members and customers to contribute ideas this will help to ensure topicality as well as indicate what others would be happy to read.

✓ Use a photograph to enhance your chances of getting printed. Editors like to break up space with pictures, so have a good press photograph taken for each key member of your team. Colour and action are in. Formal passport-type head and shoulders are less welcome.

✓ Write a specific release date on all press material.

✓ Write: 'BEGINS' at the beginning and 'ENDS' at the end. This may sound daft, but editors work fast and it is the quickest way for them to check that they have it all.

✓ Double-space your copy for easy editing. Editors do edit and, speaking for myself, much of what I write is all the better for skilful editing.

✓ Keep it brief. Be as concise as you are able. When journalists want more information they call you.

✓ Mention your website in your heading along with your telephone number and the basis of your authority to write on the subject. Where possible offer more information or some 'goodie' in the text so that the journal has a motive for telling its readers how to contact you.

✓ After the word 'ENDS' have a note: 'For further information ring Fred Smith on 44 (0)1765 698477' and make sure that Fred Smith or someone who is fully briefed will be available on that number any time that the journalist makes the call.

✓ Find the name of the appropriate editor (news, features, sport, business, law, accountancy – whatever) check in *Willings Press Guide* or *Rates and Data*. Always send releases to named individuals where you can, not to 'the editor'.

✓ Remember that a good percentage of editors these days are women. Do not use the salutation 'Dear Sir'. If you are too inept or too lazy to identify the recipient do not expect your release to be printed.

✓ Use e-mail to send news. Journalists are great users of e-mail and an attachment can quickly be trimmed if necessary without unnecessary keyboard work.

✓ Provide useful information to the press. Before you know it you will be an authority. If you are perceived as an authority the press will come to you when they want information and coverage is assured.

✓ There are lots of awards about these days. If you win one tell the world, but slant your copy to indicate what is in it for the reader. The only person who really cares about you is you. (Unless you are very famous.) Assume that others are always lazy and short of time and you are unlikely to go wrong.

✓ Test your press coverage by the cost of equivalent space in advertising and the value of additional business that each brings in. Your time is precious. Coverage is nice, but it is all about business in the end.

✓ More and more people are going for news online. Jupiter Research suggests that 61 per cent want national/international news, 39 per cent look for business news, 34 per cent and 31 per cent are interested mainly in sport and entertainment respectively.

✓ Web users are increasingly migrating to online newspaper sites. So find them and send them your releases.

✓ Almost as many online readers check out the advertisements as they look for news and/or weather, so advertising is by no means dead. But be careful if you think of combining advertising with editorial in the same publication. It can work, but it can cause the reader to believe that if you paid for the advertisement you paid for the editorial coverage, and that makes editorial no more credible than advertising for most readers. (Recently some search engines have begun providing 'top of page one listing' to those sites willing and able to pay for the privilege. I am delighted to report that research suggests that, for the present at least, such high listings are viewed with a strong degree of scepticism by sophisticated Internet users who tend to bypass them and go straight to the normal listings.)

*See also:* Is the online customer a different sort of animal?

# THE PROPER USE OF E-MAIL

With opt-in e-mail the potential customer or the loyal customer each say to you, 'Please sell to me.' This is an essential of e-commerce, one of the two legs of what I call 'mandate marketing'. If it is done well it will ensure that the intelligent customer will never risk their time or energy looking for alternative sources of supply. They will be bound to you and your business by chains of pure gold.

## Why do I need to use an opt-in e-mail facility for my customers?

The truly unique feature that web technology brings to the market is the ability to personalize and tailor communications to thousands of customers.

Unsolicited mail, however, is no more welcome on the Internet than elsewhere. In fact, it is often more irritating. Junk mail that drops onto your doormat or into your mailbox is quickly and easily sorted and thrown away without trouble. Unsolicited e-mails that clog up your files and may threaten you with viruses will make you mad. People differ, but as a rule of thumb 'it ain't good business to do unto others anything that drives you crazy when they do it to you'.

E-mails are flame-proof when the customer specifically asks you to keep in touch, looks forward to hearing from you, finds what you send is relevant and timely. Anything else is just spam.

## How do I get the customer's mandate to keep in touch?

✓ Make sure that your site is informative and attractive.

✓ Offer visitors the facility of having regular updates delivered into the e-mails.

✓ Run competitions with valuable prizes and ask for the e-mail addresses of entrants. If you do this, also offer the facility as above. Unsolicited material is still unsolicited even if you are a prizewinner.

✓ Make sure that entrants who do not want to be placed on any e-mail list can indicate their wish with a simple code, and be resolute in respecting their wishes.

✓ Offer a freephone (toll free) or online service to answer urgent questions between mailings.

✓ Make it clear that you do not sell e-mailing lists and that personal privacy and confidentiality are always respected.

✓ Avoid all temptation to sell lists of customer's e-mail addresses – ever.

*Test and go on testing your service*

✓ Are you achieving greater and greater conversion of enquiries into sales by better targeting of potential and actual customers?

✓ Are you getting better response rates than you did with traditional marketing?

✓ Do customers tell you and prove through their buying habits that you are giving them something that they value?

✓ Are more and more potential customers opting in to your offer of information?

✓ Do they want to continue to communicate with you?

✓ Are you able to leverage the initial mandates in order to get closer and closer to customers' changing needs?

✓ Do you know more about your customers than before?

✓ Are you getting more referral business?

✓ Is your internal decision making and product development improving?

✓ Are you increasingly better able to concentrate on those customers who give and receive the best value?

✓ Are you getting a bigger share of the best customer's buying?

✓ Is profitability improving?

✓ Is your staff more committed and anxious to stay with you?

✓ Are growing cost savings becoming evident?

✓ Are sales per person employed showing healthy growth?

*Things to avoid*

● Pushing too hard for the sale.

● Asking for the sale too early.

● Presenting obvious advertising puff as if it was information.

● Messages that are too loud, too long and too insistent.

● Messages that are not relevant to the customer needs.

● Messages that are too frequent.

● Messages that are not relevant to customer wants.

● Deception and fraud.

● Sale of personal information to others including the hated spam merchants.

● Exaggerated claims.

● Invasion of privacy.

Never ask questions that can be seen as irrelevant to the customer's needs or impertinent.

# CAN I GET BY WITHOUT A WEBSITE?

## How can I market online without the cost of a website?

You may want to have some of the advantages of marketing online without the need to build or pay for a website. Can it be done? The answer is 'yes and no'. With a little creativity you may make it rather more 'yes' than 'no', but you may need to be warned that 'here there be dragons!' Banner advertisements on someone else's website can be bought and do not have to be 'clickable'. In fact the smart people do not want 'clickable' advertisements on their sites. The old familiar banner advertisement is an invitation that reads, 'now that you've just arrived here, why don't you go somewhere else?' An advertisement on someone else's site can simply give your e-mail address or, better, ask for the visitor's e-mail details so that you can send product or service updates.

Better than advertising is a recommendation from someone the buyer trusts. So it is possible to have your product or service promoted by others. This works best on the basis of 'I'll scratch your back' and we will deal with this later, but it is possible to piggyback on another's site as long as there is enough value in it for your host.

You can use your e-mail facility. It is perfectly possible to buy and use e-mailing lists from brokers online. If unsolicited mail is timely, relevant and interesting it will get results. If it is sent to the wrong people at the wrong time it will be regarded as 'spam', but I realize that if you favour sending out junk mail you may wish to avoid having an expensive website that your ISP can pull the plug on. (Strangely I find that there is a strong correlation in business between those whom it is unwise to trust and those who believe that they have nothing less than a genius for producing junk mail that gets results.)

The Internet has developed its own culture in which spam is detested as mentioned above. The most effective way of dealing with spam is not to ignore it. The web is a two-way communications operation and recipients of unwanted information can readily 'flame' the sender, that is, they can organize a blitzkrieg of e-mails that can grind all your activities to a halt if they choose to do so. If you send unsolicited e-mails you may not be ignored. You may be put out of business in the short term at least, if you have a website. The quality of the list and the relevance of the message remain critical.

You need to also bear in mind the simple but sad fact that consultants have to find their next bandwagon. As I write, they are trying to create a new disease of 'information overload'. They are suggesting that the poor overworked worker suffers stress because he or she receives e-mails. This nonsense is being promoted by the news media that seem to have nothing better to report. The Institute of Management are getting in on the act with their advice: 'Don't send any internal e-mail to your poor stressed colleague. Waste your employer's time and money by strolling down the corridor for a chat.' (I paraphrase, but I am 'on message'.) Have these people never thought of the obvious. If I do not want to read an unsolicited letter I throw it into the bin unopened. If I do not want to read an e-mail I click on 'delete'. No spam, no flaming, no problem.

There was a time when e-mails suffered a little by being a print-only medium. This is no longer the case. A friend sends me very pretty stuff which takes a little longer to download, but which brightens my day, and my American friends constantly send me multimedia delights across the Atlantic. At the very least you can include hyperlinks so that the recipient can choose to get further information from your strategic ally's website.

*See also:* The chairman wants a website. What do we need to think about?

## How can I use information groups or chat rooms?

✓ E-mail discussion groups the members of some of which may have an interest in your services, products or ideas are out there. As a first step take a look at www.liszt.com to get a list of the lists.

✓ Newsgroups exist so that those who share an interest can 'talk' to each other online. Most have noticeboards on which information of general interest can be 'posted'.

✓ You can post messages that, as long as they are not perceived as 'too commercial', can attract business. Unfortunately each newsgroup has its own idiosyncratic view of what is, or is not, 'too commercial' so this is a case of 'taste and try before others buy'.

✓ Spend some time reading postings to see what is acceptable before you unwittingly cause offence.

✓ For no risk entry into the world of newsgroups look for those that begin their addresses with uk-adverts, alt-forsale, uk-forsale or biz-marketplace. These are far more likely to carry advertisements and may possibly even welcome them.

✓ If you decide, despite warnings, to advertise on newsgroup bulletin boards, use AD or FS at the start of the headline and tell the world that it is an advertisement and that only those who are interested in reading commercial information should open it.

✓ You can, if you can afford it, go in for sponsorship. Just as Coca-Cola can sponsor the Olympics, Euro 2000 or Little League Baseball, you can sponsor a website that attracts a whole lot of visitors such as sports or news sites. Be careful though. This is generally a 'brand-building' exercise beloved of the big advertising agencies. It does little to build immediate sales. Never believe the advertising agency's doctrine of 'reach' unless you can afford to invest vast sums in 'tombstone advertising'.

✓ 'Tombstone advertising' was once defined by the late, great Howard Shenson as: 'Advertising that builds trust because it is so expensive and so frequent that it tells the world that you must be successful enough to pour money into something that does no more than to say, "Hi guys, we're under here – somewhere".' Tombstone advertising is usually pretty. It is sometimes clever. It takes a long time for it to become useful. It is best left to those who have deep purses and long memories.

✓ Before coming to a final decision you may wish to garner a little more professional information. As an idea starter why not take a look at:

www.emap.com/internet/hot

☞ *See also*:   How can I use PR to bring business to my website?

## BACK TO THE REAL WORLD

### Is going online workable without a solid distribution system where the customer lives in the real world?

Bad reputations take a very long time to be forgotten, unless you are very lucky. One of the major complaints about doing business or attempting to do business online is that it is often too complicated and difficult to place an order. According to much replicated research more than 80 per cent of would-be customers leave a site, never to return, because they could not place the order that they wished. Almost as many complain that, having placed an order and paid for the goods, the delivery service was no service at all. There is a new beatitude: blessed are they that can deliver online for they shall not be let down by their carriers.

The purpose of an e-commerce web presence is to build business by having people visit your site, stay long enough to like what they see, complete an initial purchase, be delighted and return again and again to buy. Anything less and you have an electronic white elephant.

## How do I maintain my success online in the face of ever-growing competition?

Once you are enjoying success online you cannot afford to take your eye off the ball. Unlike a pop singer, when you get into the top ten you need to stay there.

At the very least use all the main search engines to check out where you site is with regularity. Better yet automate the business of checking. One service that comes highly recommended is that of WebPosition Gold available online. (Check out www.coastalsitesuk.co.uk for details.)

## How can I check changing search engine results quickly and easily?

The WebPosition Gold program checks out all the major search engines with as many phrases and keywords as you have the creativity to produce. Analysis of the positioning results gives you the information that you need to keep your site among the best.

If you want more detail it can check each of your pages and indicate how each one is working for you.

Pages are subject to some strange behaviour. Sometimes a new page will shoot straight into the top ten only to sink without trace when the rules change. Conversely, pages may slowly edge their way up into a top position taking months to complete the process.

## How do I make it easy to buy from my site?

✓ Build confidence by emphasizing the security of transactions and your guarantees of customer delight.

✓ Avoid smart technologies that crash the visitor's browser.

✓ Make your guarantees clear and worry-proof.

✓ Avoid minor irritations like spelling errors, and keep your prices up to date.

✓ Where appropriate, indicate your carriers and make it easy for customers to trace shipments. If you use an internationally known and respected shipper such as FedEx or UPS, say so. The association with a well-known brand does no harm.

✓ Publish testimonials.

✓ Where appropriate join a recognized and respected regulatory or arbitration body and show their logo on your site.

✓ Arrange in advance to take the major credit cards and list those that you are able to handle. Show their logos. Again the association can build confidence and the best cards often carry their own guarantees.

✓ Show the international key icon for a secure transaction.

✓ Limit order forms to what you need to know to process the order efficiently.

✓ E-mail confirmations immediately with the fullest possible delivery details.

✓ Invite every customer to opt in for further information and offers.

✓ Invite referrals.

✓ Remember to say 'thank you' for the order.

✓ Survey customer satisfaction online by e-mail and make it worth the customer's while to respond.

✓ Consider whether it is appropriate to form customer clubs or chat rooms.

✓ Happy customers love to share ideas on the good buys that they have made.

✓ Keep your website content fresh, informative and entertaining so that customers come back and buy with increasing frequency.

# A STRATEGIC AND TACTICAL SUMMARY

✓ Your server may give you access to a log file that shows both the search engine and the keywords that visitors to your site used to find you. This is valuable information, but it is of limited use. It fails to tell you of the many who used different words and failed to find you.

✓ Statistics are crucially important in running a successful Internet business, so ask your server what statistics packages they are able to offer you. To get an idea of what is available as part of the hosting package or as an add-on you might like to take a look at http://www.kudos.com/.

✓ As a start to your own web success you will probably make a well-educated guess at the keywords that people are most likely to use to find you.

✓ In my business I might choose a series of simple generic terms and keywords from my book titles that I hope and expect that people will think of when they are looking for the kind of services that I offer, for example: consultant, consultancy, mentor, mentoring, coaching, high income, power, influence, psychology, dominance, sales, marketing, transformation, winning, culture, culture change. This list is only limited by your, or my, imagination.

✓ Most searches are completed using very simple words and phrases and, although the professional may learn the key differences between placing a phrase within inverted commas or using Boolean logic, the general public prefers to keep it simple.

✓ In fact, the general public tends frequently to get the spelling wrong. So, if there are known popular misspellings of any words on your list, you should consider including those in addition to their correct versions. It is a question, in a way, of trying to get into the customer's mind.

✓ What words would he or she choose? What misspellings is he or she likely to make?

✓ There is a shortcut to finding out the words that are being used and the most common mistakes when spelling them. One source of this vital information is a company called Beyond Engineering. Their reports go under the generic title of WordSpot. You can subscribe to a full report and, to save you valuable time, to specific keywords (including their expansions, derivatives and misspellings). Words are ranked in order of popularity enabling you to track changes and amend your site as necessary.

✓ If you sell specific brands, you can subscribe to see which are subject to most enquiries and design additional web pages for the most popular as well as looking seriously at those that you stock.

✓ You may also want to look at www.go2.com a search engine website that offers the facility of typing in a keyword phrase and checking how many times it was used by their visitors.

✓ You need to prioritize your keywords and key phrases. The algorithms keep changing, but as a general rule of thumb the earlier a word or phrase appears the better your chances of being listed in the mystical top 20.

✓ Do not discount the value of very ordinary words and phrases. Some of the most popular words used include: shop, find, where, shopping, for, buy, buying . . . information, compare . . . me, get . . ., etc. People really like to keep it simple.

✓ Write the information on your website, especially the home page, with this important thought in mind. People use simple language. They are not inclined to look for the 50-dollar word when the 5-cent word pops readily into their mind.

✓ Just to make your life and mine a little more exciting, every search engine looks for keywords in its own idiosyncratic way.

✓ In general a piece of complex software, usually called a spider or crawler, 'looks' at a submitted page and catalogues the important words. It takes into consideration the word's position on the page, the number of times that a word is used, the relative density of words and whatever else the clever people who design the software decide to take into account such as, for example, the number of links to (and from) other sites which may be counted as being indicators of the recognition that the site under examination receives and then compares that site with a few million others to assess what position it will get when a word or phrase is entered by a user.

✓ It does not stop there. They may emphasize link popularity – other pages linking to yours, link relevancy – the number of opportunities that you give browsers to find out more of the same from related sites and anything that in their judgement makes yours a valuable site.

✓ You are in a constant competition for prominence against very great odds, so look for and use all the reliable help that you can afford both in setting up your site and keeping it in the front rank.

✓ The people who design search engine software are very smart, as you might imagine. Smart people tend to get bored with what is and look for ways to create what might be, and so they delight in tweaking already complex programs.

✓ To stay on top of the search engines you need to plan how you will constantly tweak your own pages, develop and add new pages and drop whatever is no longer working. You really do need to get all the help that you can get. Planet Ocean Communications offer a book, *The Unfair Advantage Book on Winning the Search Engine Wars*, which enjoys an enviable reputation for steering entrepreneurs in the right direction.

You should consider getting hold of a copy.

✓ Books are, as you would expect me to say, a wonderful form of communication, but the search engine wizards can and do change the rules with great frequency and books take a while to get into print. I suggest that you back up your reading by talking to experts. My personal experts are at www.quadrantinternet.com and www.1-internet-marketing.com and www.net-profit.co.uk. Check them out and decide whom, if anyone, you need to talk with.

✓ You will need to write, or have written for you, a number of descriptions of your site to submit to the directories. This needs to be genuinely informative about your business while incorporating the keywords and key phrases that will have people beating a path to your door.

✓ Do not try to be excessively clever when composing this description as the directory and search engine wizards were on to all the best tricks years ago. Mindless repetition of a keyword that used to be a popular ploy with pornography sites a while back now simply tends to trigger the crawler to ignore the offending new site. You can be lost and unloved out there in cyberspace if you are labelled a cyber cheat. (But see below.)

✓ Link your pages and your sites together. Some search engines love links and if you choose to have a multisite operation, either to promote a range of services or simply to promote each other, the more links the better.

✓ You can sometimes get a relatively small to considerable boost to your site by inviting an editor of a directory to review it in the hope that it will be inserted under the appropriate heading on their home page.

✓ If you invite review, make the editor's work as easy as possible. Be specific about the category in which you want to be listed. Clearly state the site title. Send them a concise 'nonsense-free' description of what your site offers visitors and a brief suggestion of how your inclusion will benefit their directory. If at first you do not succeed, resubmit three or four times a year.

✓ The real expert will want to use metatags to entice the search engine to give it a high score. Metatags are keywords that appear in the page titles and body of the page, 'hidden' in graphics and the like. The temptation is to repeat the same words through the piece. This is fine but, since position of words can be critical, it can help if the same words are rotated so that they are in different positions in different locations.

✓ I hate to say this, but you will need to remain patient once you have submitted your site to the search engines. Some may have you listed within a day or so, others will take up to 12 weeks to have your site popping up and thrilling the crowds.

✓ Advertising on or off the web may bring visitors. All that was written earlier is true for dirt-world or cyber advertising. Advertising, however brief, must pull in additional business or it is a waste of money. Avoid tombstones and go for haemorrhoid advertising. (You have the pain we have the ointment.)

✓ I have warned against selling banner or button advertisements on your site. I find it impossible to understand the logic of 'now that I've got you here after considerable effort please go somewhere else at once'. That does not mean that you cannot or should not buy banner advertising space elsewhere. Many sites are happy to sell. I would strongly advise, however, against buying pop-up advertising. Pop-up advertising frequently does no more than irritate those who are trying to read something more relevant to their needs and can be enough to turn them away from you for ever.

✓ I, and many like me, get mad when, for example, AOL insist on imposing on my precious online time by thrusting advertisements that I do not want to see for products that I will never buy under my unwilling nose. I now hate AOL and all who advertise on it. A banner has the excellent virtue that I can, and usually do, simply ignore it. (I do, but who says that I am typical?)

✓ The exception to selling or swapping banner advertising is when your site is new and the search engines have not yet finished their arcane examinations. In the early days you have little to lose and anything that brings in visitors may be useful, but do not raise your hopes too high, the click rate is low – between 5 per cent and zero.

✓ If you do use bought and paid for banners, change the content frequently enough so that regular visitors are not inclined to think 'oh, that old stuff again'.

✓ On a banner advertisement you have room for little other than a headline, so make yours compelling.

✓ Bright colours help to catch attention, but it is the offer that brings about click through.

✓ Positioning of advertisements has for many years been an important area of research in newspapers and magazines. If you want to catch the attention of most men place you advertisement on the sports page. Online things are easier. We read from left to right and start at the top, so top left-hand corner is a logical place to position advertisements.

✓ If you cannot get the left-hand top, go for the bottom of the page. Some gurus have tested positions and found that the bottom draws 30 per cent better because people have read what they want to and then are happy to click through to somewhere else.

✓ You may not want to stop at little banners and buttons. Some are now trying half-page and even full-page advertisements. They say that they work for them, but research runs at present from non-existent to there is not any.

✓ Before you get overexcited, however, take a cool look at costs.

✓ Suppose that a great many people visit your attractive site but few actually buy. Then paying for a great many new visitors may very well mean that you lose money on what seems to be a very attractive price per click. Work out the detail before you invest.

✓ A substantial number of those who shop online do so for convenience and price. So, make purchasing easy for people and make special offers a key feature of your advertisements.

✓ Always test the effectiveness of your advertising – preferably before you invest a small fortune in it. Measure accurately the response in terms of sales not visitors. If an advertisement is working with you please do not change it for change sake.

✓ With online advertising testing is made easier for you. You can set up a separate folder for each offer and readily test which pulls best.

✓ If you see a site in the form www.tomfib.com/offer/bum21/htm, it simply means that Tom, who happens to live and love in Illinois (fib), is tracking an offer by popping responses into a folder, which he advertised or e-mailed under the code bum21. Please do not try to link onto this site; it does not exist.

✓ Data are important. Start collecting statistics about your site as soon as you can. But statistics are of little use until you turn them into information by relating them to your knowledge of the business world. Information assumes real value when you combine it with your creativity, beliefs, hunches and values to create knowledge, and knowledge when intelligently applied is wisdom.

✓ Improving your position with a search engine will not affect how well you do with a directory or vice versa. You need to work with both.

*Some websites to help you to keep ahead of the game*

www.trellian.com

www.aadsoft.com

www.topdogg.com

www.signposter.com

# Glossary

In an emerging discipline new words or new uses of old words are invented almost daily. Too often they are used as a barrier to enable specialists to pursue their speciality without 'undue' interference from line management. With this in mind this glossary goes a little wider than the text and offers some additional food for thought for thoughtful businesspeople.

**Above the line**  Marketers love talking of above-the-line and below-the-line activities to confuse the unwary. Above the line is mass marketing, such as advertising; below the line is addressed to individuals. Since the 'mass market' is made up entirely of individuals the difference has little meaning to the businessperson.

**Activity-based costing**  The key to effective costing of business activities is to separate those that add to customer delight and to regard such costs as an investment. The old approach of allocating costs to products tends to produce a product-centric rather than customer-centred approach and is being replaced in forward-looking companies where everything is related to the customer.

**Address**  An address in a unique identifier assigned to a web page. The address is more commonly referred to as the URL (Uniformed Resource Locator).

**Adjacent sector/segment**  A market segment or sector that could be serviced with existing products or services at relatively small cost and that is often used to extend the life cycle of a product or service.

**ADN**  Advanced Digital Network often refers to 56 kbps leased line for computers in different location to share information and contact the Internet.

**ADSL**  The British Telecom version of Advanced Digital Network (Asymmetrical Digital Subscriber Loop).

**Affinity marketing**  Having your product or service recommended to their customers by an honest broker that has a similar customer base, but completely non-competitive products or services.

**Anonymous FTP** Users may gain access to a remote server using File Transfer Protocol without actually having an account on that server. The user's e-mail address is usually given as a password and the user name 'anonymous' is assigned to the user by systems supporting this service.

**Applet** A multimedia application written or embedded in the Java language such as animation or sound, viewable only in a Java-enabled browser such as Netscape 2.0 or HotJava.

*See also:* HotJava, Netscape Communications

**Archie** A database of anonymous FTP sites and their contents, 'Archie' keeps track of the entire contents of these sites, and allows users to search for files on those sites using various different kinds of filename searches.

**Archive** Often compressed, archives are usually large files containing several smaller files. Commonly used archive file formats are ZIP, TAR, ARJ, LZH, UC2.

**Archive site** Contains archived files of many kinds, available for users to download either by FTP or e-mail.

**ARJ** Allows the user to store one or more files in a compressed format in an archive file. This saves space both in the compression and in the saving of disk sector clusters. Particularly strong compressing databases, uncompressed graphics files, and large documents. Named after the creator, American programmer Robert Jung.

**ARPA** The Advanced Research Projects Agency is a US governmental organization responsible for creating an experimental network which heralded the beginning of the Internet. Now known as Defence Advanced Research Projects Agency.

**ARPAnet** Network created by ARPA in 1969, primarily allowing data transfer between Government laboratories. Now defunct predecessor to the Internet.

**ASCII** American Standard Code for Information Interchange, a file containing only text characters: numbers, letters and standard punctuation.

**Asset stripper** The massive, often short-lived cash assets of some dot coms are becoming a happy hunting ground for a new breed of asset stripper who seeks cash rather than stuff.

**Assets** Anything of value owned by the business and recorded on the balance sheet. In modern theory the market value of the company should be a high multiple of the assets because knowledge and competencies add value.

**ATM** Asynchronous Transfer Mode is a new communications standard that is currently in the later stages of development. The ATM is designed to transfer voice, video, and other multimedia data that requires short bursts of large quantities of data that can survive small losses but must be broadcast in real time.

**ATM** Automated teller machine or cash machine.

**Attachments** Multimedia files that are 'attached' to an e-mail; can be text, graphics, sound, video, spreadsheet, database, or even an entire application.

**Auschwitz syndrome** Feelings of guilt experienced by the survivors of downsizing that lead them to covertly damage the firm that they see as making them complicit in their colleagues' job loss.

**Backbone** A central high-speed network established by a company or organization for connecting independent subnetworks.

**Balanced product offering** The assurance that a product:

✓   works as it should

✓   is available when required

✓   has the unique and recognizable qualities of the brand.

**Bandwidth** In simplistic terms, bandwidth is the amount of information travelling through a single channel at any one moment.

**Barriers to entry** The quality of your service to customers online or off should be a barrier to entry for your potential competitors that causes them to overspend, lose money and withdraw. That is e-market dominance.

**Baud Rate** Speed at which data travels through a modem, measured in bps (bits per second). Most modems today range from 2400 to over 50 000 bps.

**BBS** Bulletin Board System is a computer system usually run by local users making files available for downloading and setting up electronic discussion forums.

**Below-the-line marketing** Public relations, point of sale, demonstrations and similar activities aimed at buyers one at a time.

**Binary** Binary data is a direct representation of the bits stored in RAM on a computer. Much more compact and accurate than ASCII.

**Bit** Binary DigIT is the smallest unit of computerized data, comprising of either a 1 or 0. A combination of bits can indicate an alphabetic character, a numeric digit, or perform a signalling, switching or other function. Bandwidth is usually measured in bits per second.

**Body** In e-mail terms, the part of the message containing the most textual content, sandwiched between the header and the signature.

**Bookmark** Virtual bookmarks work pretty much the same as the real ones. They record a URL or web page to enable you to refer back to at a later date.

**Boston Consulting Group Matrix** The categorization of product, services and even customers (in private) as cash cows, stars, question marks or dogs. Cash cows should be looked after with loving care. Stars and question marks should be market tested and should attract investment. Dogs should be helped to die.

**bps** Bits per second is the speed at which data transfer is measured.

**Brand** Is the accumulation of highly visible qualities of a product or service that are promoted to differentiate the offering and assure consumers of consistent and high quality. In a marketing strategy, branding is intended to be used to assure the company of customers who are also of high and consistent quality. Branding is important, but too often those without the will or the capability to do otherwise produce fancy but impractical websites to 'build the brand'.

**Brand awareness** The self-indulgent measurement of the percentage of consumers who recognize a brand. This is usually reported by advertising agencies who omit the essential information of whether the consumers who recognize the brand are prepared to buy it. In a hypothetical brand awareness study if every consumer said, in effect, 'Yes we recognize that brand, but we wouldn't buy the product because it's rubbish', the marketing department would be congratulating themselves from here to Carey Street.

**Browser**  Often called a 'web browser' this allows the user to search the World Wide Web and other Internet facilities using a Graphical User Interface. Examples are Mosaic and Netscape.

**Business process re-engineering**  Is an approach that, at its best enables a company to improve processes and remove duplications of effort. At its worst it has become an excuse to reduce headcounts, damage morale and loyalty, damage the long-term viability of the business and make huge bonuses for hatchet-wielders who have the good sense to abandon each sinking ship that they leave behind every 18 months or so.

**Budget**  A tactical plan expressed in financial terms.

**Business to business (B2B)**  Providing goods or services to other businesses rather than to the consumer.

**Byte**  A unit of data, generally formed from 8 bits. Example: 01101010.

**Captive demand**  Creating a market advantage such that the customer has no choice but to come to you. If Amazon had exclusive rights to a Tom Lambert book all my many fans would have no choice but to go to them. (Sadly no one offers me millions to write exclusively for them.)

**Cash cow**  A mature product that offers high revenues with little investment usually in a low growth market. Cash cows should have unstinting protection when they still have potential, but when they grow too old they should be recognized as 'dogs' and dumped.

**CERN**  (Conseil Europeen pour la Recherche Nucleaire) A laboratory located in Geneva, Switzerland, where the concept for the World Wide Web was first developed.

**CGI**  (The Common Gateway Interface) is an interface-creation scripting program that allows you to make World Wide Web pages on the fly, based on information from fill-in forms, checkboxes, text input, etc.

**Change agent**  A process consultant who 'acts as a catalyst' to bring about change in a company. What worries me about such worthies is that like the catalyst to which they compare themselves they induce change in others without experiencing any change themselves. (Another way of saying that some of us never learn.)

**Change management** The process (usually expensive and protracted) of changing the culture of a business. Research in the USA and the UK suggests that between 1970 and 1995 75 per cent of such attempts failed to achieve their objectives.

**Client** In a client–server relationship, the client is a computer running programs or applications from the server, or accessing files from it.

A 'posh' word for a customer intended to denote that the user is in a 'profession' rather than a trade.

**Competencies** What the firm is good at doing. A key part of strategic planning for market dominance should be devoted to assessing: what competencies will enable us to best exploit current markets? Which do we have and which must we build? What competencies will we need to exploit the most exciting markets of the future? What competencies do we need to build in order to create the rules by which others have to play if they wish to compete?

**Competitive advantage** Usually taken by marketers to be a cost advantage, a price advantage or both. On the Internet savings can produce major cost advantages that can be applied to ensuring that customers are so delighted that they see no need to even look elsewhere for what they buy from you.

**Compress** The act of discarding redundant or semi-redundant information from a file, thereby making it smaller.

**CompuServe** A US Internet Service Provider; one of the oldest and biggest. Taken over by AOL.

**Consortium** A strategic alliance, sometimes short term, to offer a better range of competencies to the marketplace than any one member is able to offer alone.

**Cookie** A cookie is a piece of software which records information about you. It holds this information until such time as the server requests it. For example, if you are browsing around a virtual shop, each time you place an item in your basket the information is stored by the cookie until you decide to buy and the server requests the purchase information.

**Core workers (knowledge workers)** Those who have the capacity to make a major contribution to the success of the firm. Core workers have too often been limited in some company-think as the technical experts. This is fine as long as it does not lead to a low estimate of the worth of others.

**Corporate Alzheimers** The loss to a company of essential, but unrecorded, knowledge when downsizing has occurred and those with the most experience have left taking their understanding of customers, markets and systems with them.

**Culture** How we do things around here.

**Customer proposition** Why a particular segment or sector should buy your product or service in preference to any other. The customer proposition should always be clearly stated online or off.

**Customer retention** Research by Reichheld of Bains and Company has shown that customer retention is the key to employee retention, investor satisfaction and profitability. The essential is to attract and retain the right customers.

**Cybercafe** A café or bar allowing customers to explore the World Wide Web whilst having a drink or snack, usually charged per half-hour of usage. Increasingly in USA and UK libraries are permitting free access to the Internet without the need to buy a coffee and a bun.

**Daemon** A program that runs in the background whenever needed, carrying out tasks for the user. They 'sleep' until something comes along which needs their help; most commonly found on Unix systems.

*See also:* Unix

**Database** Details of your customers and the computer software that facilitates the keeping and updating of the records. Properly speaking, the software is a databank.

**Delayering** An ugly word usually taken to be the removal of unnecessary levels of bureaucratic management. In e-commerce it can also mean the removal of unnecessary intermediaries.

**Development capital** Investment that is intended to fund growth rather than start-up of a business.

**Dialup** 'Dialup Access' or a 'Dialup Account' is when a modem is used to gain access to the Internet via a network.

*See also:* Modem

**Domain Name** Unique address identifying each site on the Internet, usually of two or more segments separated by full stops.

**Domain Name Server** Computers connected to the Internet whose job it is to keep track of the IP Addresses and Domain Names of other machines. When called upon, they take the ASCII Domain Name and convert it to the relevant numeric IP Address.

*See also*:    IP Address

**Domain Name System** Allows users to relate to computers on the Internet by using textual addresses (eg. www.theplanet.net) for ease of use, rather than the IP Address system.

**DOS** The Disk Operating System is a simple operating system developed by Microsoft, allows extensions by other programs. Originally known as QDOS (quick and dirty operating system).

**Download** When you transfer information off a remote machine connected to the Internet onto your local machine, you are downloading data.

*See also*:    Upload

**Electronic mail or e-mail** Method of communication whereby an electronic message is sent to a remote, or not so remote (people sitting at adjacent desks have been known to send each other e-mails), location and received by another user at a specific e-mail address. Internally in many companies the novelty and convenience of e-mail has led to its use for numerous non-business communications to the degree that workers, encouraged by the press and to the delight of consultants, are complaining of 'e-mail overload'.

Opt-in e-mail where your customers invite you to keep them appraised of news about products or services on a regular basis is a key feature of e-commerce.

*See also*:    Attachments, Body, Header, Signature

**Emoticons** These are the sideways smiles and frowns used in e-mail to indicate emotions. E.g. :-) would indicate a smile and :-( would indicate a frown!

**E-tailers** Businesses on the Internet selling directly to consumers (B2C).

**Ethernet** A type of network cabling allowing theoretical data transfers of up to 10 Mb per second.

**FAQ** (Frequently Asked Question) Lists of Frequently Asked Questions (and their answers) covering all manner of topics can be found across the World Wide Web, allowing the user to search for a query that somebody has already found the answer to.

**FDDI** Fibre Distributed Data Interface is a standard for transmitting data through optical fibre cables at a rate of around 100 million bps.

☞ *See also*:  Bandwidth, Ethernet, T-1, T-3

**Filename extension** Commonly a three- or four-letter extension on the end of a file name designating the file type. There are hundreds in existence, and new ones are frequently being invented. Examples are .txt (text file) and .gif (Graphics Interchange Format).

**Finger** A Unix program which displays information about a particular user or all users logged on the system, or a remote system.

☞ *See also*:  Unix

**Firewall** Secures a company or organization's internal network from unauthorized external access (most commonly in the form of Internet hackers).

**First to market advantage** The theory that the first supplier in any market can build and sustain competitive advantage, but only if they are able to deliver high customer satisfaction rather than pursuing high short-term profits.

**Flame** An insulting or derogatory message usually sent via e-mail as punishment for breach of 'netiquette'. There have been instances of 'Flame Wars', when other people join in the heated exchanges. In either case, not recommended.

☞ *See also*:  E-mail, Netiquette

**Forms** Certain browsers support electronic fill-in forms. A form on a web page can be filled in by users in all parts of the world and the information is sent electronically to the relevant domain site.

☞ *See also*:  CGI, Browser

**Four 'Ps' of marketing** Price, place, product and promotion. To which some add a fifth, people.

**Fragmented market** A market in which there are many competitors of whom none has a dominant share.

**Freeware** Software allowed to be distributed free by the author, but often with certain conditions applying (i.e. the software cannot be modified or must be registered etc.).

*See also:*   Public Domain, Shareware

**FTP** File Transfer Protocol is one of the main ways files are transferred across the Internet. An FTP site is that which is provided by a company or organization as a depository for all kinds of files that users may download.

*See also:*   Download, Protocol

**FTPmail** The process where e-mail is used to access FTP sites.

*See also:*   E-mail

**Gateway** The interface between two opposing protocols. By means of software and hardware a gateway allows connection between otherwise incompatible networks.

*See also:*   Protocol

**GIF** Graphics Interchange Format was developed by CompuServe. GIF is a platform-independent file format, used extensively throughout the Internet for graphics files. Compresses files using a 'lossless' method that ensures picture quality is not diminished.

*See also:*   CompuServe

**.gif** Graphics Interchange Format (GIF) filename extension.

**Gigabyte (GB)** A thousand megabytes.

*See also:*   Megabyte

267

**Globalization** Where customer tastes, expectations and desires are sufficiently similar worldwide to be satisfied by a global product or service.

Having a global strategy in terms of costs, resources, people and production facilities to minimize costs and, in theory at least, maximize customer satisfaction.

**Gopher** Internet Gopher is a distributed document search and retrieval system. It takes a request for information and then scans the Internet for it. The protocol and software follows a client–server model, and permits users on a heterogeneous mix of desktop systems to browse, search, and retrieve documents residing on multiple distributed server machines.

*See also*: Protocol

**Hawthorne effect** The tendency for results to improve for no better reason than that they are being researched. A sort of placebo effect for business scientists.

**Header** In e-mail terms, this is the part of the message indicating who the sender is and some other brief details, such as the subject of the message.

*See also*: Attachments, Body, E-mail, Signature

**Hit** As used in reference to the World Wide Web, 'hit' means a single request from a web browser for a single item from a web server; thus in order for a web browser to display a page that contains three graphics, four 'hits' would occur at the server: one for the HTML page, and one for each of the three graphics.

**Home page** On the World Wide Web, this is the main navigation page owned by a company, organization, university, individual, etc., from which hyperlinks are made to other pages on the site (or other sites).

*See also*: Hyperlink

**Host** You usually connect to a host computer whenever you use the Internet.

**HotJava** A web browser developed by Sun Microsystems expanding traditional browser capabilities by allowing dynamic functions instead of just static text and images.

*See also*: Applet, Java

**HTML** HyperText Markup Language is the tagging language used to format web pages. Allows pictures and text to be combined to create web documents, and the most important feature – hypertext – making it possible for links to be made between different documents.

*See also*:   GIF, JPEG, Tag, World Wide Web

**HTTP** HyperText Transport Protocol has been used on the World Wide Web since 1990. This application-level protocol is essential for the distribution of information throughout the web.

**Hub and spoke system** A distribution system where a central facility supplies a number of smaller warehouses that in turn supply customers or distributors.

**Hyperlink** In World Wide Web pages, hyperlinks are highlighted text or images which, when selected (usually by clicking the mouse button), follow a link to another page. Hyperlinks can also be used to automatically download other files as well as sounds and video clips.

*See also*: Download

**Image map** An image with clickable 'hot spots', allowing several hyperlinks from a single image file. For example, the image could be of a country, split into different areas, each of which could be clickable and hyperlink to a larger view of that specific area.

*See also*:   Hyperlink

**Inertia selling** The practice of sending unsolicited goods through the mail in the expectation that the recipient will pay for them rather than take the trouble to send them back. It seems to work for charities and book clubs.

**internet** When spelt with a lower case i, it is a group of two or more networks connected together.

**Internet** With a capital I, it is the collection of all the interconnected networks in the world, and is often simply referred to as the 'net'.

**IP** Internet Protocol is the main protocol used on the Internet.

*See also*:   Protocol

**IP Address**  Unique four-number code designated to every Domain on the Internet. Each Domain also has a Domain Name as well as an IP address to make site addresses easier to remember.

**IRC**  Internet Relay Chat is a real-time world-wide electronic chat program allowing the user to communicate with other people across the globe.

**ISDN**  Integrated Services Digital Network is a digital telephone line allowing faster data transfer rates than existing analogue lines. Allows simultaneous transfer of voice, data and video information.

**ISP**  Internet Service Provider is a company or organization, such as Planet Online, dedicated to providing businesses or home users access to the Internet, usually for a fee.

**Jargon**  Like all other specialized subjects, the Internet has its own jargon; a somewhat cryptic language describing technical details. Some jargon is explained in this glossary (hopefully enough to enable you to 'bluff your way' through e-commerce so that those who would blind you with jargon are inhibited and begin to talk English).

**Java**  Developed by Sun Microsystems, Java is a web programming language supporting online multimedia effects, such as simple cartoon-like animation, background music and continuously updated information in web pages.

*See also:*   Applet, HotJava

**JPEG**  Joint Photographic Experts Group is a standard of image compression developed especially for use on the Internet. Most photographic images can be highly compressed using this method, without greatly diminishing image quality.

**.jpg or .jpeg**  Filename extensions given to JPEG graphics files.

**Kilobyte**  1024 bytes, usually rounded down to a thousand bytes for simplicity.

**Knowledge industry**  A business in which the key competitive advantage lies in having knowledge denied to others.

A business that exploits the Internet to publish and sell information online at virtually zero cost.

**LAN**  Local area network (see below).

**Leased line**  A rented, high-speed phone link for private use, available 24 hours a day.

**Lifelong learning**  In a rapidly changing world lifelong learning is no longer an option; it is a prerequisite for survival. Learning that is not used, however, is rapidly lost, so forward-looking companies develop a learning strategy that delivers 'Lifelong Learning – Just in Time'.

**Link**  Link puts the hyper in hyperlink. Links are the connections between hypertext pages. Every time you click on highlighted text to go to another page you are following a link.

**Local area network**  Usually referred to as a LAN, this describes a group of computers commonly in the same building, connected by network cables.

**Login**  When a user tries to gain access to the Internet through their host computer, they must login with their password and user ID.

**Loss leader**  Goods sold at a loss or at a reduced profit to attract customers. E-tailers should be careful not to repeat the annoyance of the bricks and mortar world where bargain offers are made to new prospects and denied to loyal customers.

**Mailserver**  The computer (and software running on it) that allows sorting and retrieval of e-mail messages.

*See also*:   E-mail

**Market leader**  What every firm should aspire to be, whether globally, locally, in a carefully chosen segment or a niche. Market leaders must remember, however, that they are there to be 'shot at' and they should be consistently looking to improve their customer service at lower cost in order to make it difficult for others to compete. The value of the 'customer for life' is that they provide employees with the knowledge, motivation and opportunity to do more for the customer with less cost.

**Megabyte (MB)**  The unit of measurement for a thousand kilobytes; a million bytes.

*See also*:   Gigabyte, Kilobyte

**MIME** Multipurpose Internet Mail Extensions is a format designed originally to include images, sounds, animations and other types of documents within Internet mail messages.

**Mirror site** An FTP site containing exactly the same files as the site it is mirroring. Sites may be mirrored several times, often in different countries around the world. They relieve the load that can be placed on a very popular FTP site, making it easier for users to gain access and download files faster.

*See also*:   Download, FTP

**Mission** What a firm is in business for; what customer desires it exists to satisfy; what makes it different and superior; how it treats its stakeholders; what challenges it to be the best of the best; the values that drive and guide the decisions of all employees.

**Modem** A MODulator-DEModulator allows the transmission of digital information over an analogue phone line.

**Mosaic** Web browser written by a group of people at NCSA. Provides a Graphical User Interface for accessing data on the World Wide Web.

*See also*:   Browser

**MPEG** Motion Picture Experts Group is a video compression format used for movie or animation clips on the World Wide Web.

**.mpg or .mpeg** Filename extension for MPEG movies.

**NCSA** The National Center for Supercomputing Applications is a powerful organization that launched the Mosaic Web Browser in 1993 for Windows, x-Windows and Macintosh platforms.

**Netiquette** Informal, largely undocumented set of rules designed to make the web a polite and civilized 'society'.

**Netscape Communications** Creators of Netscape Navigator, one of the most popular web browsers. Became notorious after introducing several HTML 'extensions' that were unsupported by other browsers.

*See also*:   Browser

**Network** Two or more computers linked together and able to share resources constitutes a network.

**Network Time Protocol** Internet protocol ensuring that the correct time is transmitted.

*See also*:   Protocol

**Network time server** Using Network Time Protocol, you access this machine to get the right time.

**Newsgroup** Thousands of newsgroups exist, distributing information on different subjects using Usenet. Some newsgroups offer opportunities for marketing products and services of interest to their members.

**Newsreader** Program that allows the user to read newsgroup messages via Usenet.

**NIC** The Network Information Center is the location where all the data is organized for a certain network.

**NNTP** (Net News Transport Protocol) Usenet news uses this transfer protocol for shifting files around the network.

*See also*:   Usenet

**Node** Any single computer connected to a network.

*See also*:   Network

**Offline** When your computer performs an operation when it is not connected to any other computers, it is working offline.

**Online** Your computer is working online when it performs an operation and is connected to other computers.

**Packet** Information moves around the Internet in 'packets' – chunks of data each with their own destination address. Think of packets as sealed envelopes containing data, with addresses written on them. They all go through the system, and usually end up at the correct destination. The more envelopes the system must handle, the slower the process becomes.

**Page** A World Wide Web 'page' is the name given to a basic web document.

**PEST+ analysis** A useful technique for assessing the business environment that includes specification of the political, economic, social, technological and legal factors that might impinge on the business in any market.

**PKZIP or PKUNZIP** Utilities for easily compressing and uncompressing DOS and Windows files. They use the .zip filename extension.

**Plug-in** There are many things that your browser can do such as displaying images and web pages. Other things are beyond its capabilities and that is where the plug-ins are introduced. Shockwave and RealAudio are examples of plug-ins required for audio and video.

**POP** Post Office Protocol provides a store-and-forward service, intended to move e-mail on demand from an intermediate server to a single destination machine, usually a PC or Macintosh.

**Positioning** Finding a market position for a product that emphasizes what makes it different from competition.

**PPP** Point to Point Protocol is a kind of Internet connection that allows a computer to use Internet protocols to become a part of the Internet. Requires a modem, a standard telephone line and an account from a service provider.

**Pricing strategy** Price is an important strategic issue that few seem to optimize. The customer should drive the price, and simple demand curves beloved of economists are not always borne out in practice. Some people prefer to pay a price premium if they perceive it as being indicative of quality and desirability. When I was a youngster in Harpenden there were those motorists who parked on double yellow lines not because of any shortage of parking spaces, but as an indication that they could afford to pay traffic fines.

**Protocol** Method by which computers communicate to each other over the Internet in order to provide a service.

*See also*: FTP, HTTP, IP, NNTP, POP, PPP, SLIP, SMTP, TCP

**Public access provider** An organization that provides Internet access for individuals or other organizations, often for a fee.

**Public domain** Refers to software that anybody can use or modify without authorization.

*See also:*   Freeware, Shareware

**Quake** The first major game designed for online play and a small piece of history of the web for many surfers.

**Question marks** The fruits of research and development that require major investment and that have yet to prove themselves in the marketplace.

**Relationship marketing** Knowing customers well enough to be able to satisfy their desires more quickly and economically than competition can hope to.

**Relative market share** Your share of your chosen market divided by the share enjoyed by your largest competitor. When your share is a considerable multiple of that of the best of the others you are on your way to market dominance.

**Repeat purchases** The cost of winning the first order is relatively high. Companies in e-commerce and in the real world should be focusing on encouraging repeat purchases that are both more frequent and bigger as the key to low-cost growth.

**Resource** A particular object of information provided on the Internet. Can be anything from a picture through to a video or application.

What some dot coms appear to believe should be irresponsibly wasted.

**Router** A special-purpose computer (or software package) that handles the connection between two or more networks. Routers concentrate on looking at the destination addresses of the packets passing through them and deciding which route to send them on.

*See also:*   Network

**Sales force** People whose views should always be listened to, but never acted on without verification.

**Scripting language** Series of programmed commands that designate how one computer communicates with another computer.

**Sector** A carefully defined part of the market with needs and desires that you have, or can readily acquire, the competencies and strengths to fulfil.

**Segment** A specified part of the total market with needs or desires that are satisfied by your product or service.

**Self-extracting archive** An archived file with the filename extension .exe, indicating that when downloaded and run it will be extracted by the decompressing program around it, without user intervention.

**Server** Within a network, a server makes files available to client programs located on other computers when requested.

**Service Provider** Freeserve are currently the largest Internet Service Provider in the UK. The role of a Service Provider is to provide subscribers a gateway to the Internet.

**Shareware** Software distributed freely, but with certain conditions applying to it. Either the software is released on a trial basis only, and must be registered after a certain period of time, or in other cases no support can be offered with the software without registering it. In some cases direct payment to the author is required.

*See also:* Freeware, Public Domain

**Signature** The automatic addition of a few lines at the foot of an e-mail. These usually consist of the sender's e-mail address, full name and other details.

*See also:* Body, E-mail, Header

**SLIP** Serial Line Internet Protocol, like PPP, lets you use a modem and phone lines to connect to the Internet without connecting to a host computer.

*See also:* PPP, Protocol

**Smileys** Characters often used in news messages, e-mails and on web pages to offer some degree of character or emotion. Example :-)

**SMTP** Simple Mail Transport Protocol, often referred to as sendmail, is designed to allow the delivery of mail messages to Internet users.

**Snail mail** Write a letter. Buy a stamp, put stamp on letter. Walk to the postbox and post letter. Wait a day or two and hopefully it will have reached its intended destination . . . that's snail mail.

**Star** A relatively new product in a high-growth market that is showing considerable sales growth, but requires serious investment in order to achieve its full potential.

**Strategic alliance** An agreement between two companies to cooperate, sharing knowledge and sometimes resources to achieve a predetermined set of business objectives.

**Surfing** A popular metaphor used for describing someone exploring the World Wide Web.

What some at least of your employees waste your money doing.

**T-1** Network link used on the Internet allowing speeds of up to 1.54 megabits/second.

*See also*:  ADN

**T-3** Higher speed (45 megabits/second) network link used on the Internet.

*See also*:  ADN

**Tag** In HTML terms, a 'tag' is used for marking-up text in various ways so that it is formatted in a web document. They are sometimes called 'Markup Tags'.

*See also*:  HTML

**TCP** Transmission Control Protocol works in conjunction with IP to ensure that packets reach their intended destinations.

*See also*:  Packet, Protocol

**TCP/IP** Transmission Control Protocol/Internet Protocol are the two fundamental protocols which form the basis of the Internet.

*See also*:  Protocol

**Teleworker**  The current in-word for what used to be called a 'homeworker' or 'telecommuter'. The Internet with its capability for almost instant communication at minimal cost enhances the opportunities to make teleworking work.

**Telnet**  Terminal emulation program allowing an authorized user to access another computer on the Internet and use that computer as if it were local (when in reality it could be several thousand miles away).

**Terabyte**  1000 gigabytes.

*See also:*    Byte, Kilobyte

**Terminal**  Piece of hardware that allows commands to be sent to a computer, usually by means of a keyboard and display unit.

**Terminal emulator**  Allows a PC to emulate several terminal types.

**Tertiary brand**  A product made by an obscure manufacturer that is designed to sell entirely on the basis of price in order to capture sales from well-known brands and retailer's 'own label'.

**Third generation idiot (TGI)**  A 25-year-old business postgraduate whose studies have been under the direction of a 30-year-old postgraduate lecturer reporting to a 35-year-old postgraduate professor, not one of whom has ever held down a real job in the real world. It is easy to spot a TGI in the workplace. They wave their hands a good deal when they talk (which is most of the time), and compare every situation to an ancient case study. 'Wow, this is just like Polaroid France –1971!'

**Thread**  In a Usenet group, this is a list of messages loosely relating to one another (using the same 'thread').

**Timeout**  The facility whereby after a certain period of inactivity the connection to a distant computer is dropped.

**Time to market**  The time taken to get a new product into the marketplace. Hamel and Prahalad recommend that a new product should be available to buyers as quickly as possible, even if it means that necessary refinements and design improvements lead to a large number of models in quick succession. (Cf Toshiba and their early range of laptop computers.)

Time taken to deliver goods or services to the online customer including any time required to answer requests for information.

**Turnover** Annual sales revenues.

The rate at which any resource of the company turns over whether labour or capital. The combination of e-commerce and a total commitment to retaining the worthwhile customer should play a major role in reducing the turnover of labour while accelerating the turnover of capital as measured in return on capital employed and return on working capital and return on investment. If it fails to improve turnover ratios it is reasonable for top management to ask: 'What are we online for?'

**Undercapitalization** The opposite of the profligate investment in daft dot coms that was the norm before the 'crash' of 2000. When seeking capital investment to cover, for example, the first year of trading, a company is well advised to assess how long it takes to obtain the capital injection and add that period of time to the date at which cash flow is forecast to become positive and profits start to accrue. This gives a buffer period during which further funding can be sought if necessary. Remember that there is no mileage in an overoptimistic forecast and, as David Myddleton has said: 'A forecast is what would have happened if what did happen didn't happen.'

**Unix** An operating system typically written in C, and designed for multiuser environments. It has TCP/IP built in, and is therefore one of the most popular operating systems for servers on the Internet.

**Upload** Transfer of files off a local computer up to a specified remote computer (as opposed to download where files are pulled off a remote machine).

*See also*:   Download

**URL** Uniform Resource Locator is the resource-addressing scheme of the World Wide Web. Assists in locating and identification of multimedia resources or multiple copies of resources.

**Usenet** Specialized network linking thousands of newsgroups covering every subject under the sun.

**USP (unique selling proposition)** The benefits of your offering that your competitors either cannot match or do not promote that will persuade the customer to come to you first and stay with you. If you fail to develop a compelling USP you may have little choice other than to sell purely on price, and those who sell on price alone are normally destined to be a follower in the marketplace rather than a leader as they try to match or beat any price reduction offered by any competitor anywhere. This approach is only viable in the long term where there exists a recognized 'low-cost niche' as, for example in the airline business.

**Value chain** The addition of identifiable customer value at every stage of production and distribution.

**Veronica** Very Easy Rodent Oriented Net-wide Index to Computerized Archives is a resource-discovery system providing access to information resources held on most (99 per cent +) of the world's gopher servers. In addition to native gopher data, veronica includes references to many resources provided by other types of information servers, such as WWW servers, usenet archives and telnet-accessible information services.

**Virus** A virus is virtual evil. It can hide anywhere where a computer stores information. They have the ability to transfer from computer to computer with the use of the Internet and various other networks. A virus can do a number of things to a recipient, such as reformatting hard drives (destroying data).

**WAIS** Wide Area Information Servers is an architecture for a distributed information retrieval system. WAIS is based on the client-server model of computation, and allows users of computers to share information using a common computer-to-computer protocol.

*See also*:    Protocol

**Wide Area Network (WAN)** Group of computers located geographically apart, usually belonging to a single company or organization, connected together using dedicated lines or by satellite to simulate a local network.

**WinSock** WINdows SOCKets is a Windows utility program allowing users connected by SLIP, PPP or other direct connection to communicate with other computers on the Internet by TCP/IP.

*See also*:    PPP, SLIP, TCP/IP

**World Wide Web ('WWW' or 'web')** Specialized Internet Service allowing users to connect to remote sites, with information presented as text with hypertext links. These links can be used to refer to almost all other resources on the Internet. Graphics can be embedded into web pages, but can only be viewed using a graphical web browser. Other applications supported are sound files and movie files.

*See also*:    Browser, HTML, Internet

**Worm** A search utility on the World Wide Web that locates resources following user-determined guidelines.

**XMODEM** A popular but slow file transfer protocol.

**YMODEM** Another file transfer protocol, slightly faster than XMODEM.

**ZIP** Files that have been compressed using the PKZIP program have this filename extension. They can be decompressed using the PKUNZIP utility. The use of a program such as Microsoft's Winzip enables e-mails to be transmitted more quickly and enables great time saving if and only if the recipient has the capability to 'unzip' what is received.

**ZMODEM** The fastest and most popular file transfer protocol, due to its efficiency and crash recovery properties.

# Appendix

## A short list of useful websites and news groups

It is an almost daily occurrence to discover a useful website. Many, however, are useful for only the day during which they were discovered. This book has been liberally strewn with web addresses of more lasting value. They have been inserted into the text in the expectation that the reader will find them most useful at the moment when the subject is uppermost in his or her mind. There are a few, however, that are more generally useful and may be needed at times when e-commerce is not the sole object of interest.

The following are a few of those of most general interest to the manager or executive and which you may want to have easily accessible on your busiest day.

## A club for chief executives

www.palsZenith.com

This site provides maximum support for the leader. In addition to providing opportunities to discuss strategic issues with your peers it provides a resource library and Boardroom Briefings to keep the busiest CEO informed of strategic issues.

## A forum or two for marketers

listserv@unc.edu

listserv@softfornet.com

The first is a resource for those interested in advertising research and education. The second provides ideas for low cost/no cost marketing – a subject always close to my heart. All that you need to do is to send an e-mail to the address given.

## Affiliate programmes

www.affiliatehelp.com

www.i-revenue.net

www.affiliatewire.com

www.affiliatetips.com

To a major degree affiliate marketing (host/beneficiary) has become the hot topic of e-commerce for the smaller company with few marketing resources. Any or all of the above will provide useful information when you are considering whether this approach is right for your business.

## Business information for busy people

www.business-minds.com

The Pearson Group, publishers of this book and many others have a website devoted to business ideas. Keep in touch in order to keep in touch with what the best business brains are doing.

## Daily news

www.silicon.com

www.firsttuesday.com

Things happen very quickly in the field of technology and e-business. Each of the above can be relied upon to provide an up-to-the-minute daily digest of news – and it's free.

## Making the most of human resources

www.pals.co.uk

Life long learning – delivered just in time – is undoubtedly the lifeblood of business now and for the future. Large or small, online or off, we all need to be considering:

- ✓ What skills, knowledge and competences do we need to develop to optimise our success in current markets?
- ✓ What skills, knowledge and competences do we need to develop to build our success in the most worthwhile markets of the future?
- ✓ What skills, knowledge, competences and behaviours do we need to acquire in order to dominate our chosen markets?

A vast amount of money has been squandered on training and development in the past. This site enables subscribers to mine resources, share ideas and post questions for their peers and external experts to ensure that they get the best out of training, coaching and supporting their people.

## Marketing for SME's

www.practicalmarketing.org

Small and Medium Enterprises sometimes lack that most essential skill of effective and low cost marketing. The Institute of Practical Marketing is in the process of being re-constituted by a group of hands-on professionals to help SMEs with more vision than resources to go from where they are to where they want to be.

## Research for serious strategists

www.jup.com

www.forrester.com

www.resourcehelp.com

www.afn.org

The only reliable antidote to media hype that seems to go from wild euphoria to deepest gloom is serious research. The above websites are worth a regular visit if only to help to put some facts in place of speculation.

## There's a big world out there

www.ft.com

www.economist.com

www.businessweek.com

Virtually every newspaper and magazine has a website. Few, however, have websites and other services to compete with those above for the serious business person.

# Index